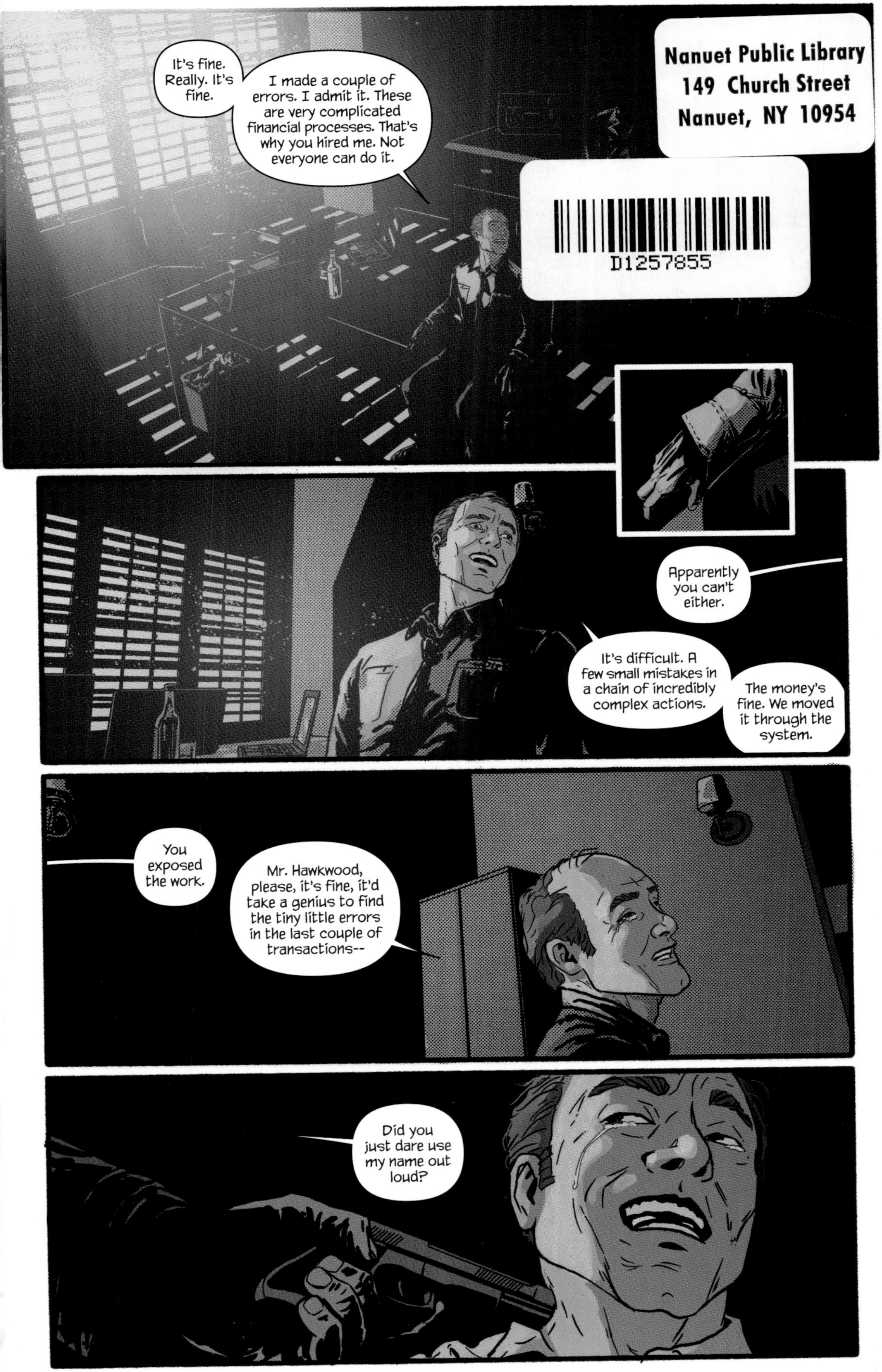
It's fine. Really. It's fine.
I made a couple of errors. I admit it. These are very complicated financial processes. That's why you hired me. Not everyone can do it.
Apparently you can't either.
It's difficult. A few small mistakes in a chain of incredibly complex actions.
The money's fine. We moved it through the system.
You exposed the work.
Mr. Hawkwood, please, it's fine, it'd take a genius to find the tiny little errors in the last couple of transactions--
Did you just dare use my name out loud?

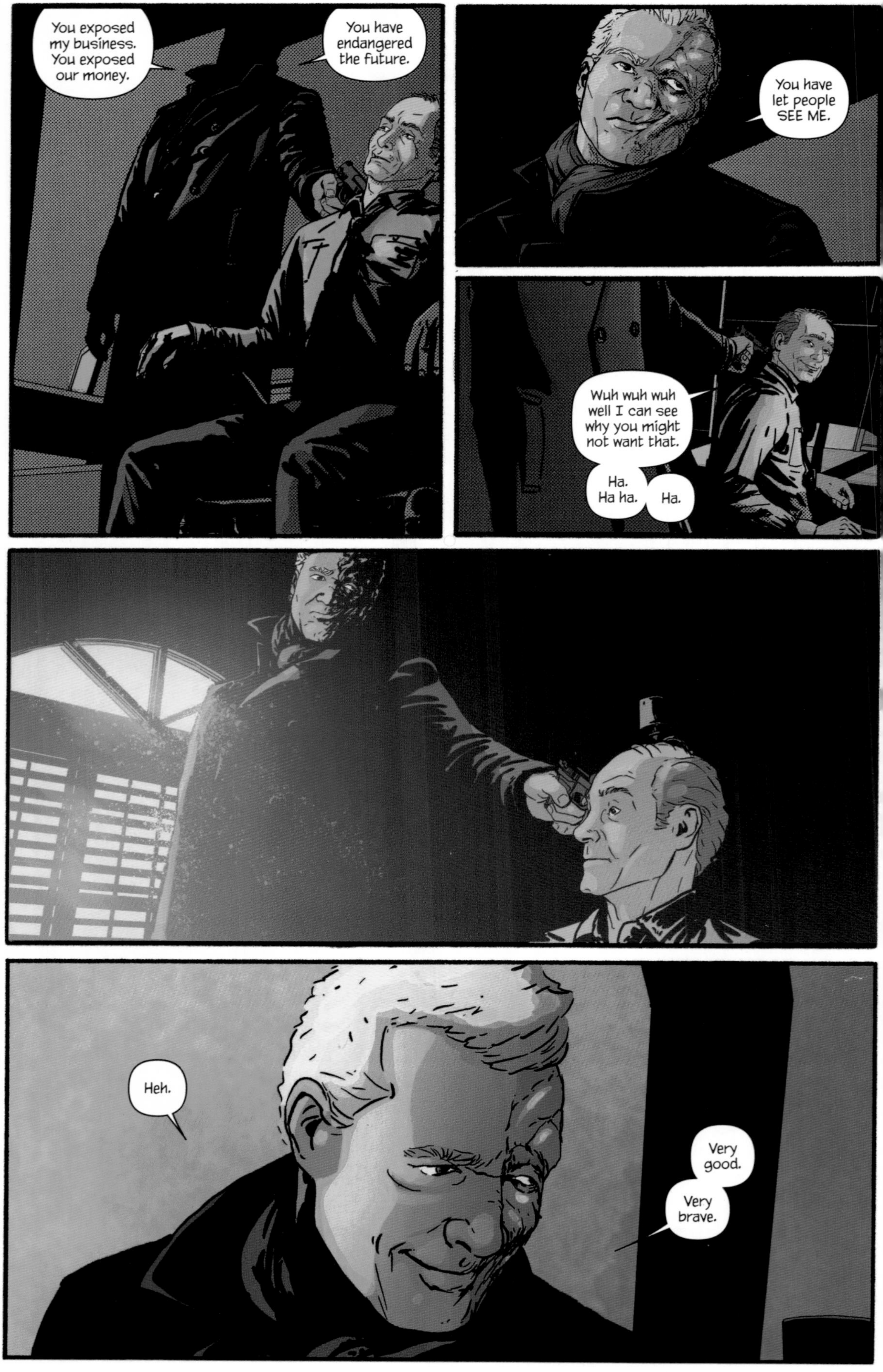
You exposed my business. You exposed our money.
You have endangered the future.
You have let people SEE ME.
Wuh wuh wuh well I can see why you might not want that.
Ha. Ha ha.
Ha.
Heh.
Very good.
Very brave.

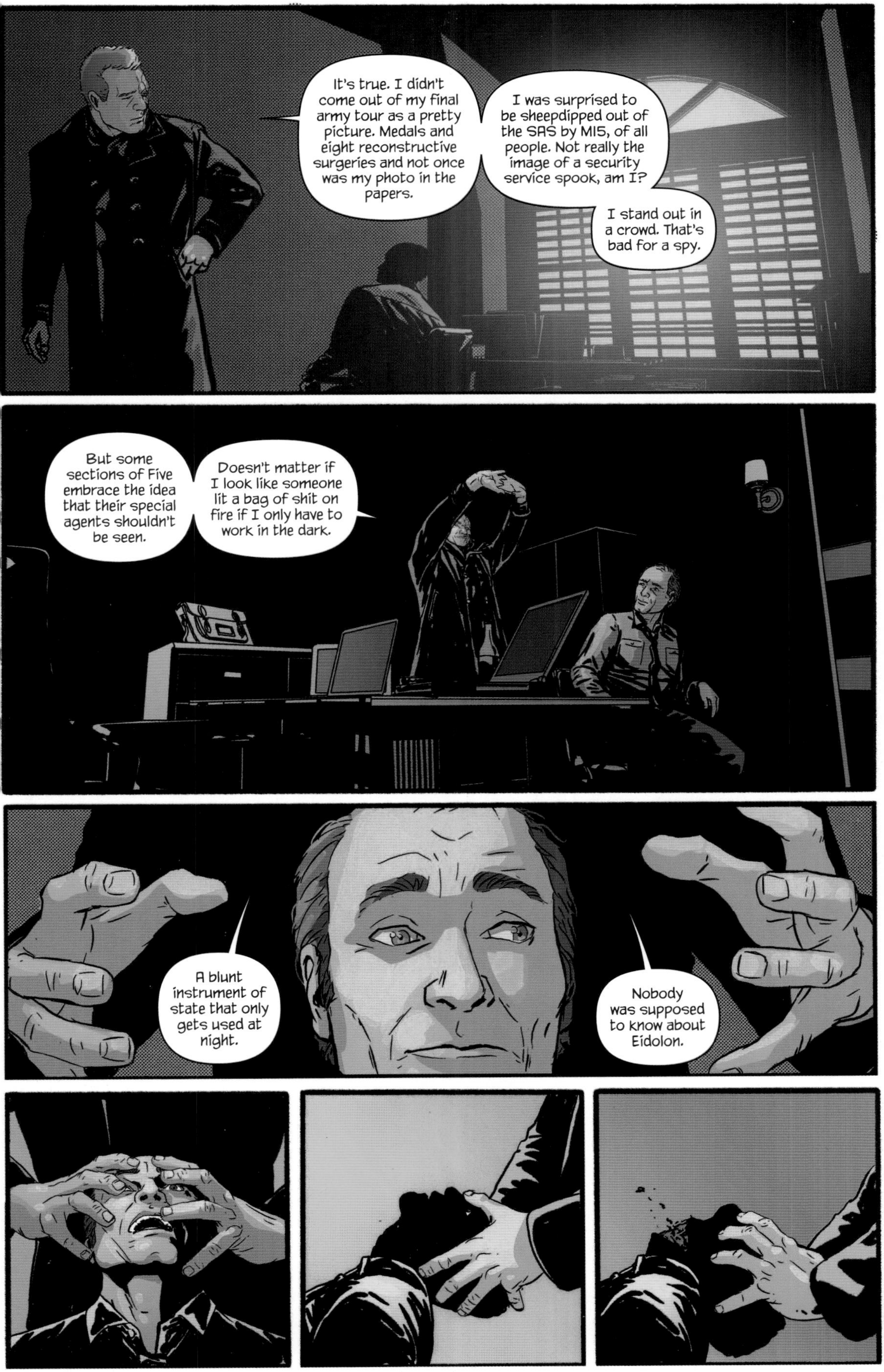
It's true. I didn't come out of my final army tour as a pretty picture. Medals and eight reconstructive surgeries and not once was my photo in the papers.
I was surprised to be sheepdipped out of the SAS by MI5, of all people. Not really the image of a security service spook, am I?
I stand out in a crowd. That's bad for a spy.
But some sections of Five embrace the idea that their special agents shouldn't be seen.
Doesn't matter if I look like someone lit a bag of shit on fire if I only have to work in the dark.
A blunt instrument of state that only gets used at night.
Nobody was supposed to know about Eidolon.

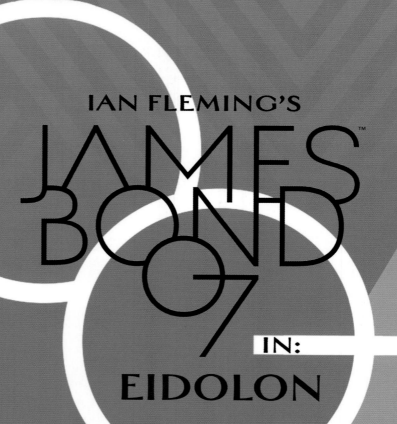

IAN FLEMING'S
JAMES BOND
07

IN:
EIDOLON

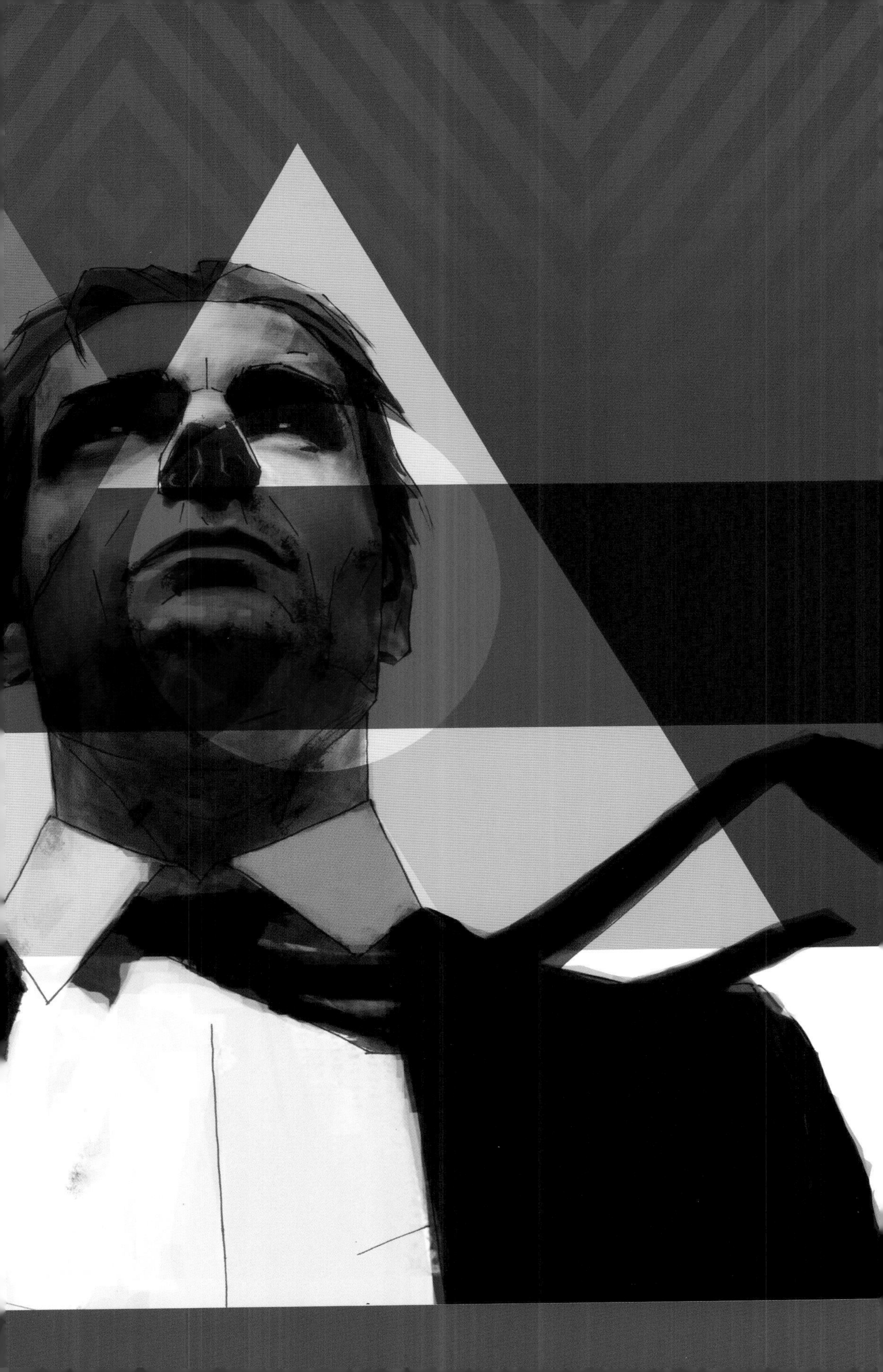

ISBN10: 1-5241-0272-2   ISBN13: 978-1-5241-0272-2   First Printing   10 9 8 7 6 5 4 3 2 1

Online at **www.DYNAMITE.com**
On Facebook **/Dynamitecomics**
On Instagram **/Dynamitecomics**
On Tumblr **dynamitecomics.tumblr.com**
On Twitter **@dynamitecomics**
On YouTube **/Dynamitecomics**

Nick Barrucci, CEO / Publisher
Juan Collado, President / COO

Joe Rybandt, Executive Editor
Matt Idelson, Senior Editor
Anthony Marques, Associate Editor
Kevin Ketner, Assistant Editor

Jason Ullmeyer, Art Director
Geoff Harkins, Senior Graphic Designer
Cathleen Heard, Senior Graphic Designer
Alexis Persson, Graphic Designer

Chris Caniano, Digital Associate
Rachel Kilbury, Digital Multimedia Associate

Brandon Dante Primavera, V.P. of IT and Operations
Rich Young, Director of Business Development

Alan Payne, V.P. of Sales and Marketing
Pat O'Connell, Sales Manager

JAMES BOND CREATED BY IAN FLEMING
WRITTEN BY:
WARREN ELLIS
ILLUSTRATED BY:
JASON MASTERS
COLORED BY:
GUY MAJOR
LETTERED BY:
SIMON BOWLAND
COLLECTION COVER BY:
DOM REARDON

EXECUTIVE EDITOR:
JOSEPH RYBANDT
ASSOCIATE EDITOR:
ANTHONY MARQUES
EDITORIAL CONSULTANT:
MICHAEL LAKE

COLLECTION DESIGN:
CATHLEEN HEARD
LOGO AND FRONT COVER DESIGN:
RIAN HUGHES

SPECIAL THANKS TO:
JOSEPHINE LANE, CORINNE TURNER,
AND DIGGORY LAYCOCK AT
IAN FLEMING PUBLICATIONS LTD.
AND JONNY GELLER AT CURTIS BROWN

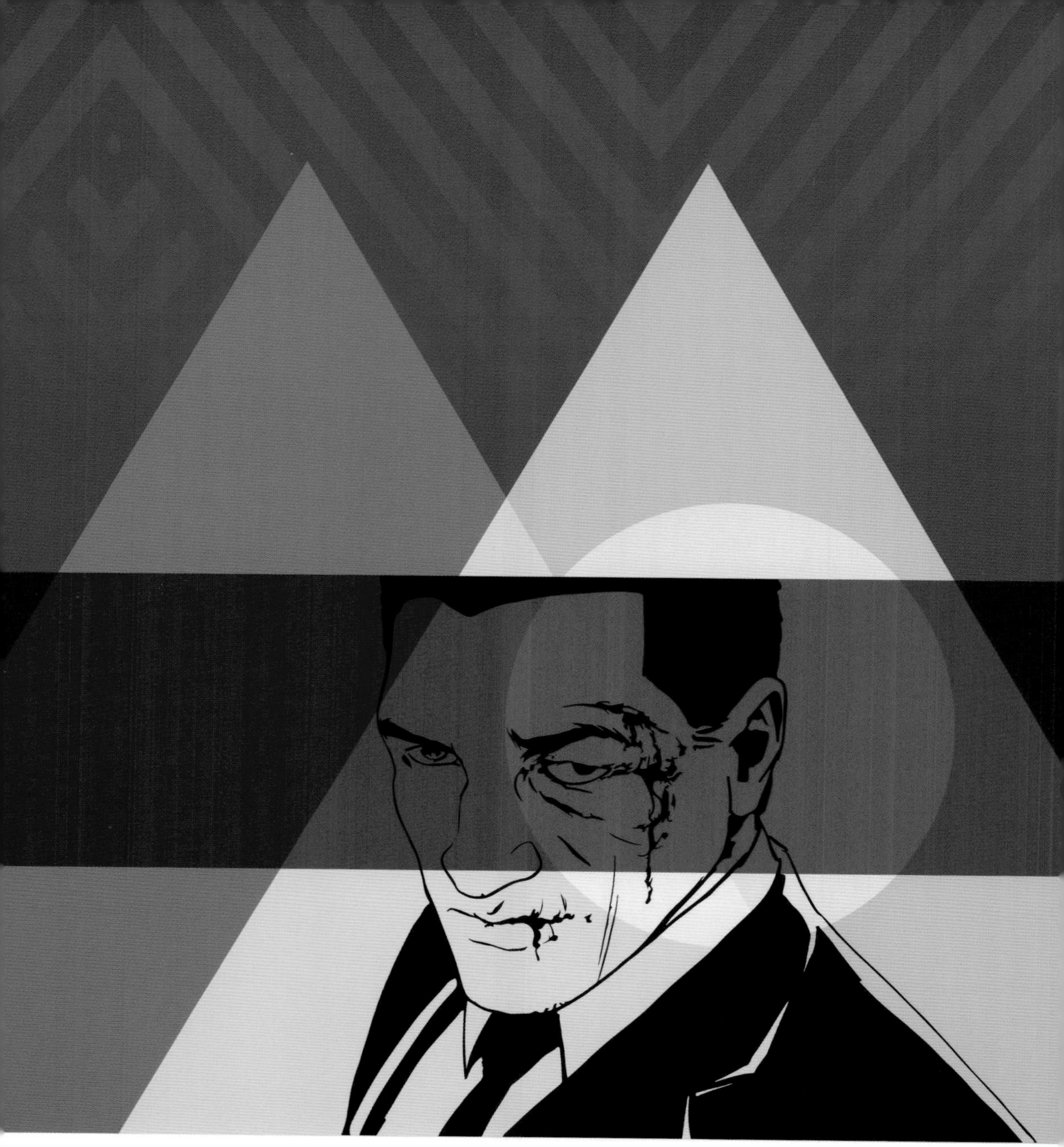

issue seven

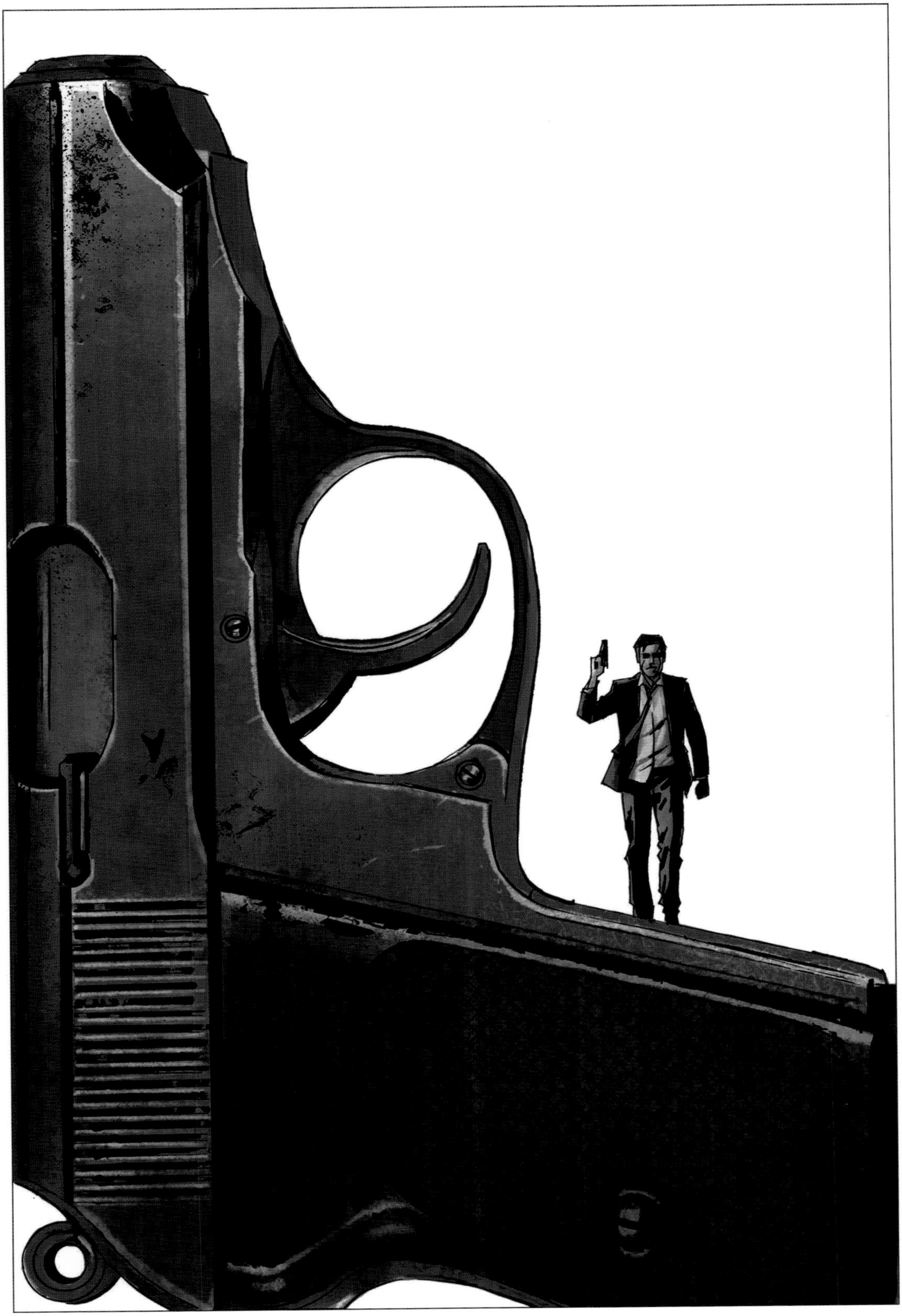

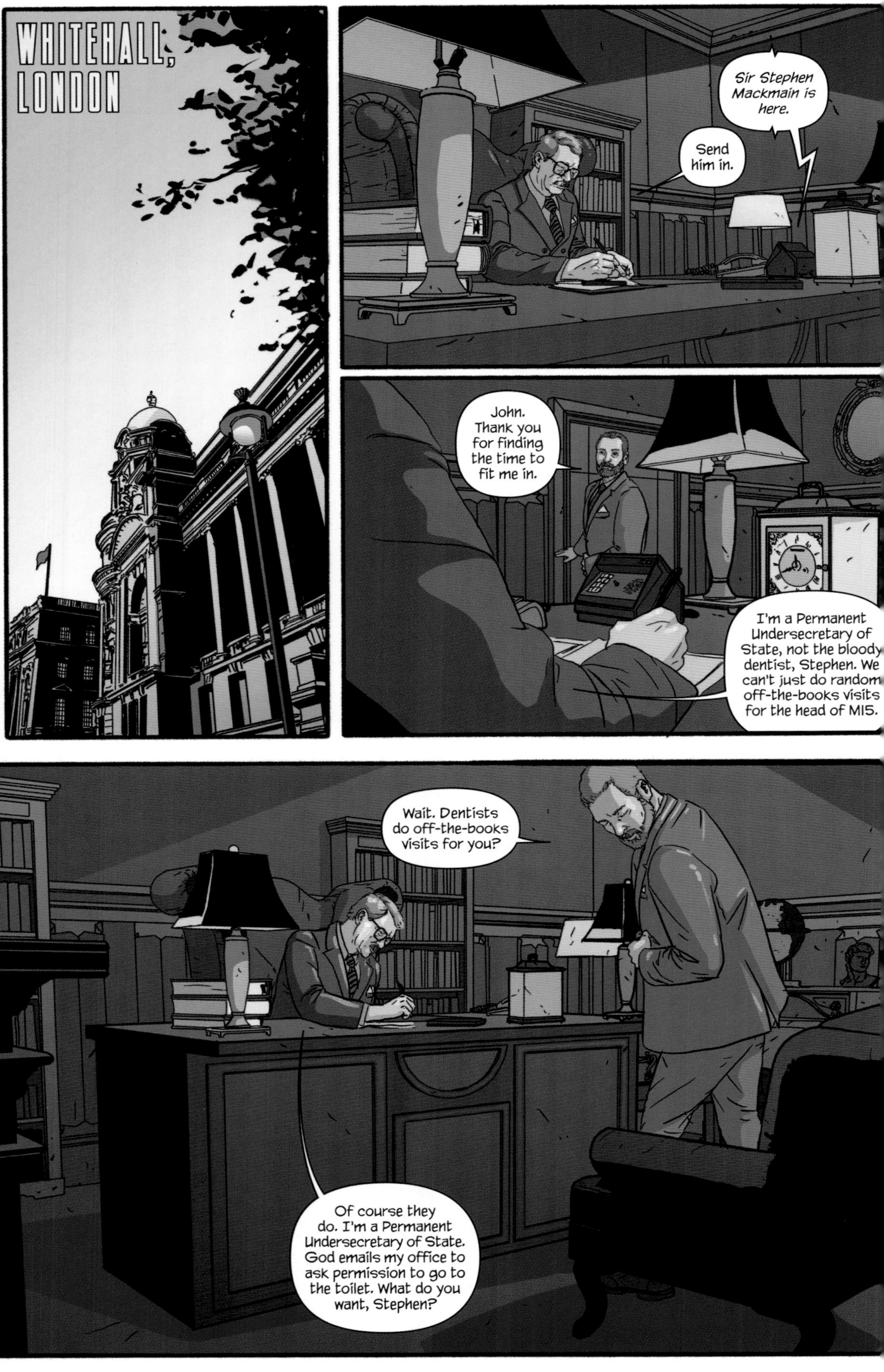
WHITEHALL, LONDON
Sir Stephen Mackmain is here.
Send him in.
John. Thank you for finding the time to fit me in.
I'm a Permanent Undersecretary of State, not the bloody dentist, Stephen. We can't just do random off-the-books visits for the head of MI5.
Wait. Dentists do off-the-books visits for you?
Of course they do. I'm a Permanent Undersecretary of State. God emails my office to ask permission to go to the toilet. What do you want, Stephen?

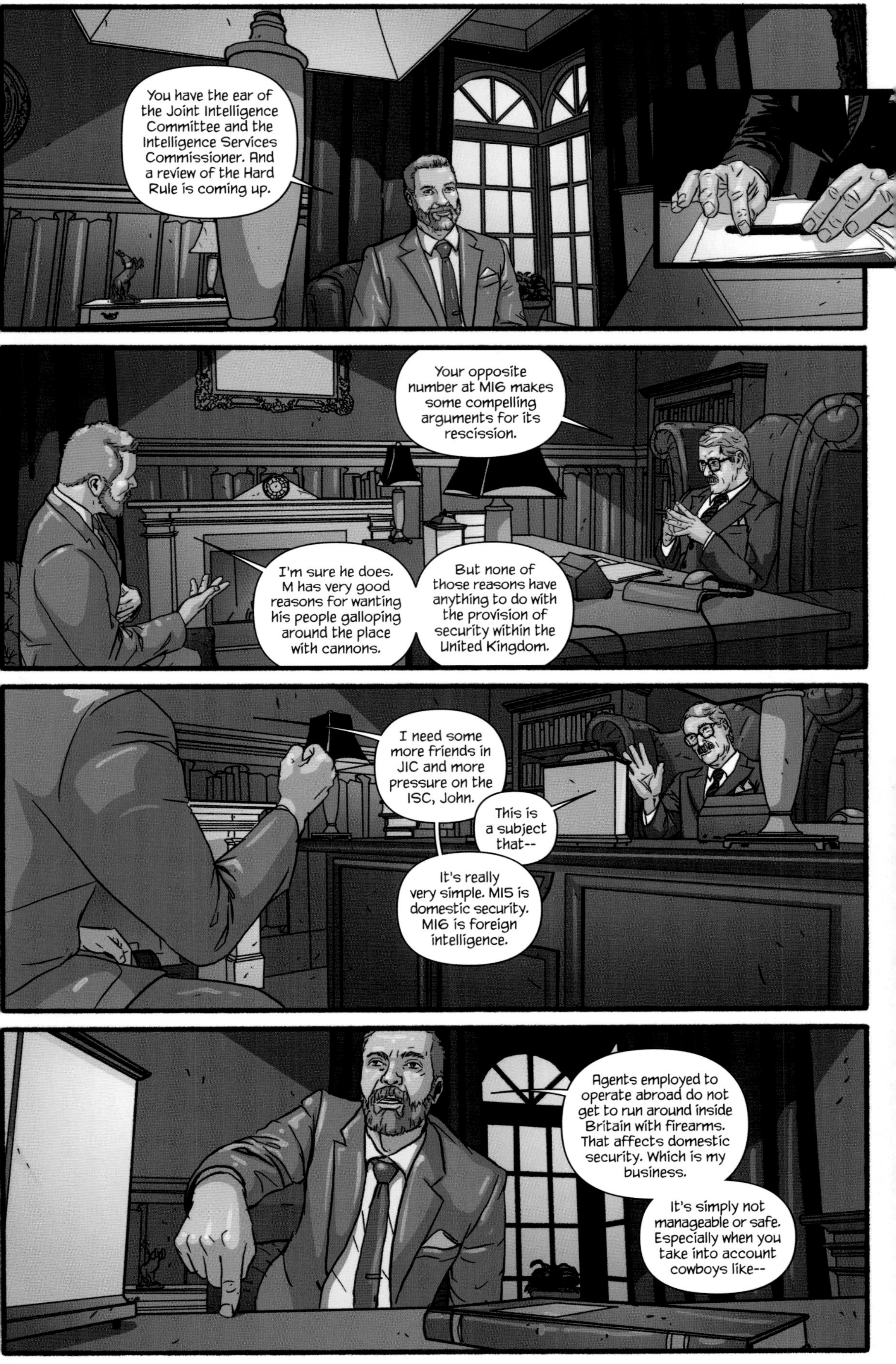
You have the ear of the Joint Intelligence Committee and the Intelligence Services Commissioner. And a review of the Hard Rule is coming up.
Your opposite number at MI6 makes some compelling arguments for its rescission.
I'm sure he does. M has very good reasons for wanting his people galloping around the place with cannons.
But none of those reasons have anything to do with the provision of security within the United Kingdom.
I need some more friends in JIC and more pressure on the ISC, John.
This is a subject that--
It's really very simple. MI5 is domestic security. MI6 is foreign intelligence.
Agents employed to operate abroad do not get to run around inside Britain with firearms. That affects domestic security. Which is my business.
It's simply not manageable or safe. Especially when you take into account cowboys like--

↑ ✈ Arrivals
← 🚗 Car Rental
→ 🚻 Toilets
→ ℹ Info
← 🚶 Check in
→ 🍴 Food

LOS ANGELES
INTERNATIONAL
AIRPORT

James.

A29   A30   TOM BRADLEY
                INTERNATIONAL TERMINAL

Felix Leiter, of all people. Why on Earth would you be waiting for me at LAX?

Consider it a very, very quiet welcome. Good to see you.

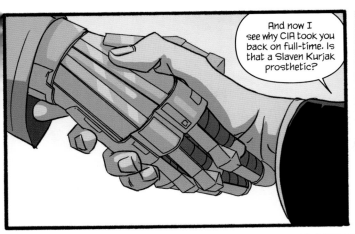

And now I see why CIA took you back on full-time. Is that a Slaven Kurjak prosthetic?

The leg, too. Though I hear that maybe I might have problems with the repair warranty in the future.

Thanks, buddy.

Sorry about that.

I don't hold grudges. It's not like I tell people it's your fault the arm and the leg got eaten by a shark in the first place.

It wasn't.

Why are you here, Felix?

We know what you're doing.

Really.

You're lifting an agent from the Diplomatic Wing of MI6 from her post in the Turkish Consulate here in LA.

We're the CIA, James.

Yes, yes, you're so special.

Her secure comms got hacked overnight. We're assuming her cover's blown, so I'm walking her out on the next flight before Millî İstihbarat Teşkilatı get involved.

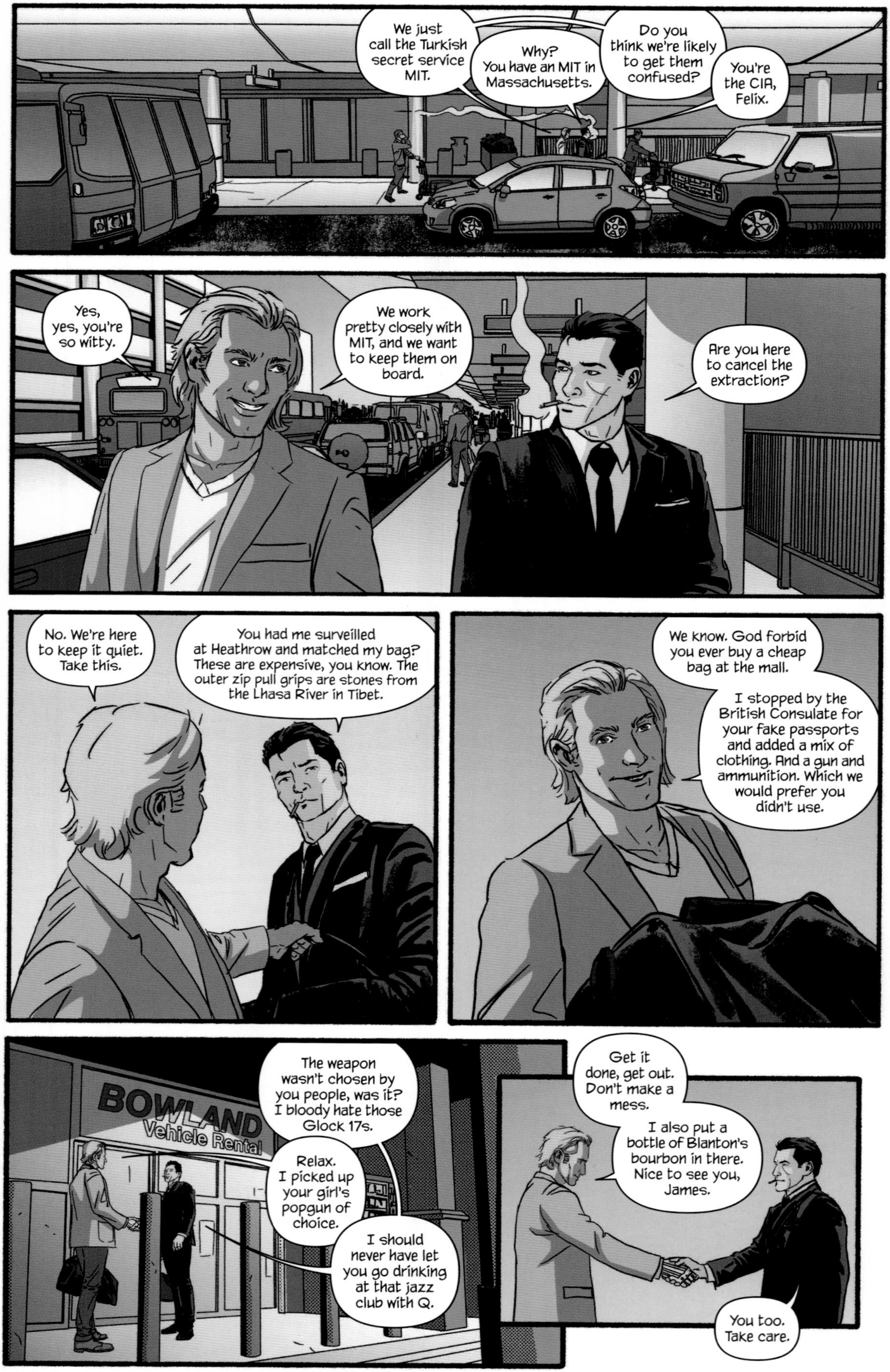
We just call the Turkish secret service MIT.
Why? You have an MIT in Massachusetts.
Do you think we're likely to get them confused?
You're the CIA, Felix.
Yes, yes, you're so witty.
We work pretty closely with MIT, and we want to keep them on board.
Are you here to cancel the extraction?
No. We're here to keep it quiet. Take this.
You had me surveilled at Heathrow and matched my bag? These are expensive, you know. The outer zip pull grips are stones from the Lhasa River in Tibet.
We know. God forbid you ever buy a cheap bag at the mall.
I stopped by the British Consulate for your fake passports and added a mix of clothing. And a gun and ammunition. Which we would prefer you didn't use.
BOWLAND
Vehicle Rental
The weapon wasn't chosen by you people, was it? I bloody hate those Glock 17s.
Relax. I picked up your girl's popgun of choice.
I should never have let you go drinking at that jazz club with Q.
Get it done, get out. Don't make a mess.
I also put a bottle of Blanton's bourbon in there. Nice to see you, James.
You too. Take care.

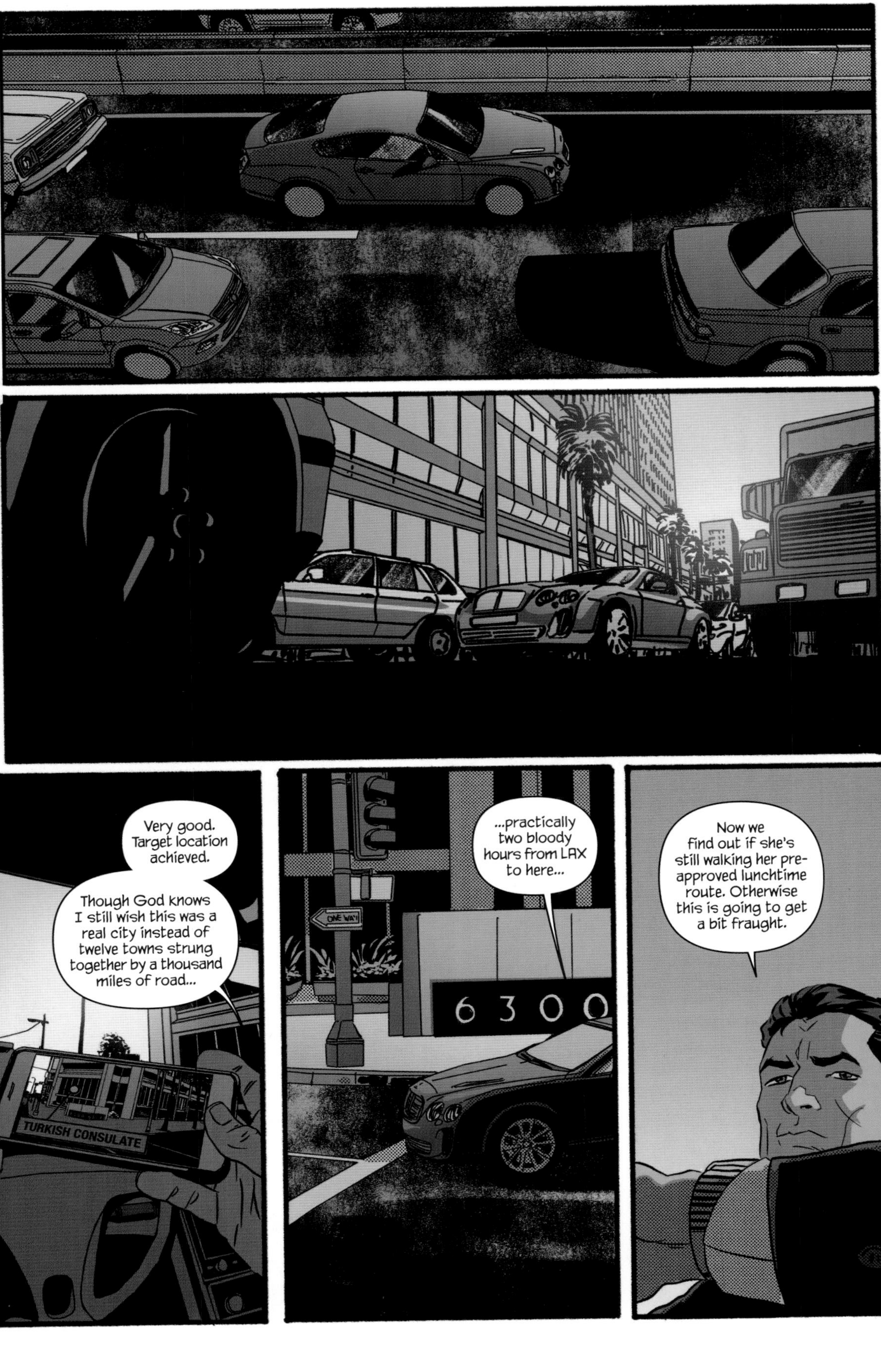
Very good. Target location achieved.
Though God knows I still wish this was a real city instead of twelve towns strung together by a thousand miles of road...
TURKISH CONSULATE
ONE WAY
...practically two bloody hours from LAX to here...
6300
Now we find out if she's still walking her pre-approved lunchtime route. Otherwise this is going to get a bit fraught.

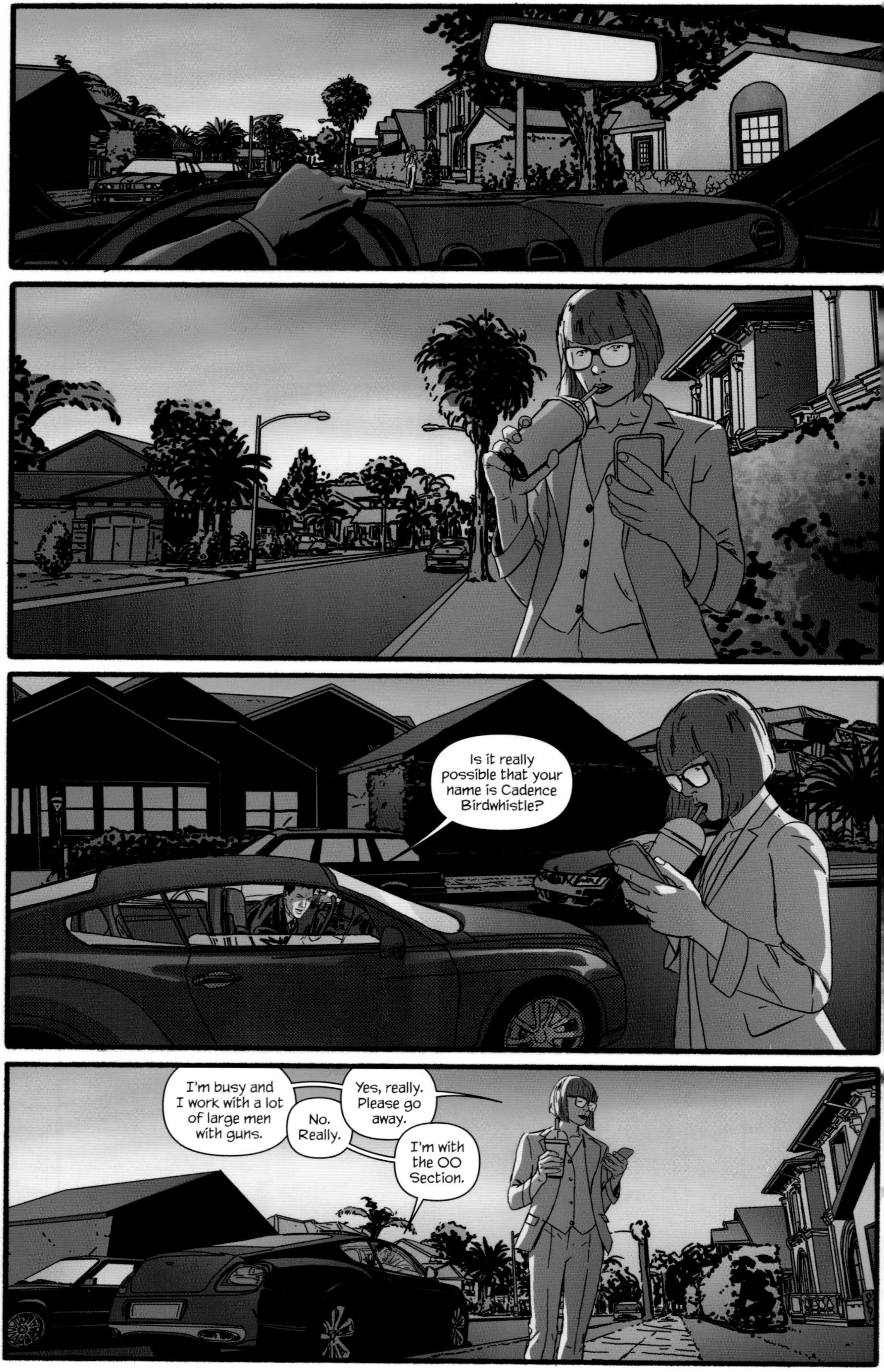
Is it really possible that your name is Cadence Birdwhistle?
I'm busy and I work with a lot of large men with guns.
Yes, really. Please go away.
No. Really.
I'm with the OO Section.

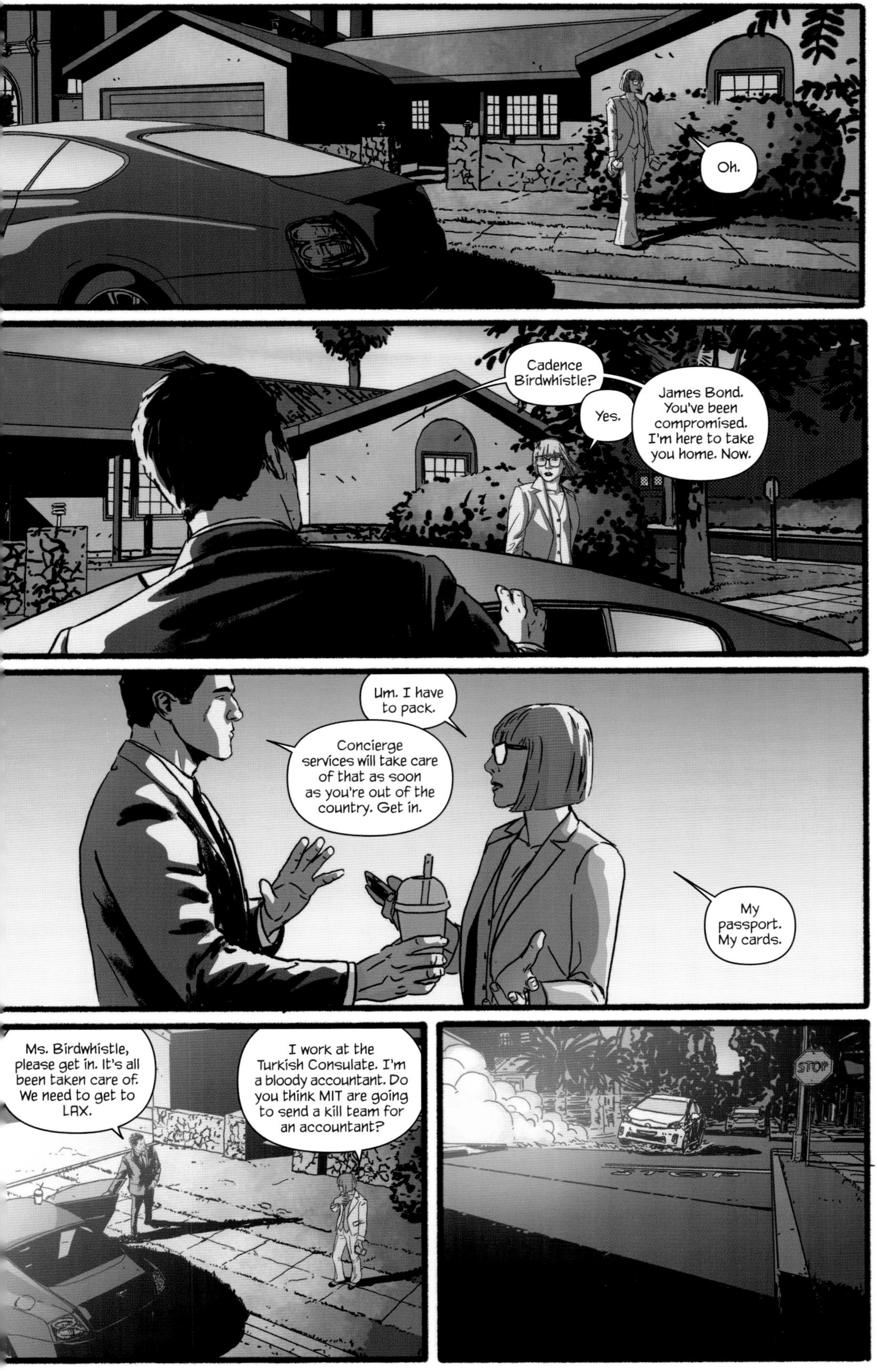
Oh.
Cadence Birdwhistle?
Yes.
James Bond. You've been compromised. I'm here to take you home. Now.
Um. I have to pack.
Concierge services will take care of that as soon as you're out of the country. Get in.
My passport. My cards.
Ms. Birdwhistle, please get in. It's all been taken care of. We need to get to LAX.
I work at the Turkish Consulate. I'm a bloody accountant. Do you think MIT are going to send a kill team for an accountant?
STOP
STOP

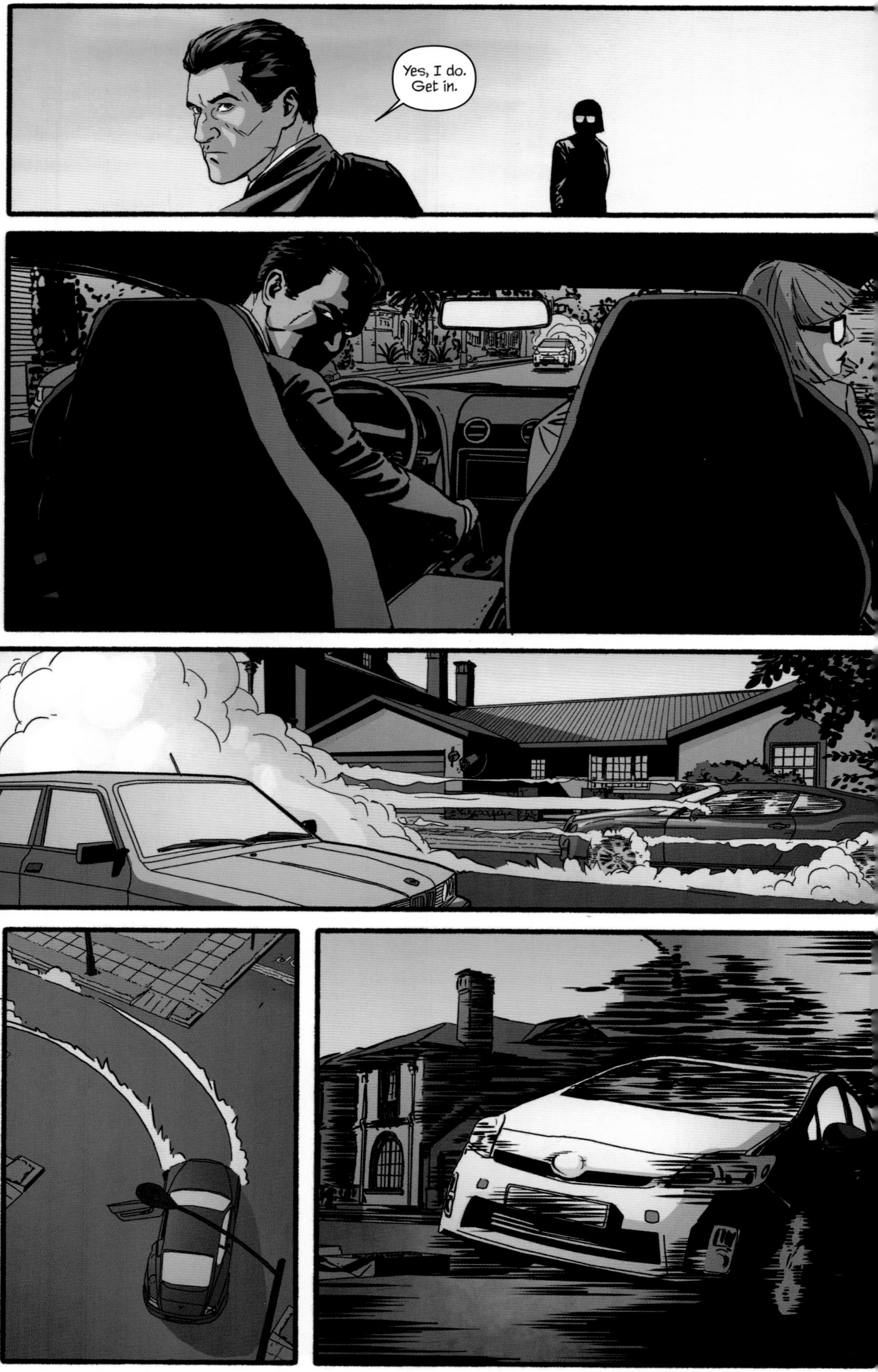
Yes, I do. Get in.

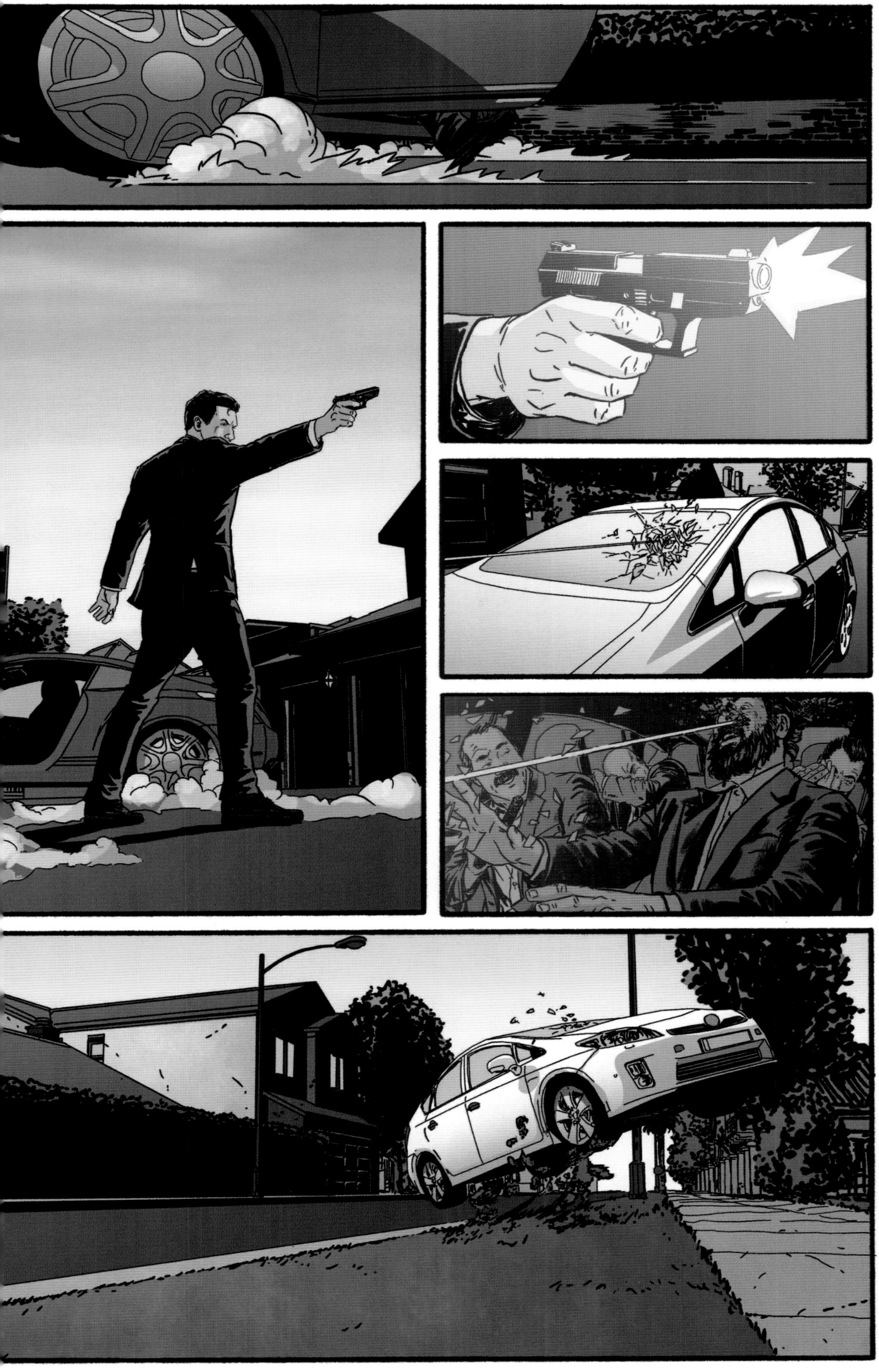

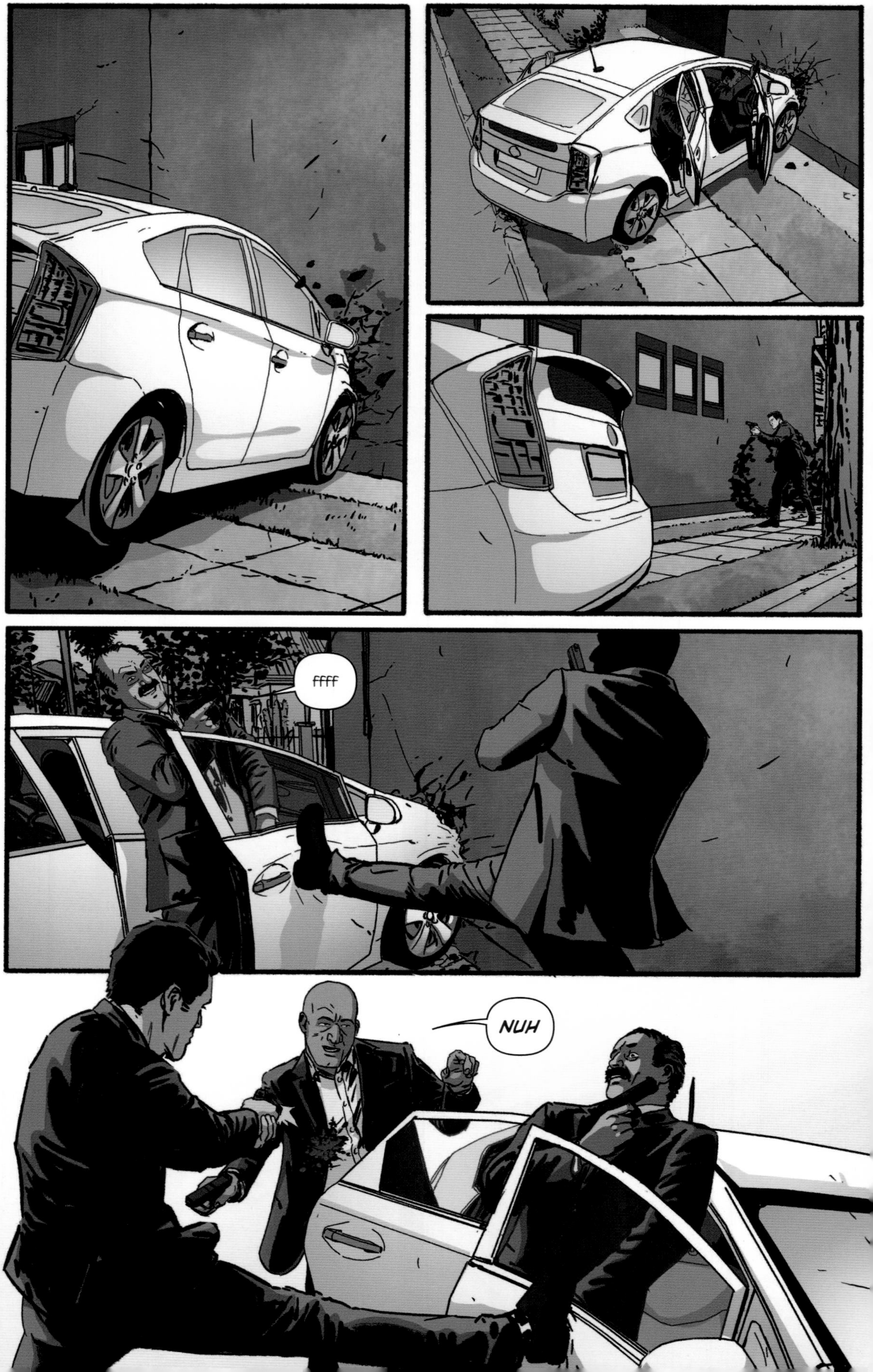
ffff
NUH

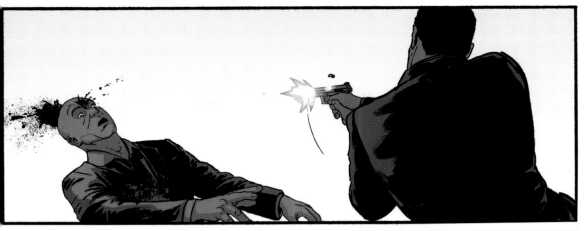

Soysuz
pezevenk--

Geri bas!

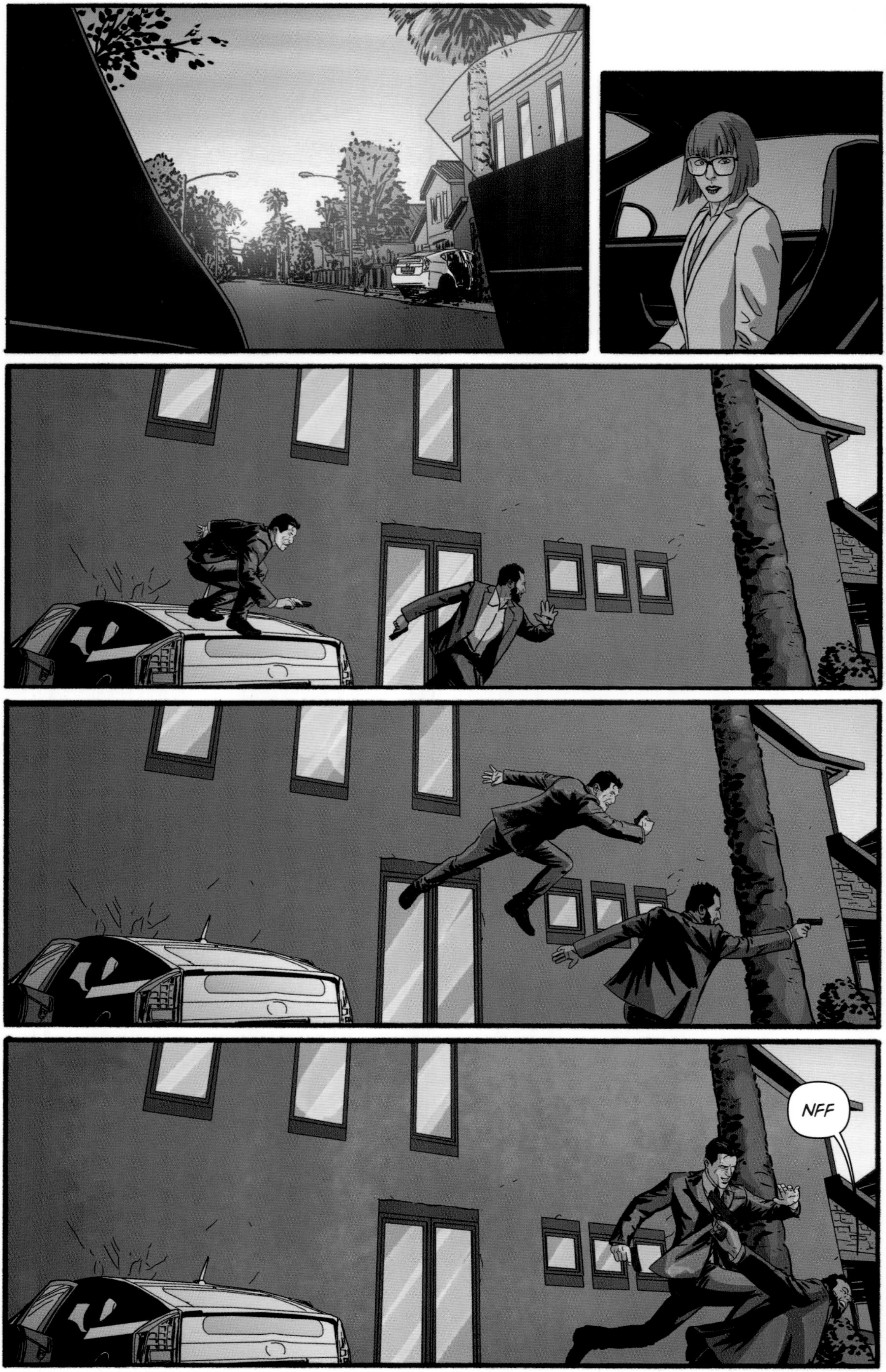
NFF

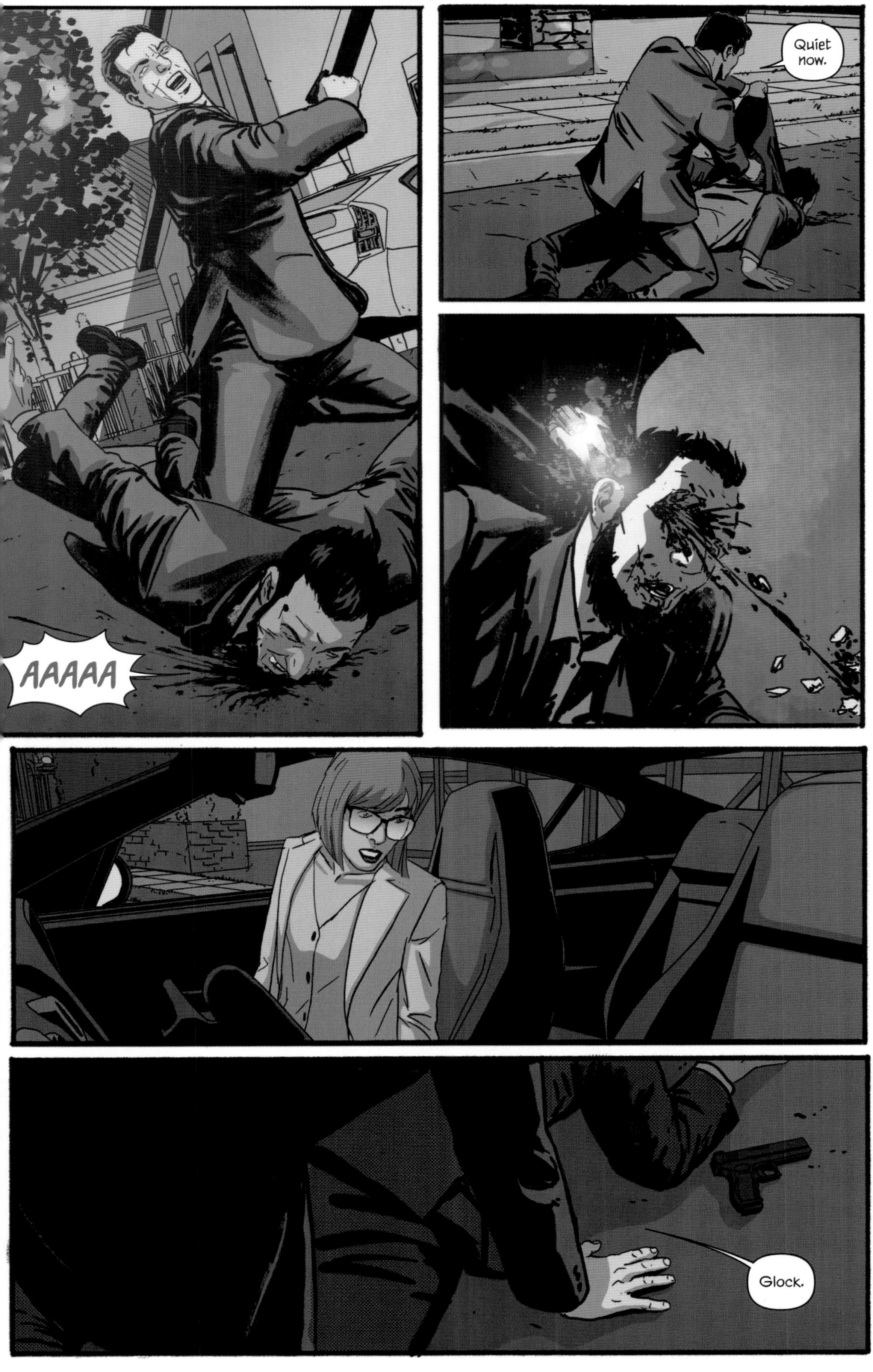
AAAAA
Quiet now.
Glock.

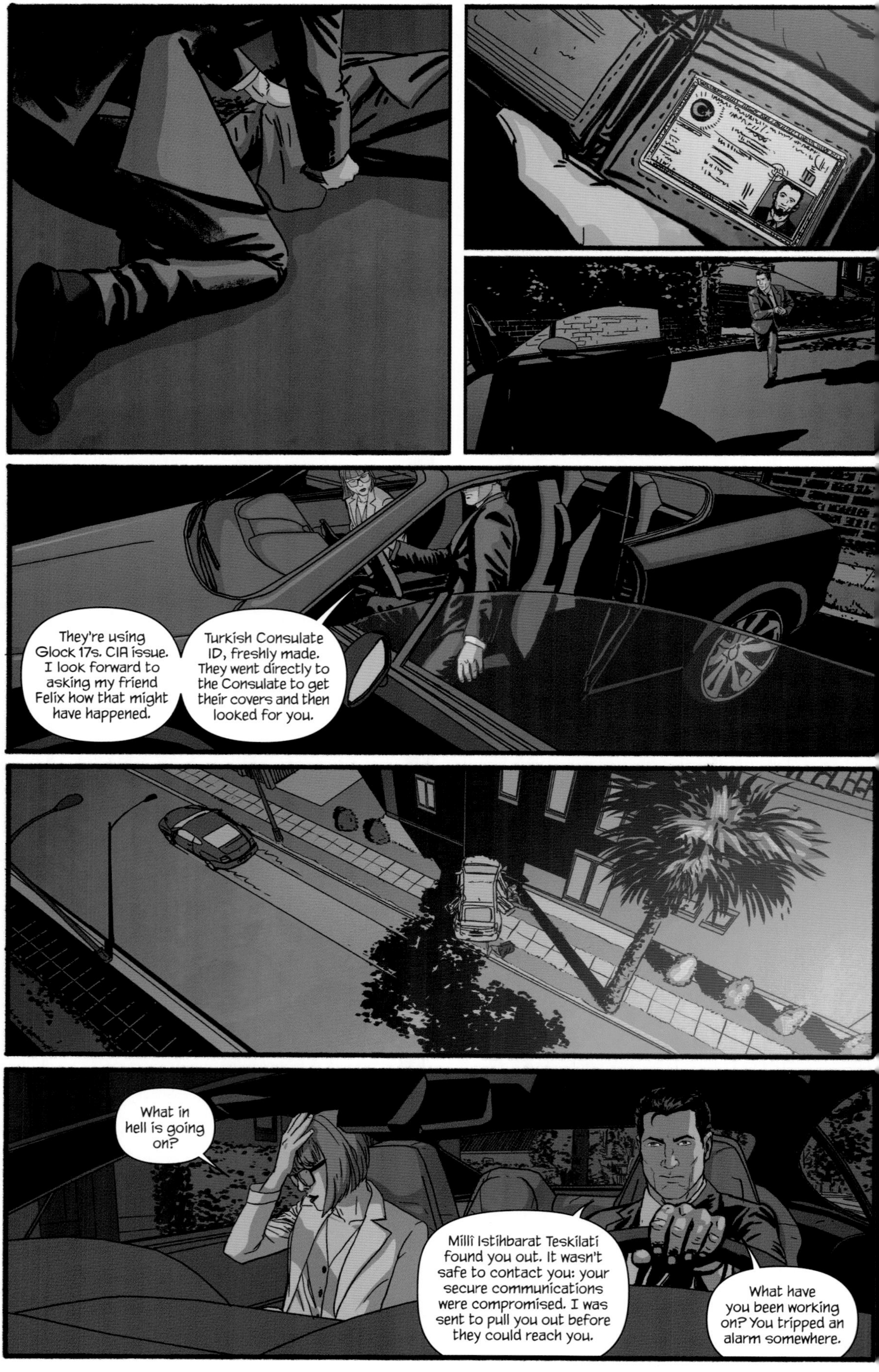

They're using Glock 17s. CIA issue. I look forward to asking my friend Felix how that might have happened.
Turkish Consulate ID, freshly made. They went directly to the Consulate to get their covers and then looked for you.
What in hell is going on?
Millî Istihbarat Teskilati found you out. It wasn't safe to contact you: your secure communications were compromised. I was sent to pull you out before they could reach you.
What have you been working on? You tripped an alarm somewhere.

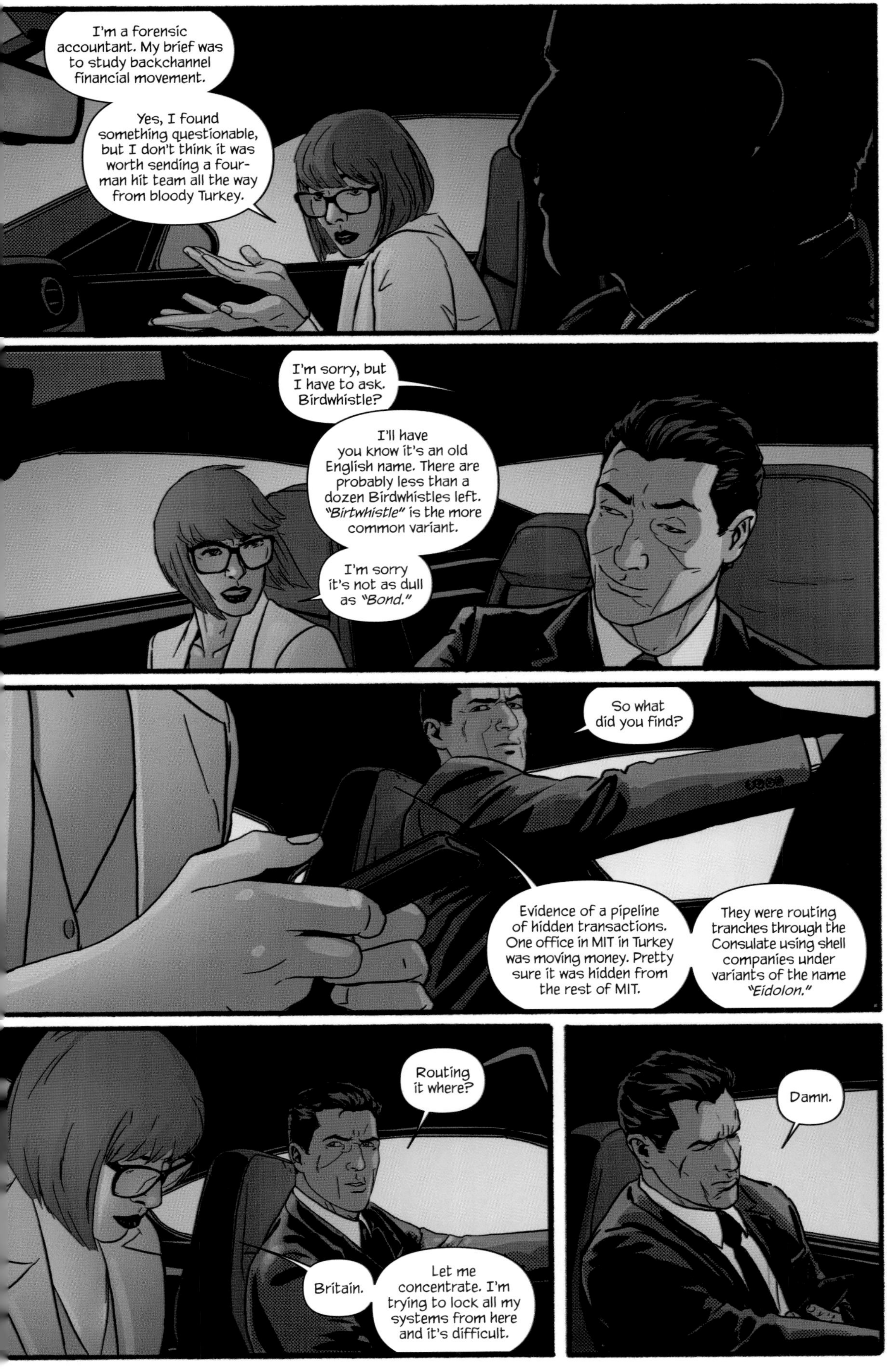
I'm a forensic accountant. My brief was to study backchannel financial movement.
Yes, I found something questionable, but I don't think it was worth sending a four-man hit team all the way from bloody Turkey.
I'm sorry, but I have to ask. Birdwhistle?
I'll have you know it's an old English name. There are probably less than a dozen Birdwhistles left. *"Birtwhistle"* is the more common variant.
I'm sorry it's not as dull as *"Bond."*
So what did you find?
Evidence of a pipeline of hidden transactions. One office in MIT in Turkey was moving money. Pretty sure it was hidden from the rest of MIT.
They were routing tranches through the Consulate using shell companies under variants of the name *"Eidolon."*
Routing it where?
Britain.
Let me concentrate. I'm trying to lock all my systems from here and it's difficult.
Damn.

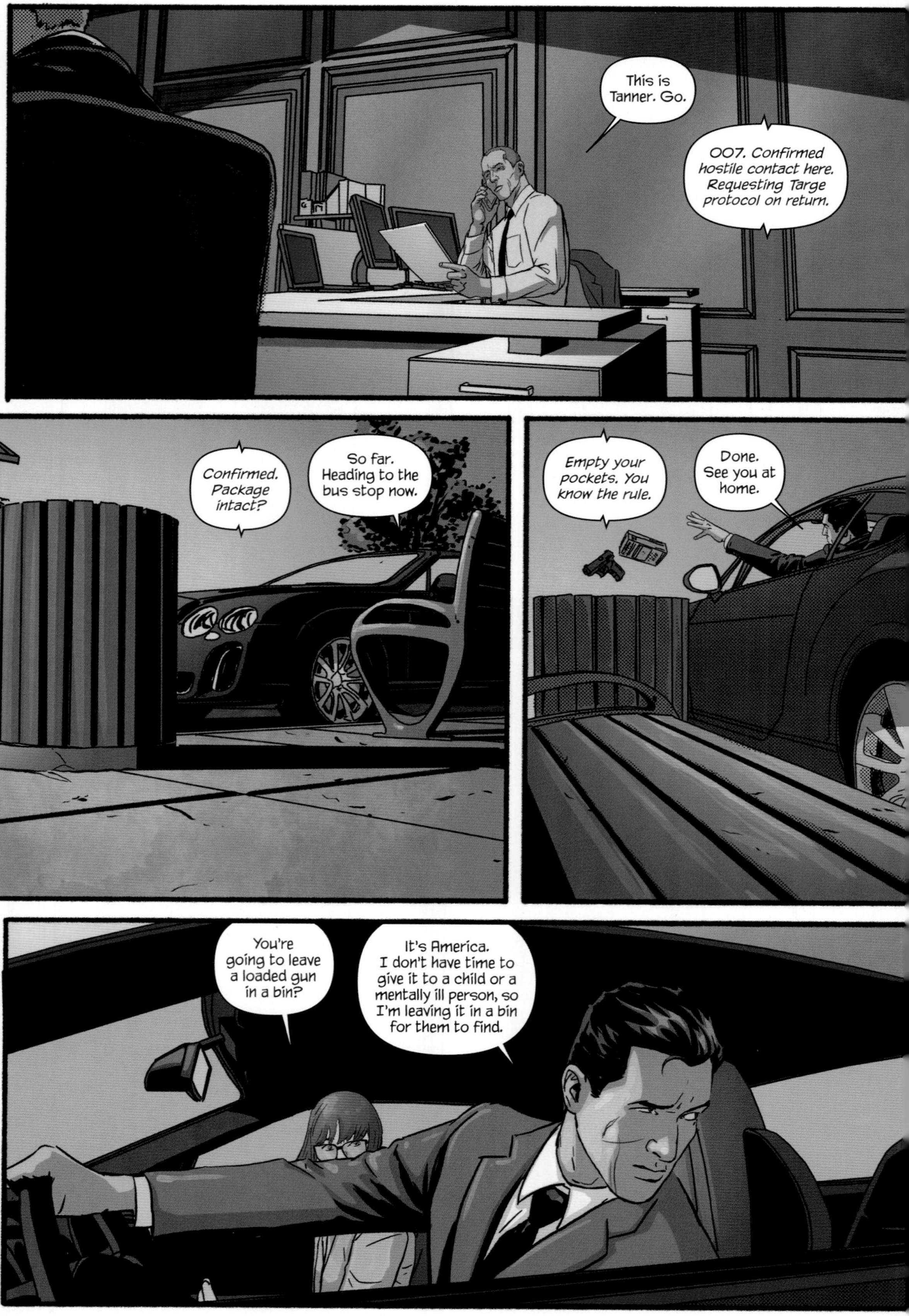
This is Tanner. Go.
007. Confirmed hostile contact here. Requesting Targe protocol on return.
Confirmed. Package intact?
So far. Heading to the bus stop now.
Empty your pockets. You know the rule.
Done. See you at home.
You're going to leave a loaded gun in a bin?
It's America. I don't have time to give it to a child or a mentally ill person, so I'm leaving it in a bin for them to find.

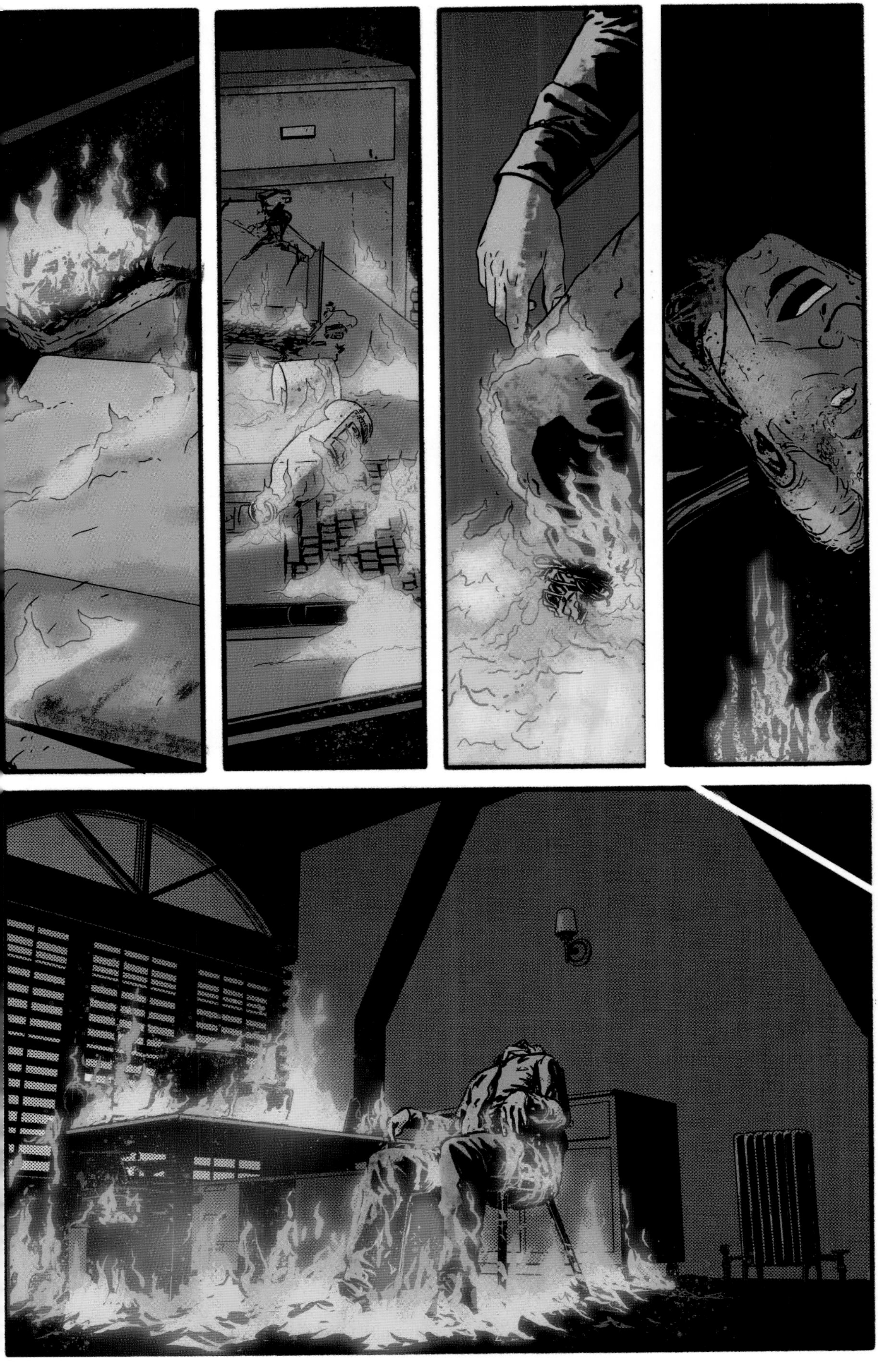

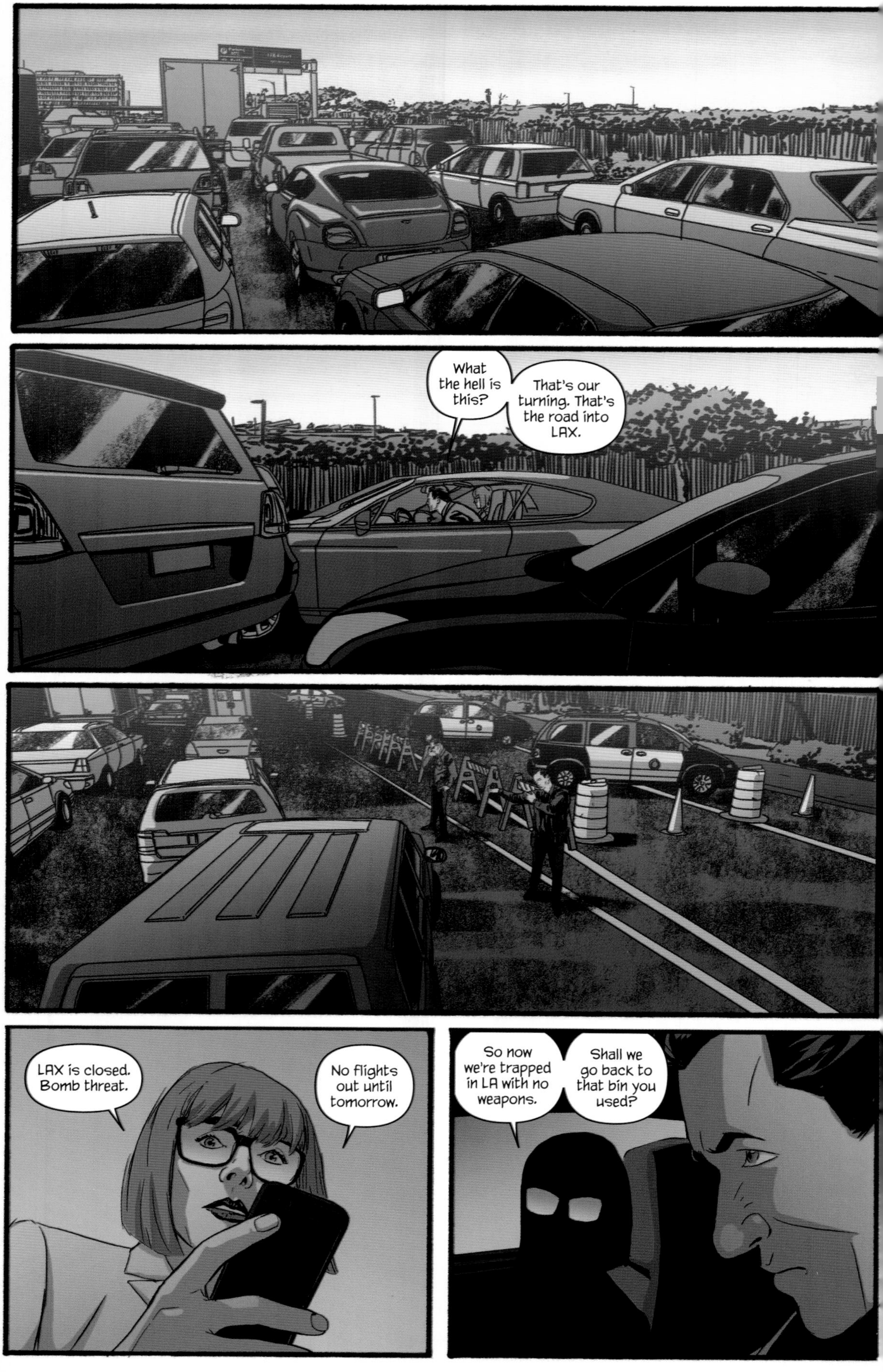
What the hell is this?
That's our turning. That's the road into LAX.
LAX is closed. Bomb threat.
No flights out until tomorrow.
So now we're trapped in LA with no weapons.
Shall we go back to that bin you used?

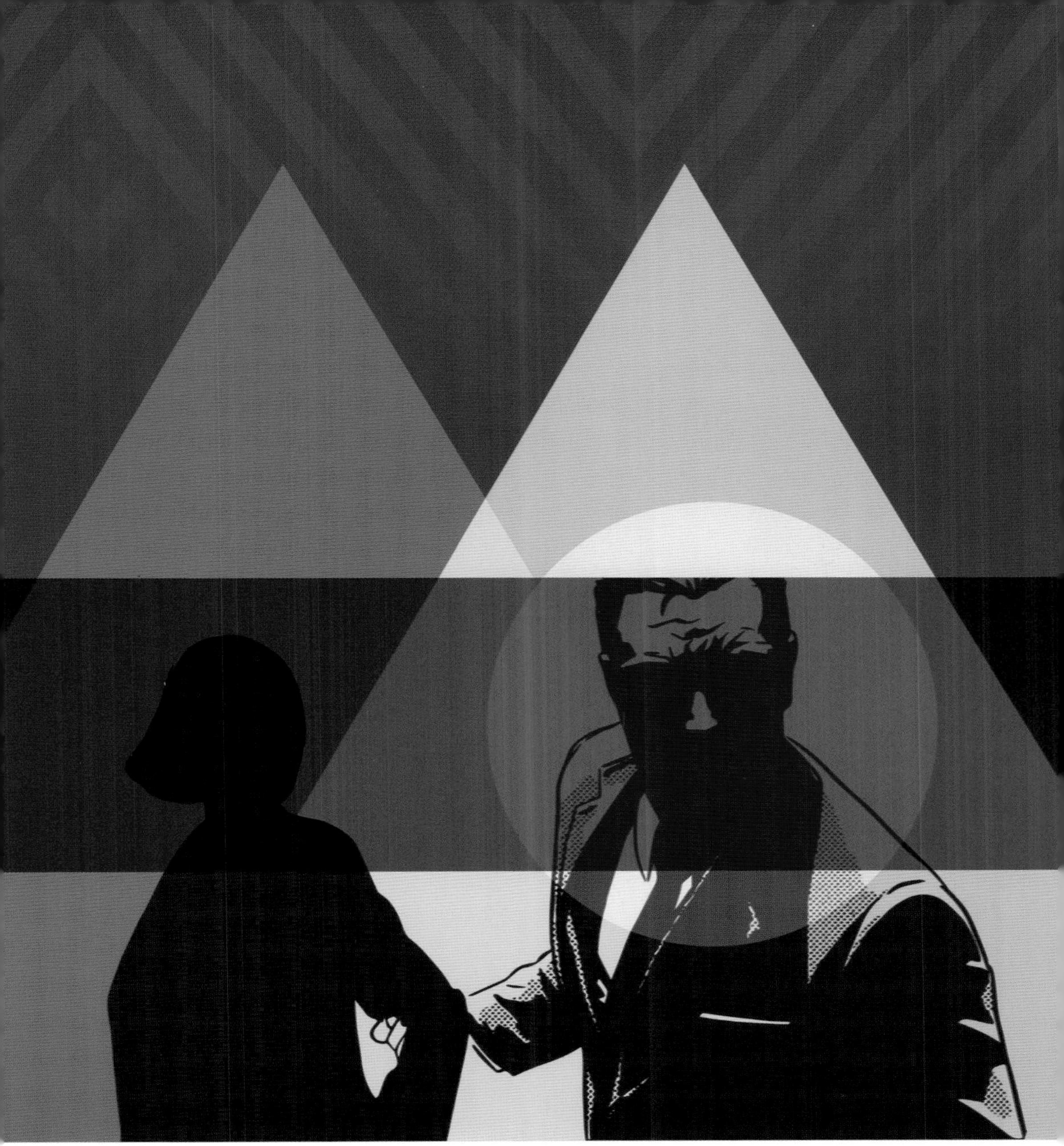

issue eight

issue #8 main cover by **DOM REARDON**

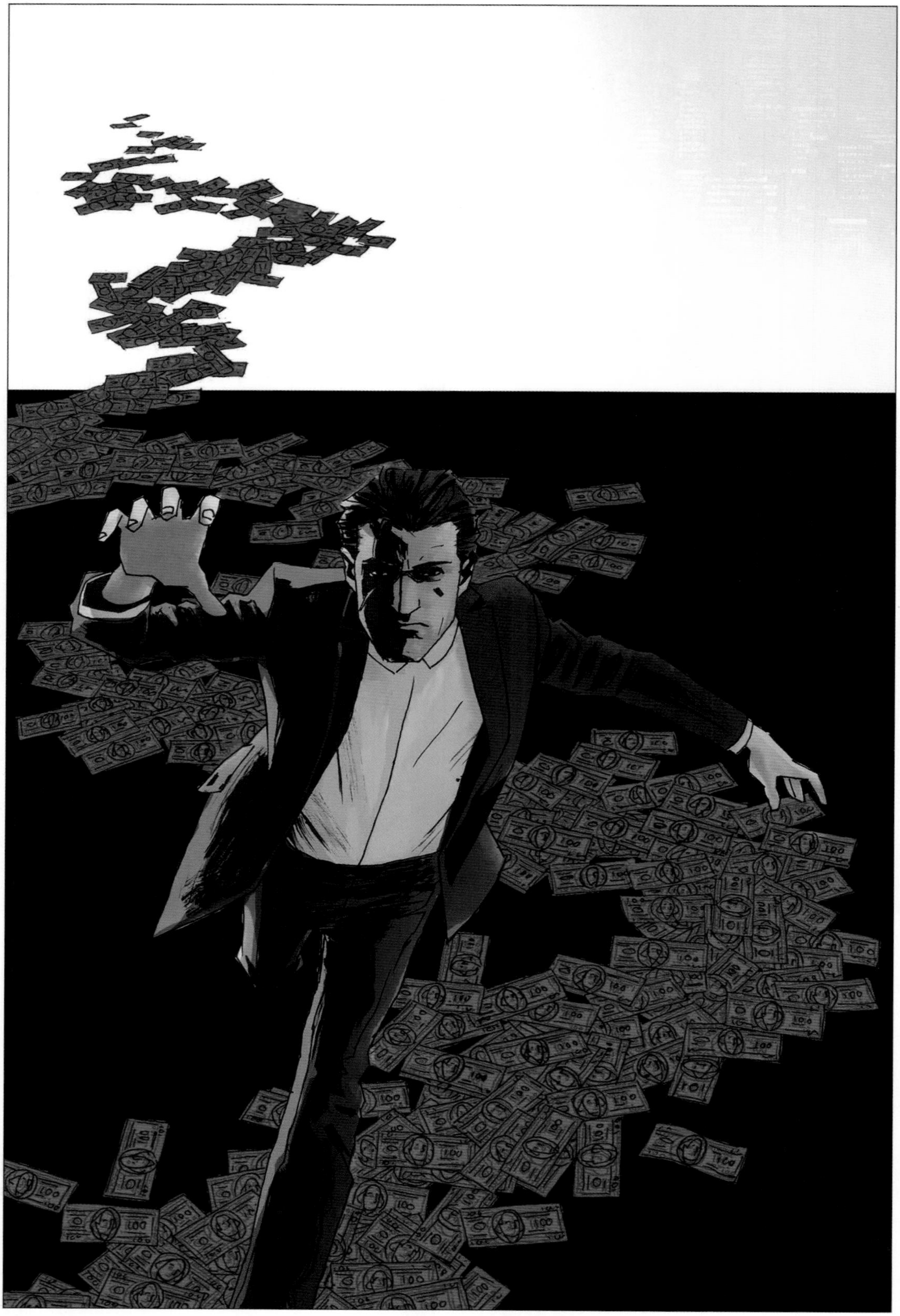

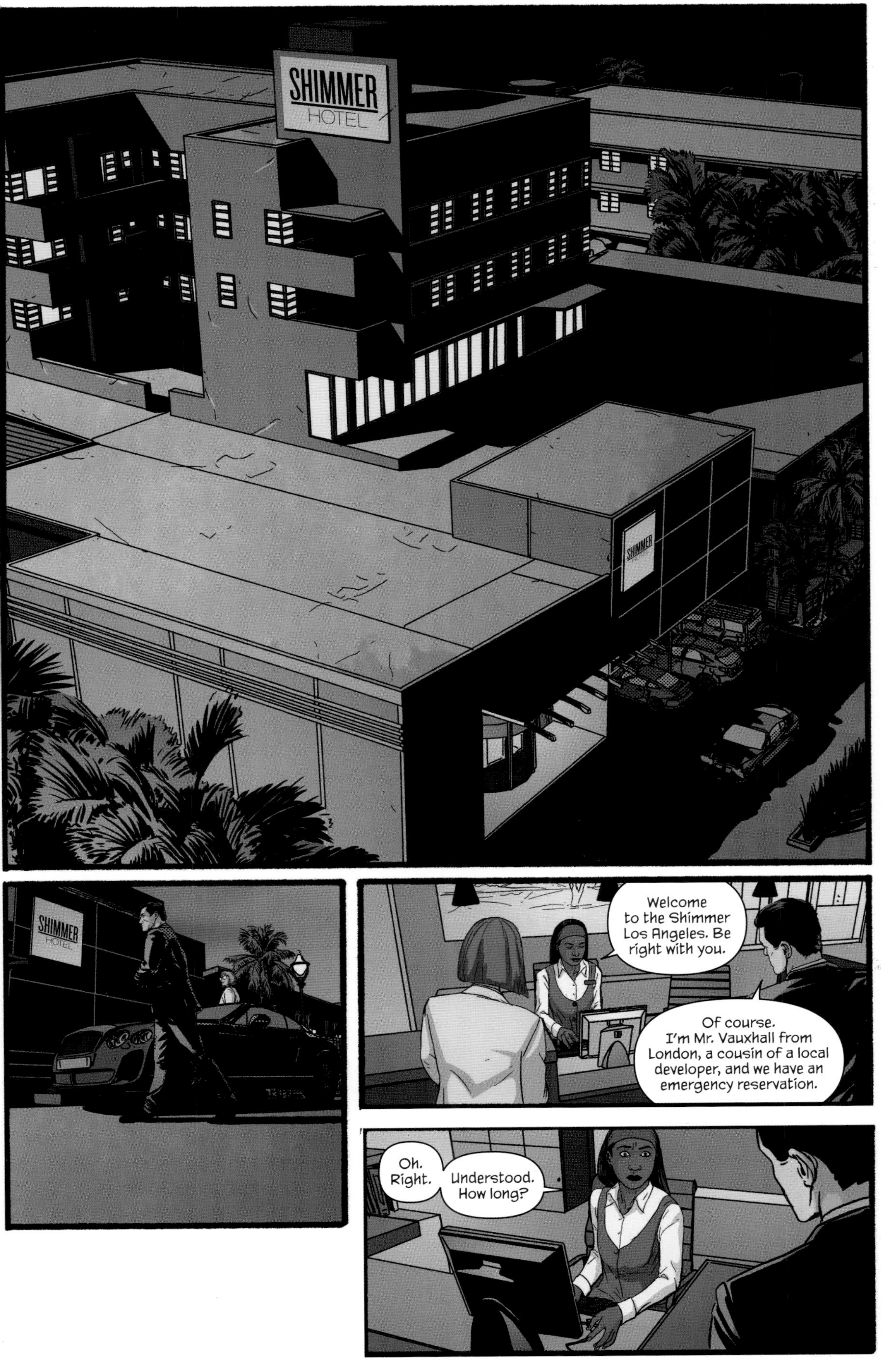
SHIMMER HOTEL
SHIMMER HOTEL
SHIMMER HOTEL
Welcome to the Shimmer Los Angeles. Be right with you.
Of course. I'm Mr. Vauxhall from London, a cousin of a local developer, and we have an emergency reservation.
Oh. Right.
Understood. How long?

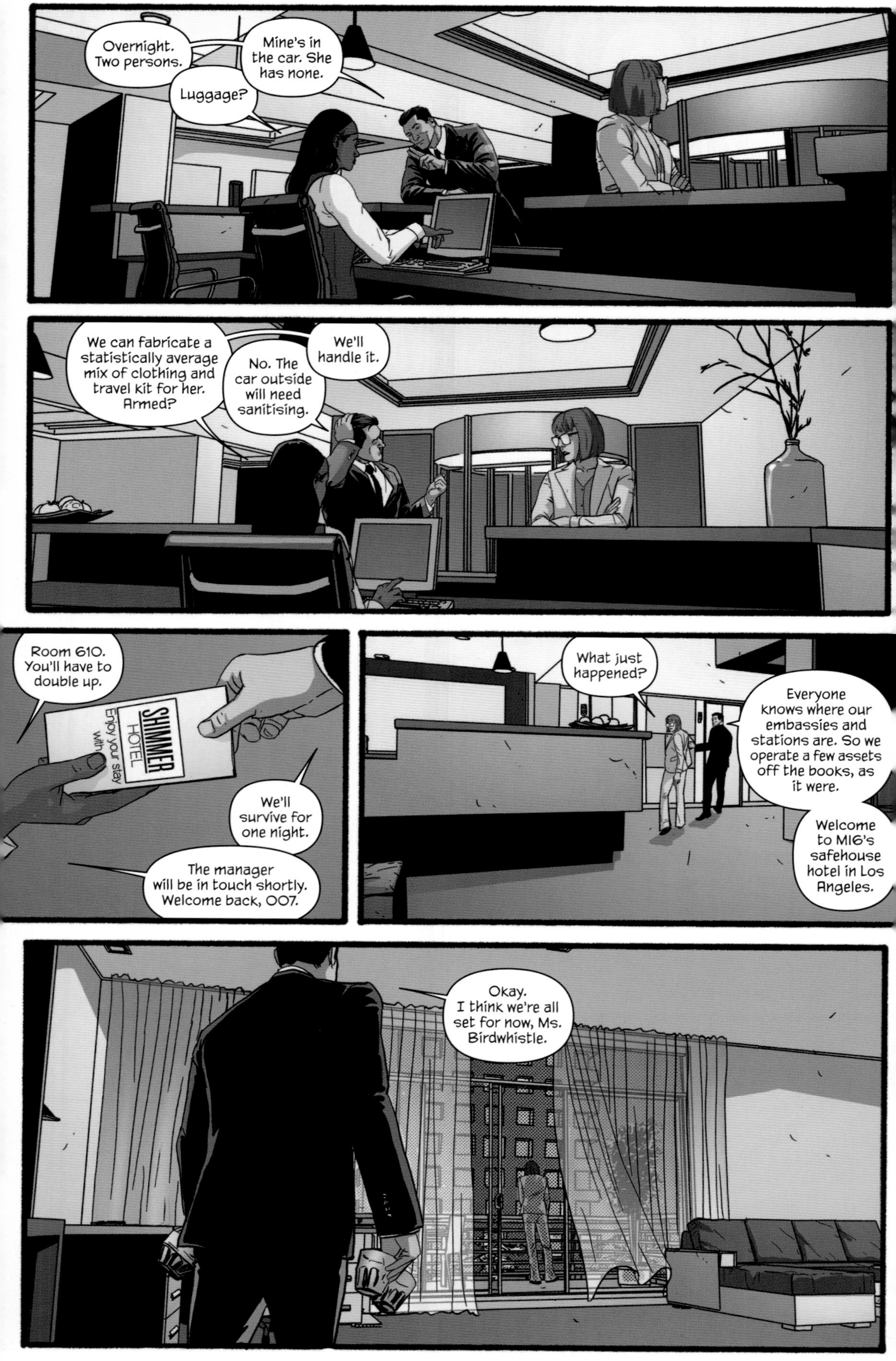
Overnight. Two persons.
Luggage?
Mine's in the car. She has none.
We can fabricate a statistically average mix of clothing and travel kit for her. Armed?
No. The car outside will need sanitising.
We'll handle it.
Room 610. You'll have to double up.
SHIMMER HOTEL
Enjoy your stay with
We'll survive for one night.
The manager will be in touch shortly. Welcome back, 007.
What just happened?
Everyone knows where our embassies and stations are. So we operate a few assets off the books, as it were.
Welcome to MI6's safehouse hotel in Los Angeles.
Okay. I think we're all set for now, Ms. Birdwhistle.

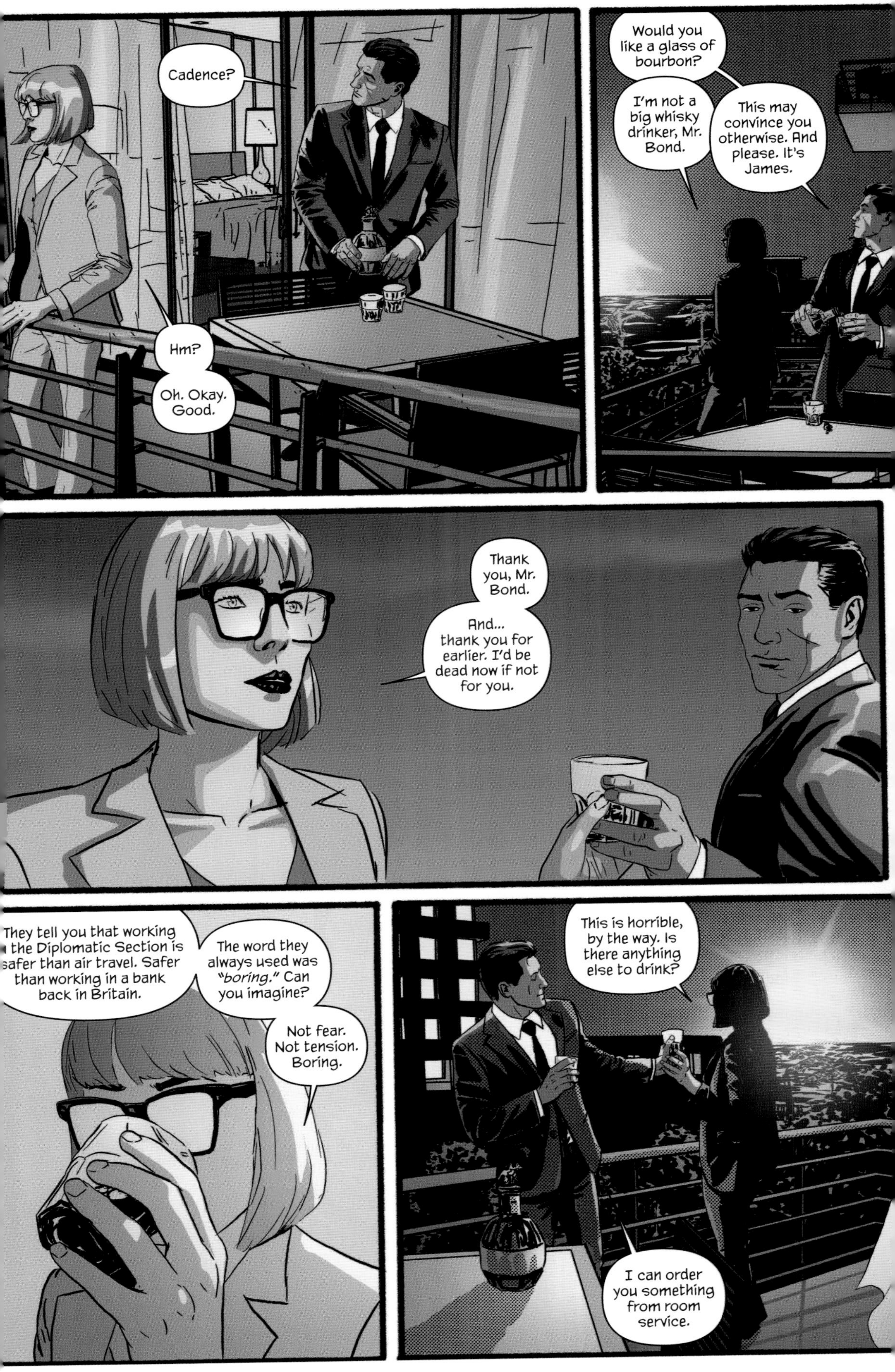
Cadence?
Hm?
Oh. Okay. Good.
Would you like a glass of bourbon?
I'm not a big whisky drinker, Mr. Bond.
This may convince you otherwise. And please. It's James.
Thank you, Mr. Bond.
And... thank you for earlier. I'd be dead now if not for you.
They tell you that working in the Diplomatic Section is safer than air travel. Safer than working in a bank back in Britain.
The word they always used was "boring." Can you imagine?
Not fear. Not tension. Boring.
This is horrible, by the way. Is there anything else to drink?
I can order you something from room service.

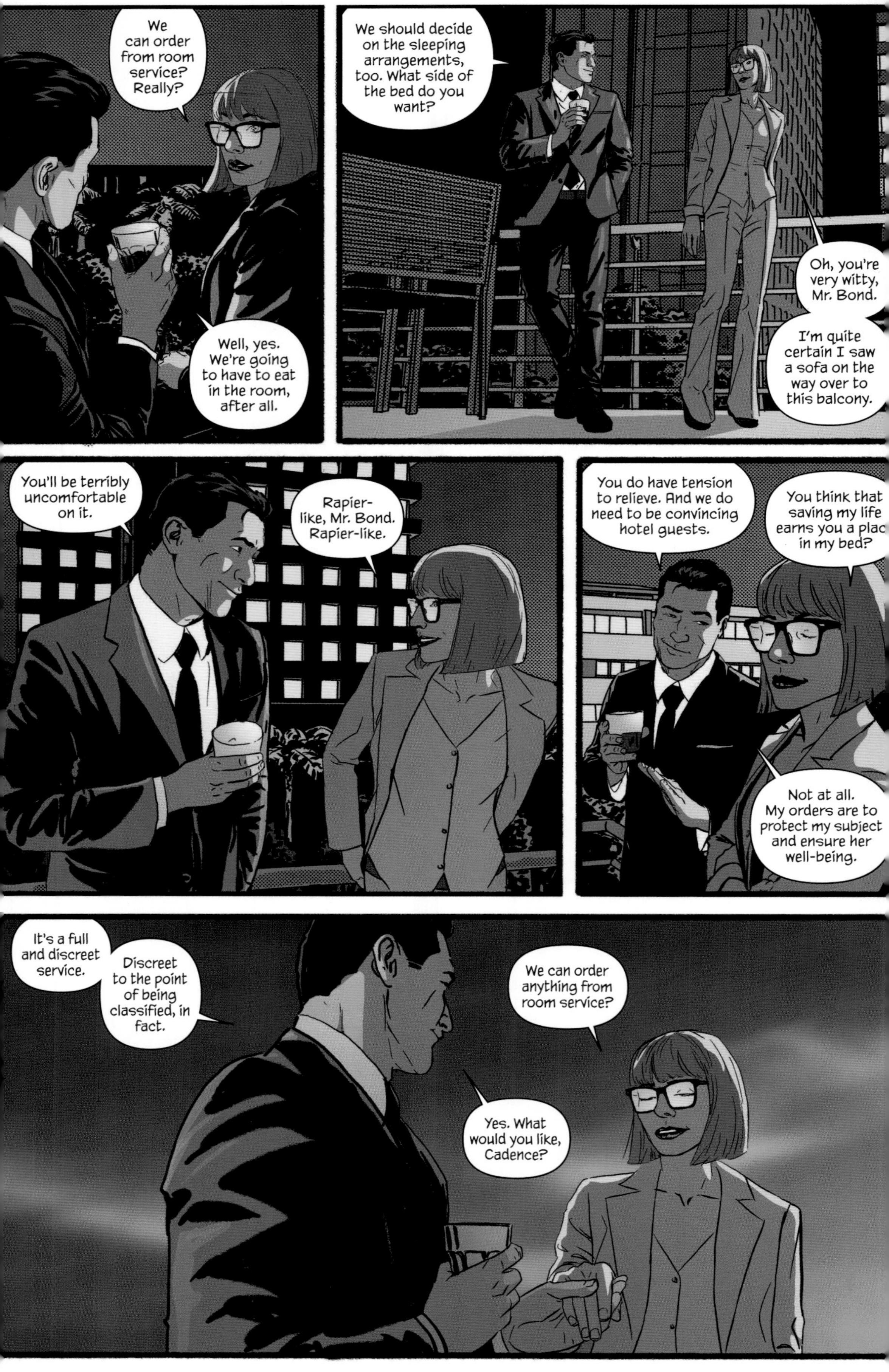
We can order from room service? Really?
Well, yes. We're going to have to eat in the room, after all.
We should decide on the sleeping arrangements, too. What side of the bed do you want?
Oh, you're very witty, Mr. Bond.
I'm quite certain I saw a sofa on the way over to this balcony.
You'll be terribly uncomfortable on it.
Rapier-like, Mr. Bond. Rapier-like.
You do have tension to relieve. And we do need to be convincing hotel guests.
You think that saving my life earns you a plac in my bed?
Not at all. My orders are to protect my subject and ensure her well-being.
It's a full and discreet service.
Discreet to the point of being classified, in fact.
We can order anything from room service?
Yes. What would you like, Cadence?

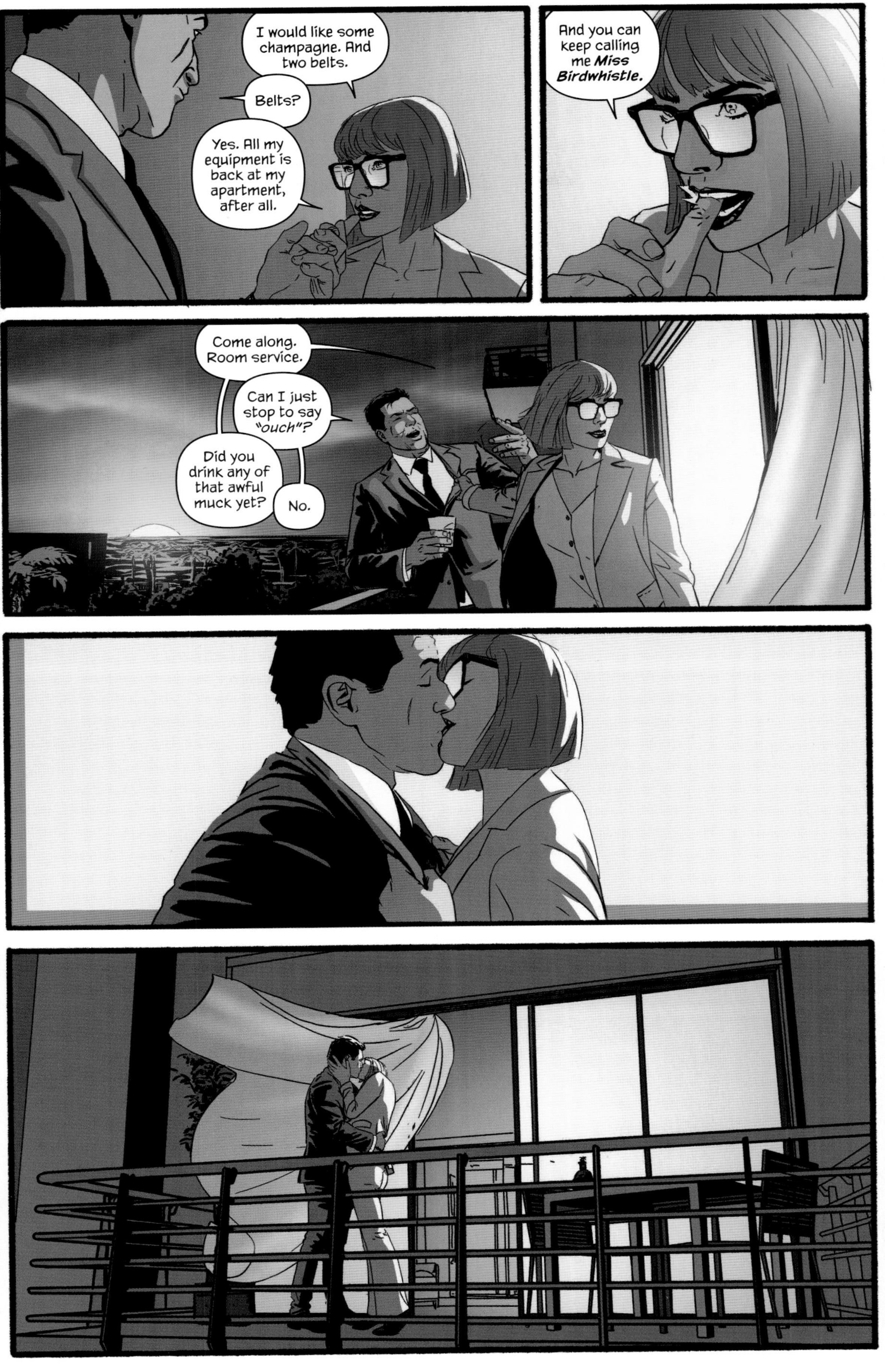
I would like some champagne. And two belts.
Belts?
Yes. All my equipment is back at my apartment, after all.
And you can keep calling me *Miss Birdwhistle.*
Come along. Room service.
Can I just stop to say *"ouch"*?
Did you drink any of that awful muck yet?
No.

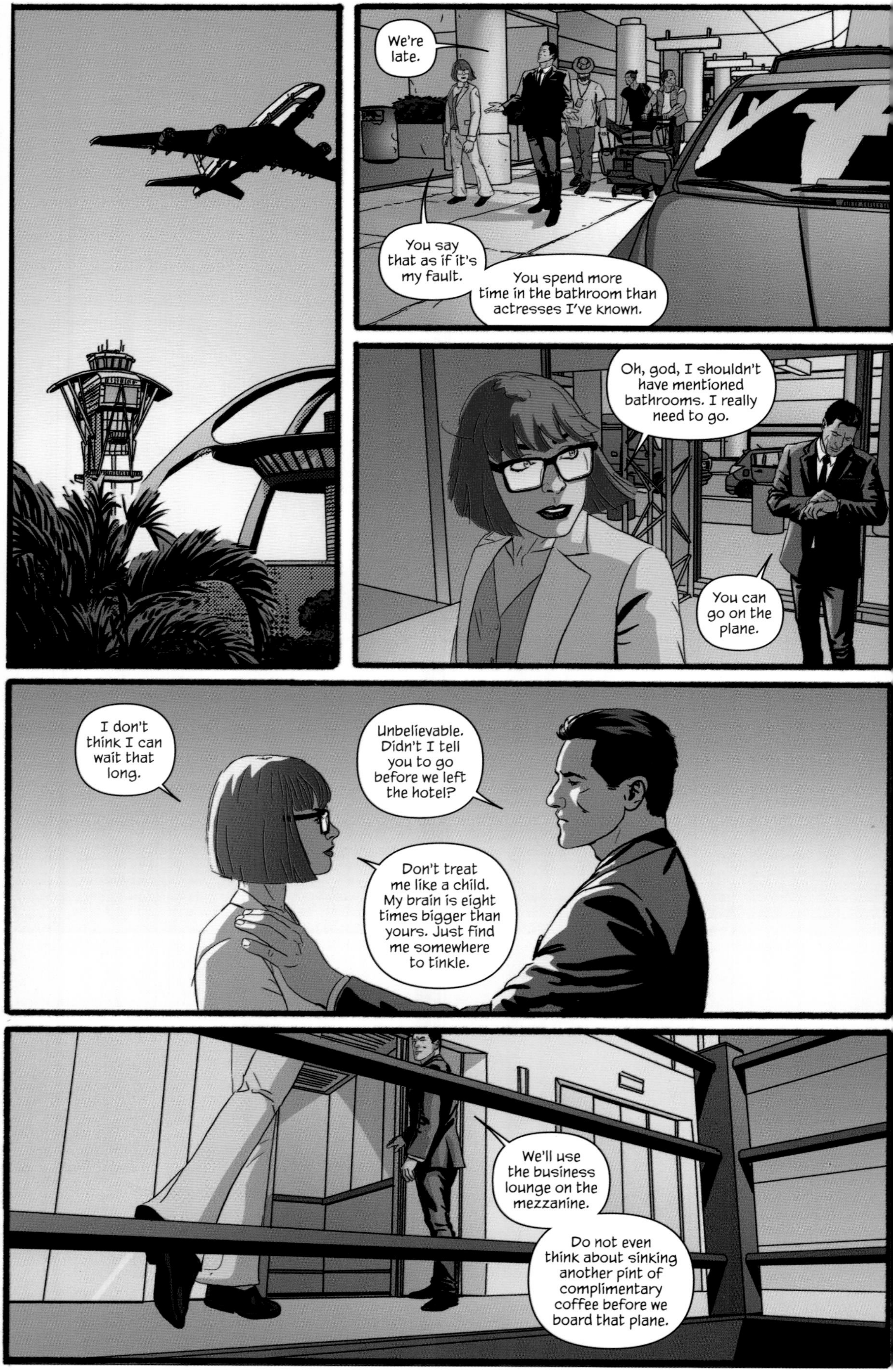
We're late.
You say that as if it's my fault.
You spend more time in the bathroom than actresses I've known.
Oh, god, I shouldn't have mentioned bathrooms. I really need to go.
You can go on the plane.
I don't think I can wait that long.
Unbelievable. Didn't I tell you to go before we left the hotel?
Don't treat me like a child. My brain is eight times bigger than yours. Just find me somewhere to tinkle.
We'll use the business lounge on the mezzanine.
Do not even think about sinking another pint of complimentary coffee before we board that plane.

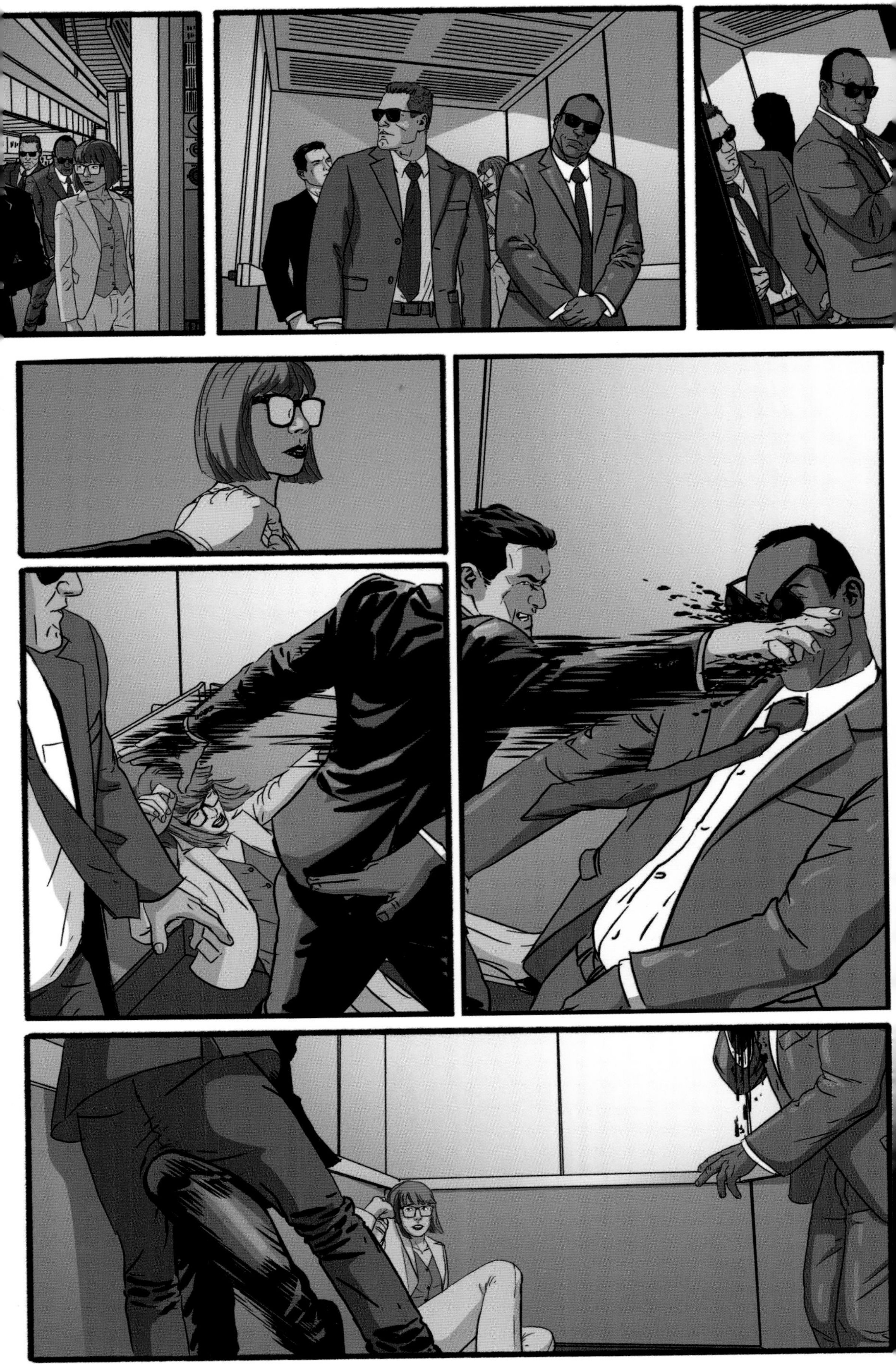

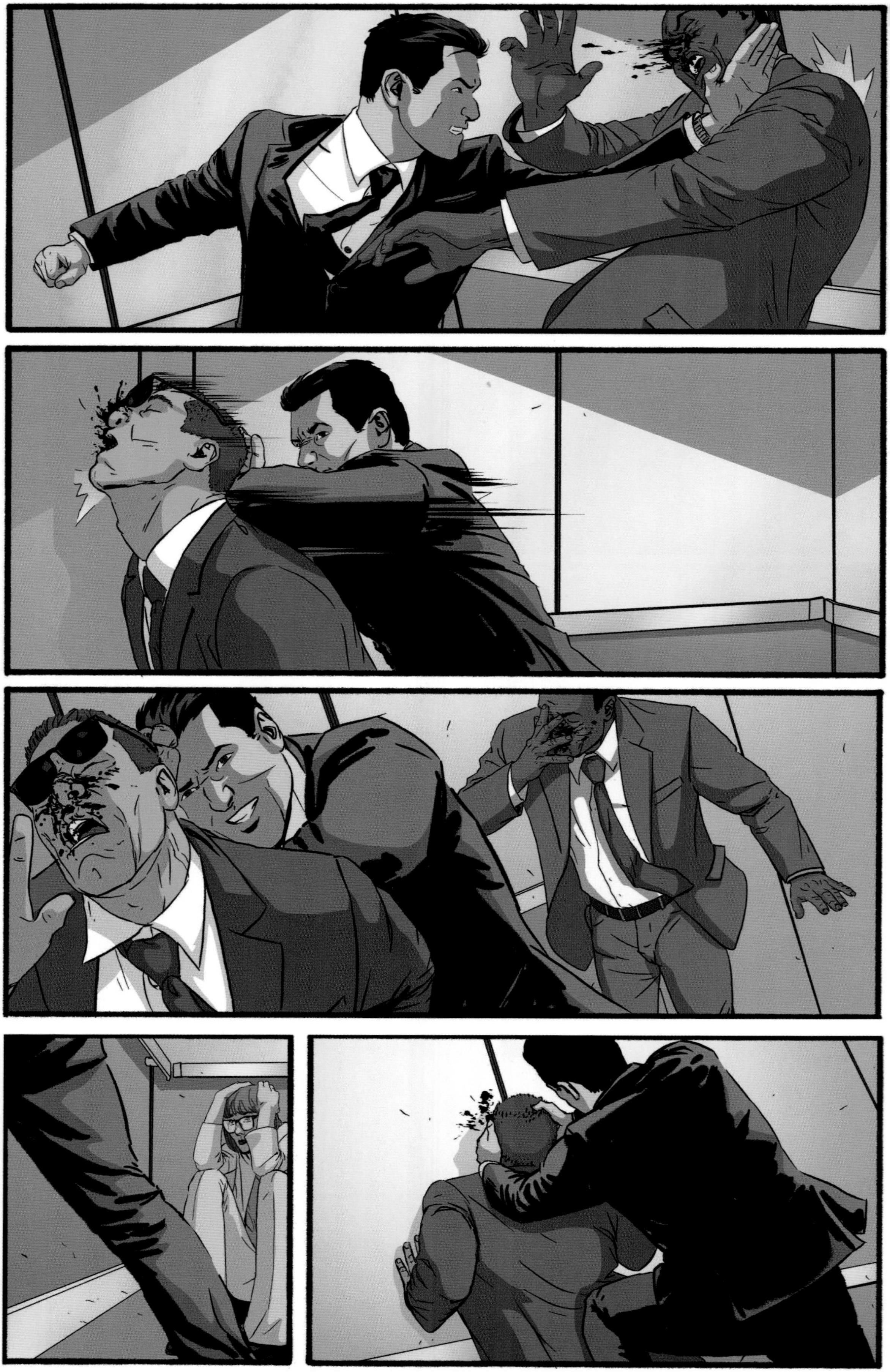

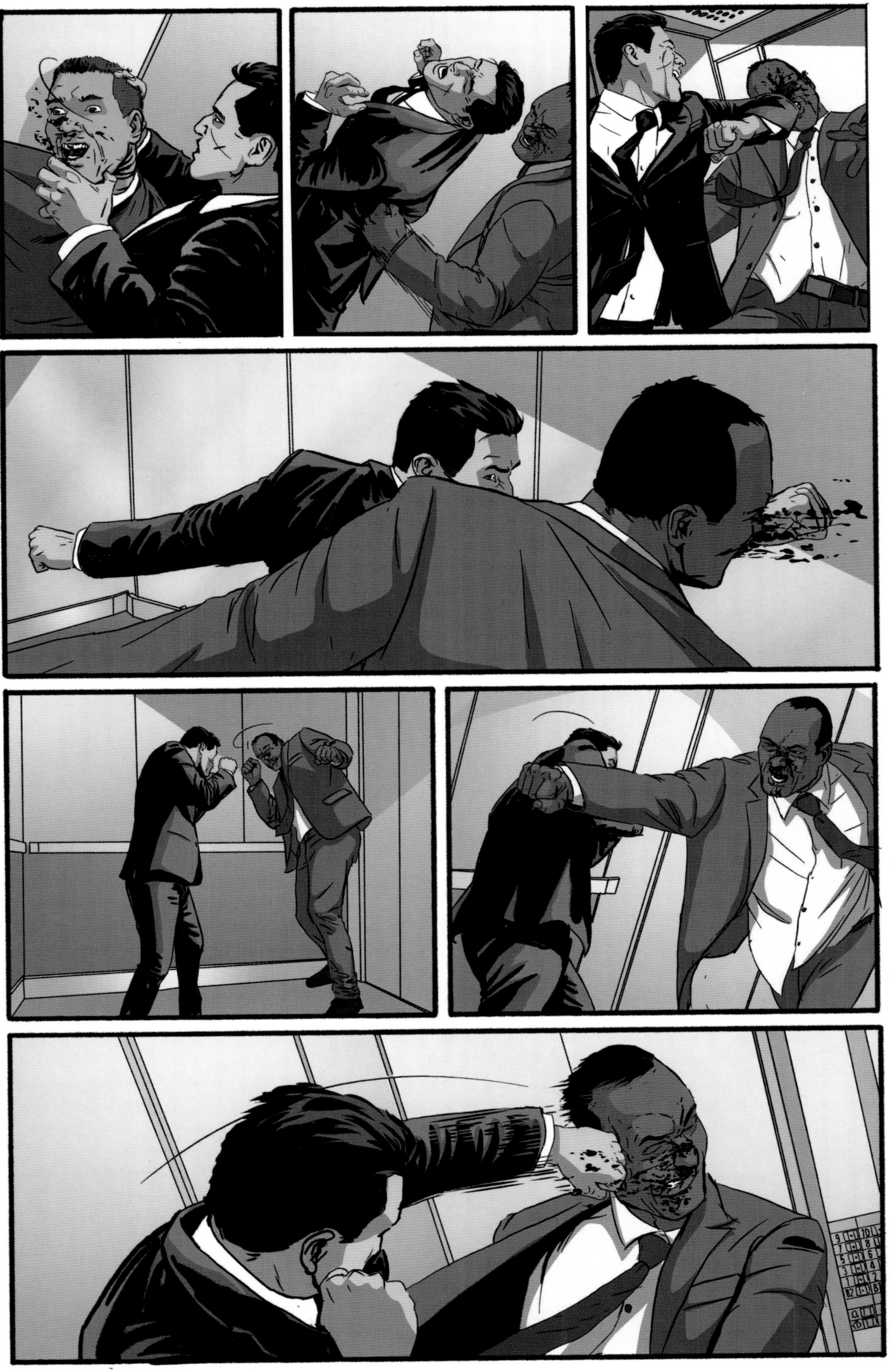

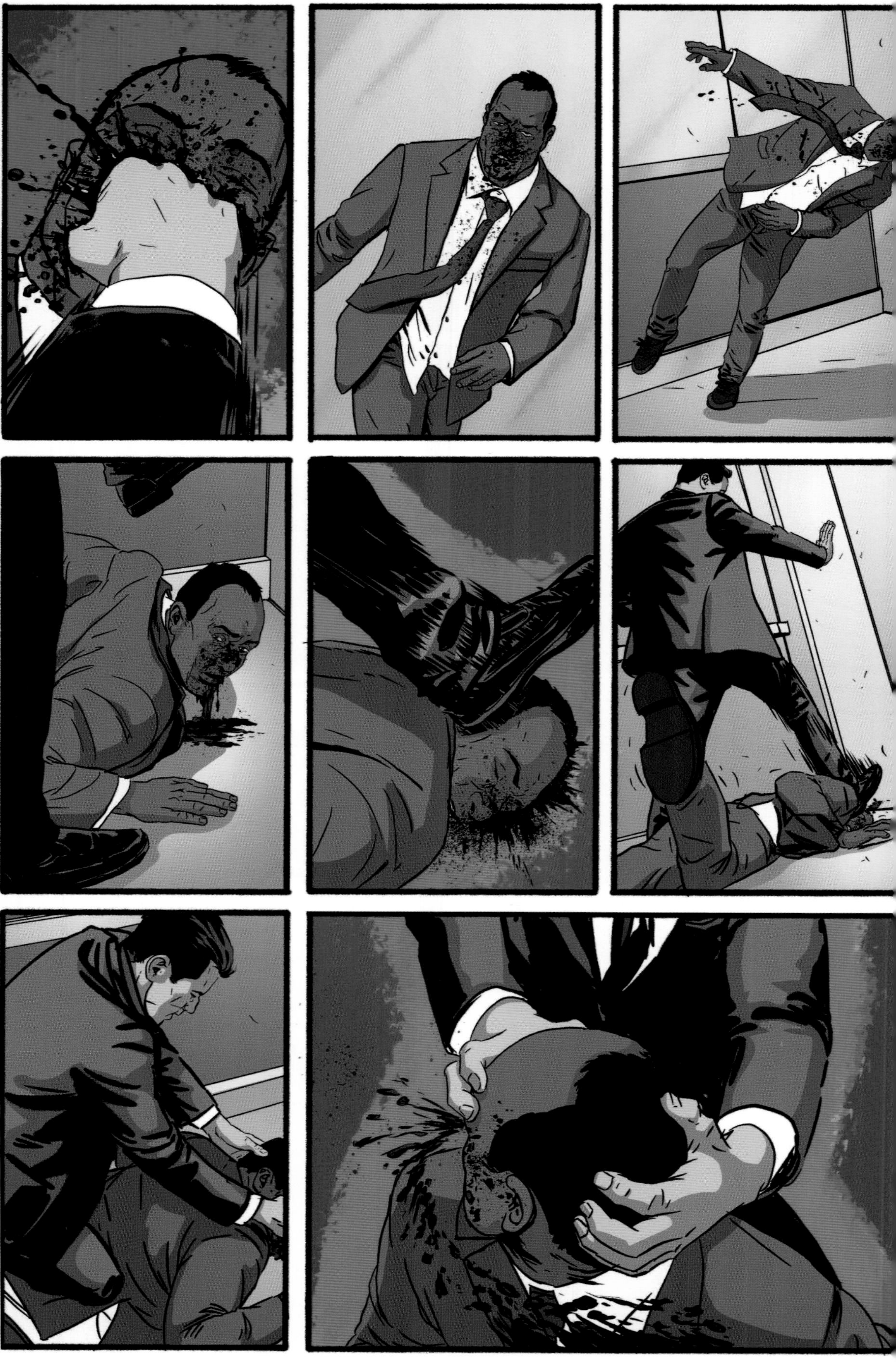

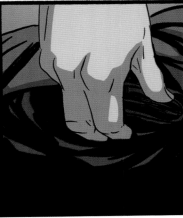

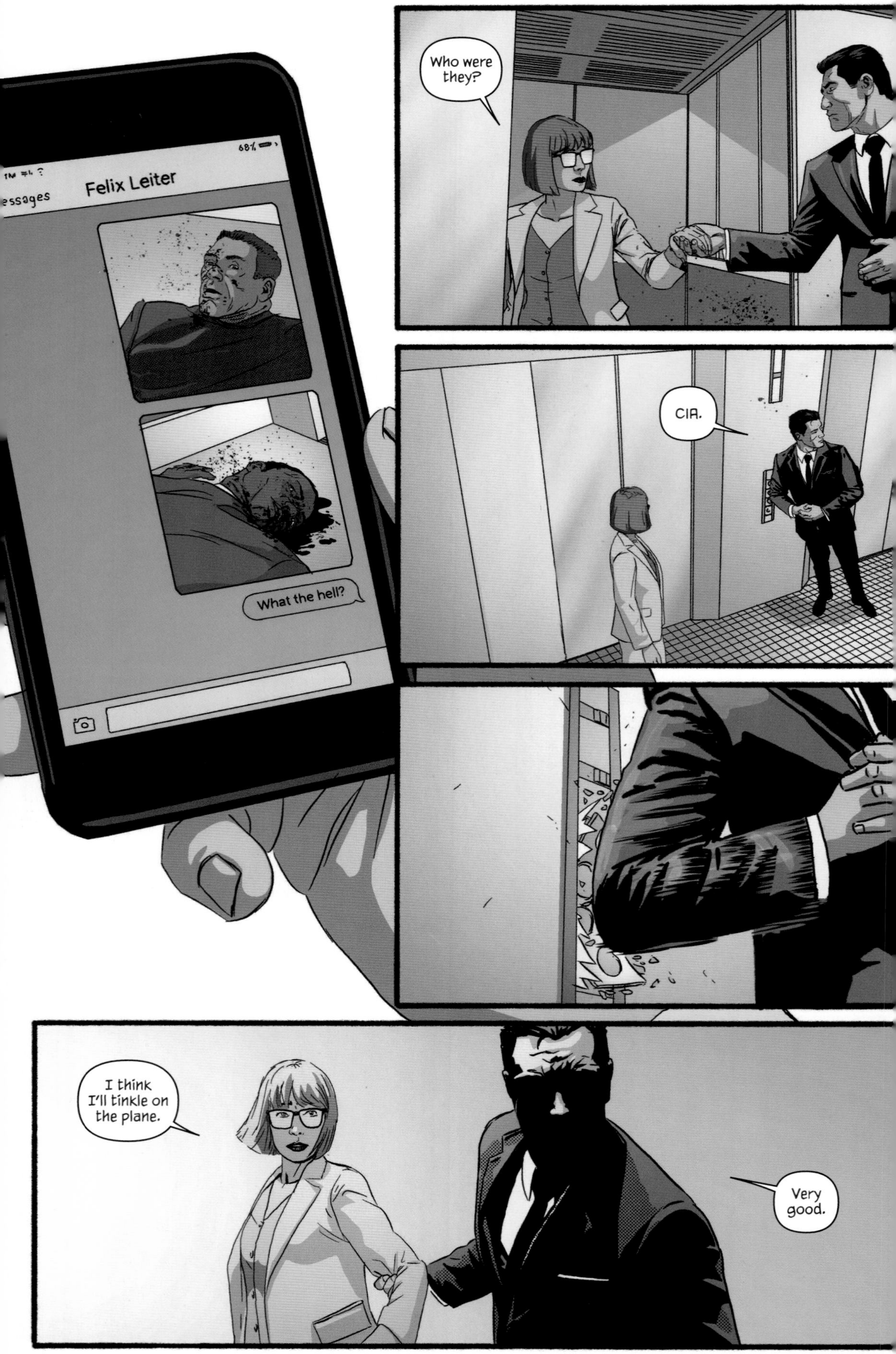
Felix Leiter
What the hell?
Who were they?
CIA.
I think I'll tinkle on the plane.
Very good.

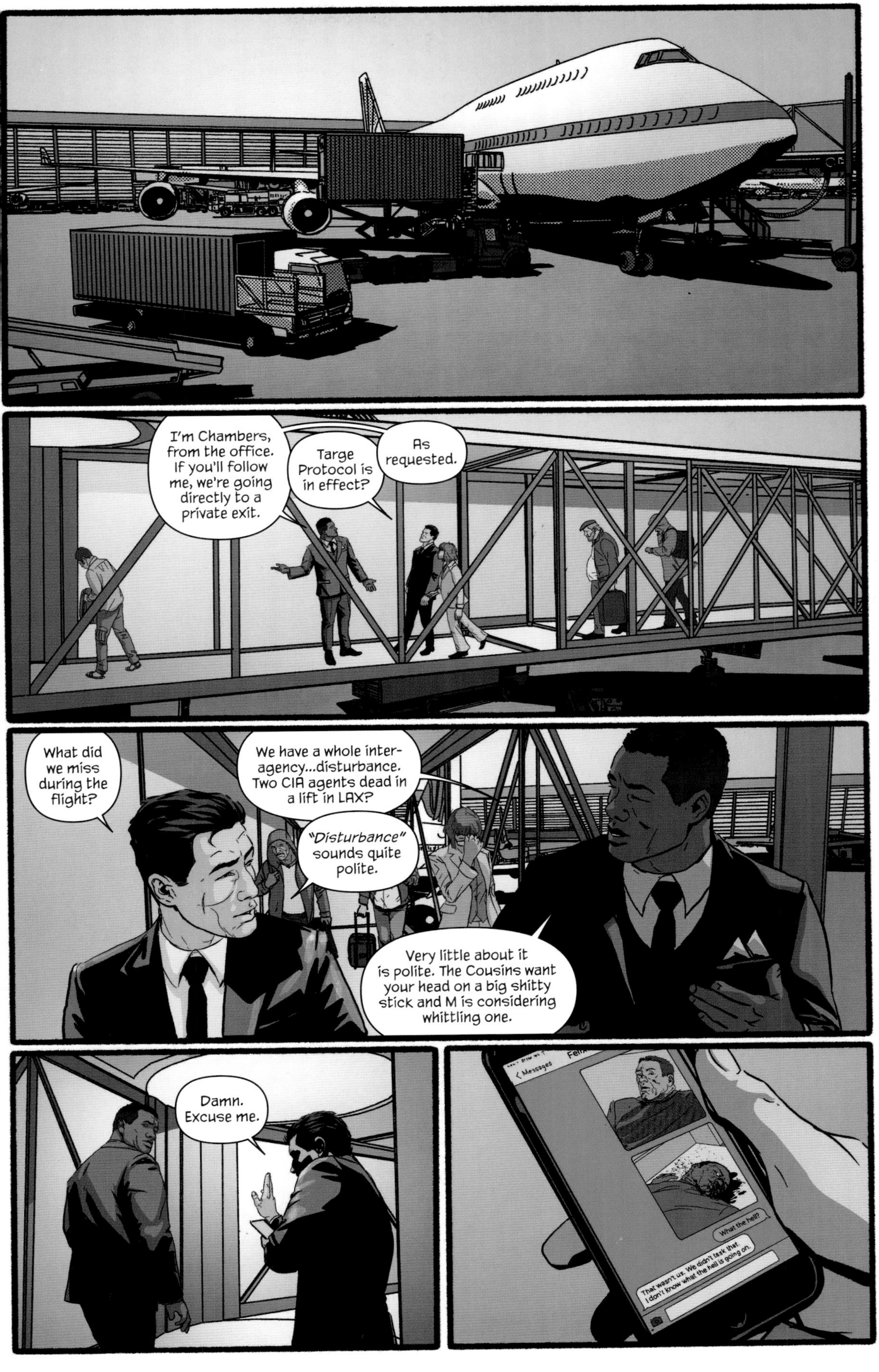
I'm Chambers, from the office. If you'll follow me, we're going directly to a private exit.
Targe Protocol is in effect?
As requested.
What did we miss during the flight?
We have a whole inter-agency...disturbance. Two CIA agents dead in a lift in LAX?
"Disturbance" sounds quite polite.
Very little about it is polite. The Cousins want your head on a big shitty stick and M is considering whittling one.
Damn. Excuse me.
Messages
What the hell?
That wasn't us. We didn't task that. I don't know what the hell is going on.

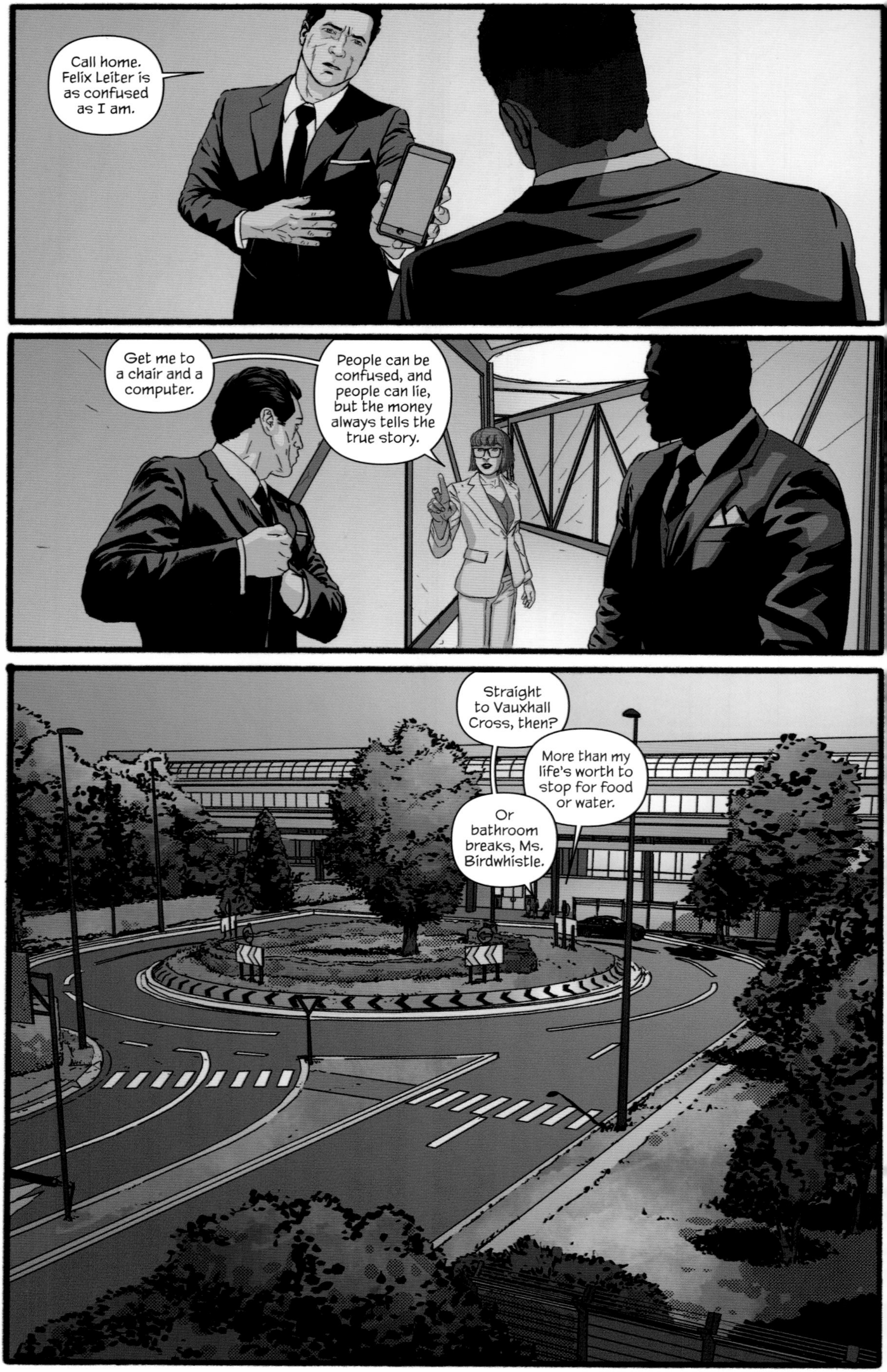
Call home. Felix Leiter is as confused as I am.
Get me to a chair and a computer.
People can be confused, and people can lie, but the money always tells the true story.
Straight to Vauxhall Cross, then?
More than my life's worth to stop for food or water.
Or bathroom breaks, Ms. Birdwhistle.

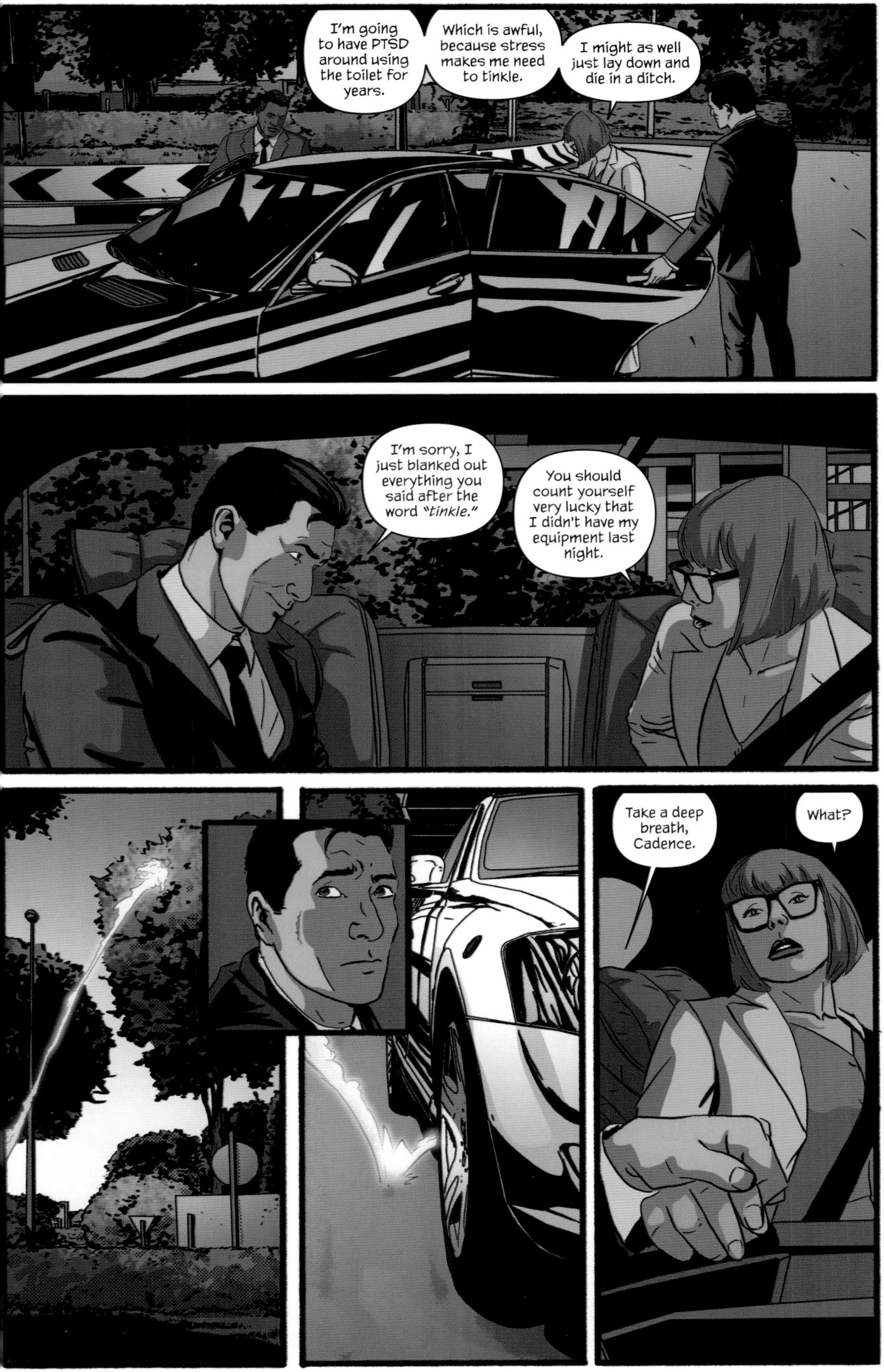
I'm going to have PTSD around using the toilet for years.
Which is awful, because stress makes me need to tinkle.
I might as well just lay down and die in a ditch.
I'm sorry, I just blanked out everything you said after the word *"tinkle."*
You should count yourself very lucky that I didn't have my equipment last night.
Take a deep breath, Cadence.
What?

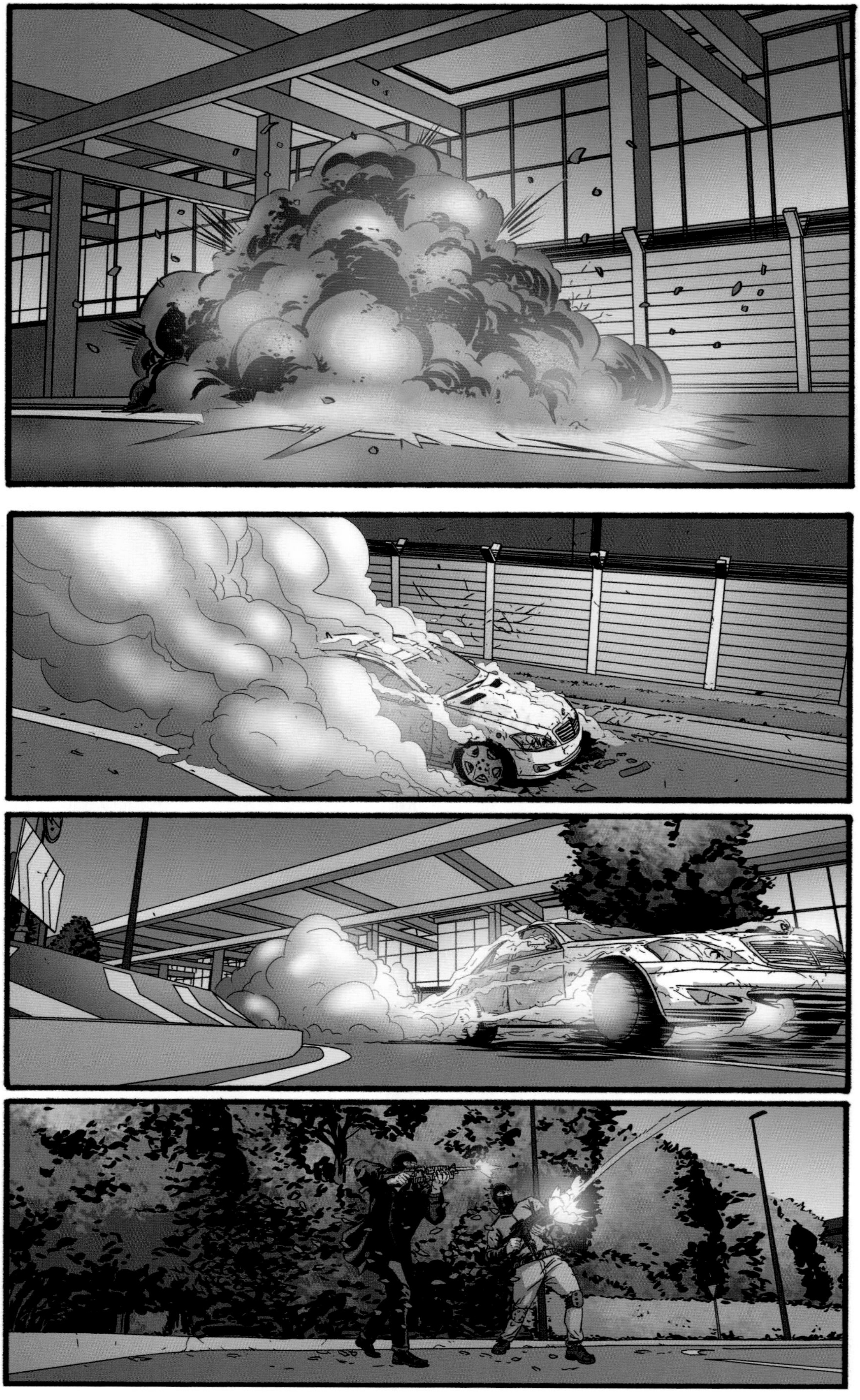

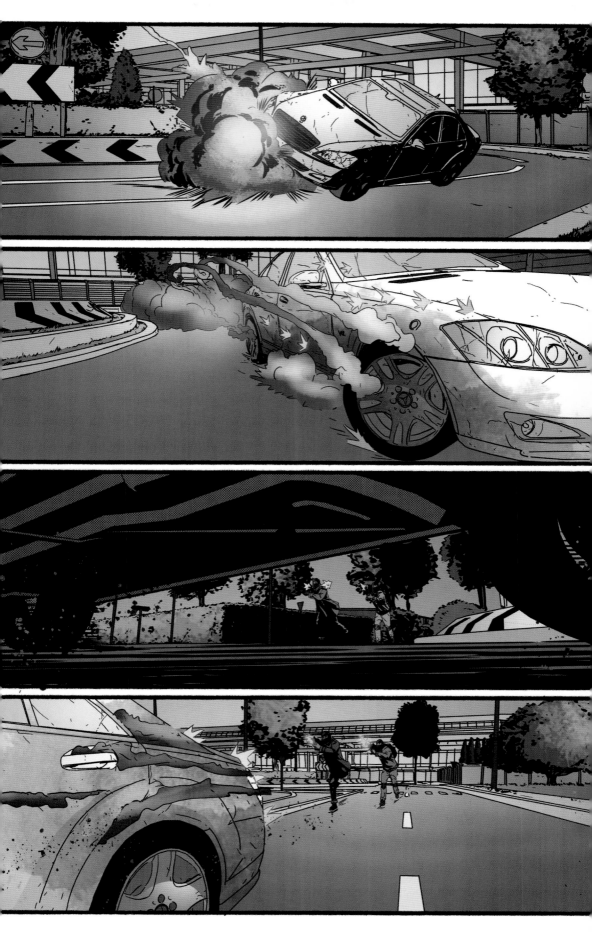

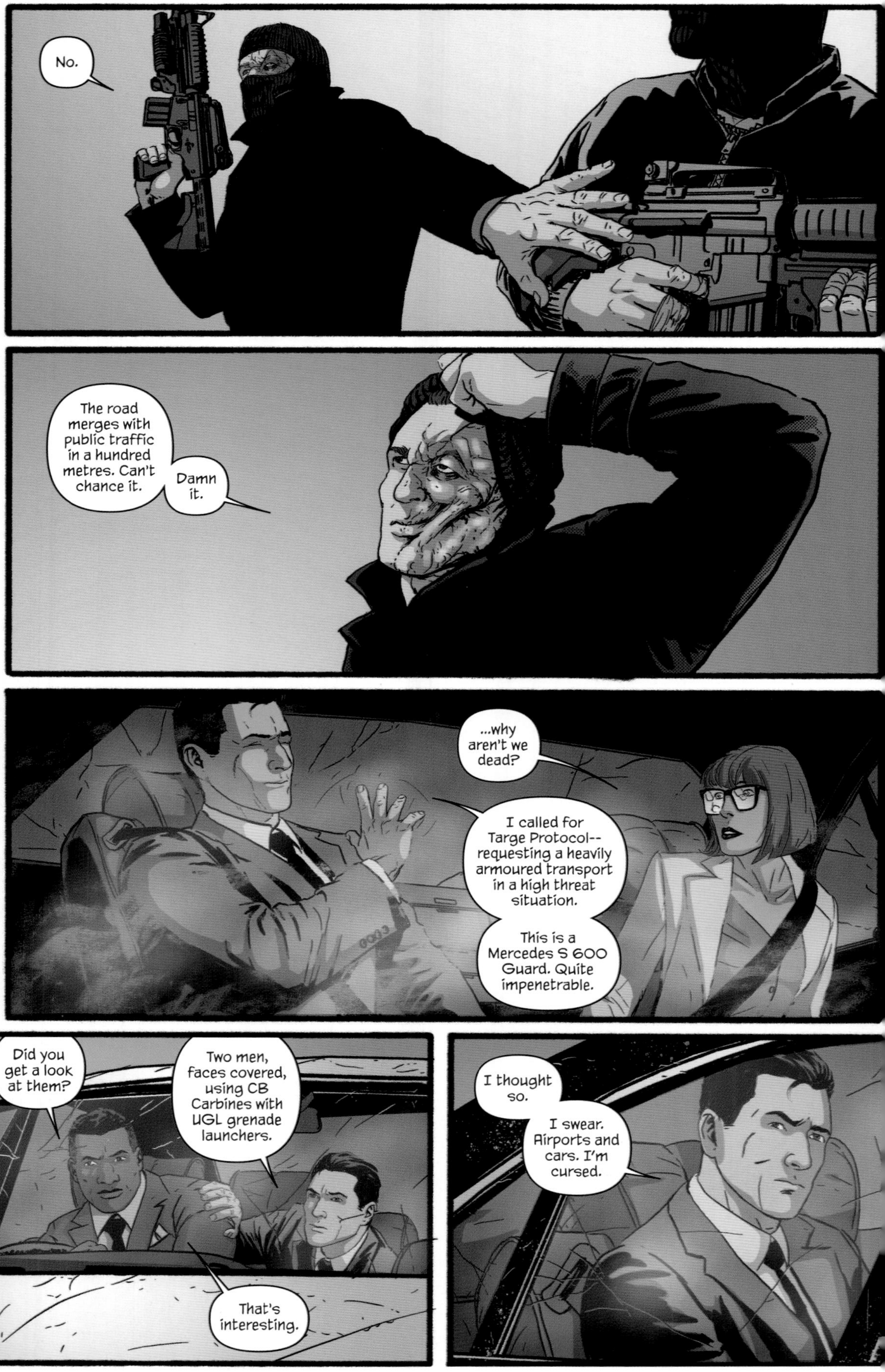
No.
The road merges with public traffic in a hundred metres. Can't chance it.
Damn it.
...why aren't we dead?
I called for Targe Protocol-- requesting a heavily armoured transport in a high threat situation.
This is a Mercedes S 600 Guard. Quite impenetrable.
Did you get a look at them?
Two men, faces covered, using CB Carbines with UGL grenade launchers.
That's interesting.
I thought so.
I swear. Airports and cars. I'm cursed.

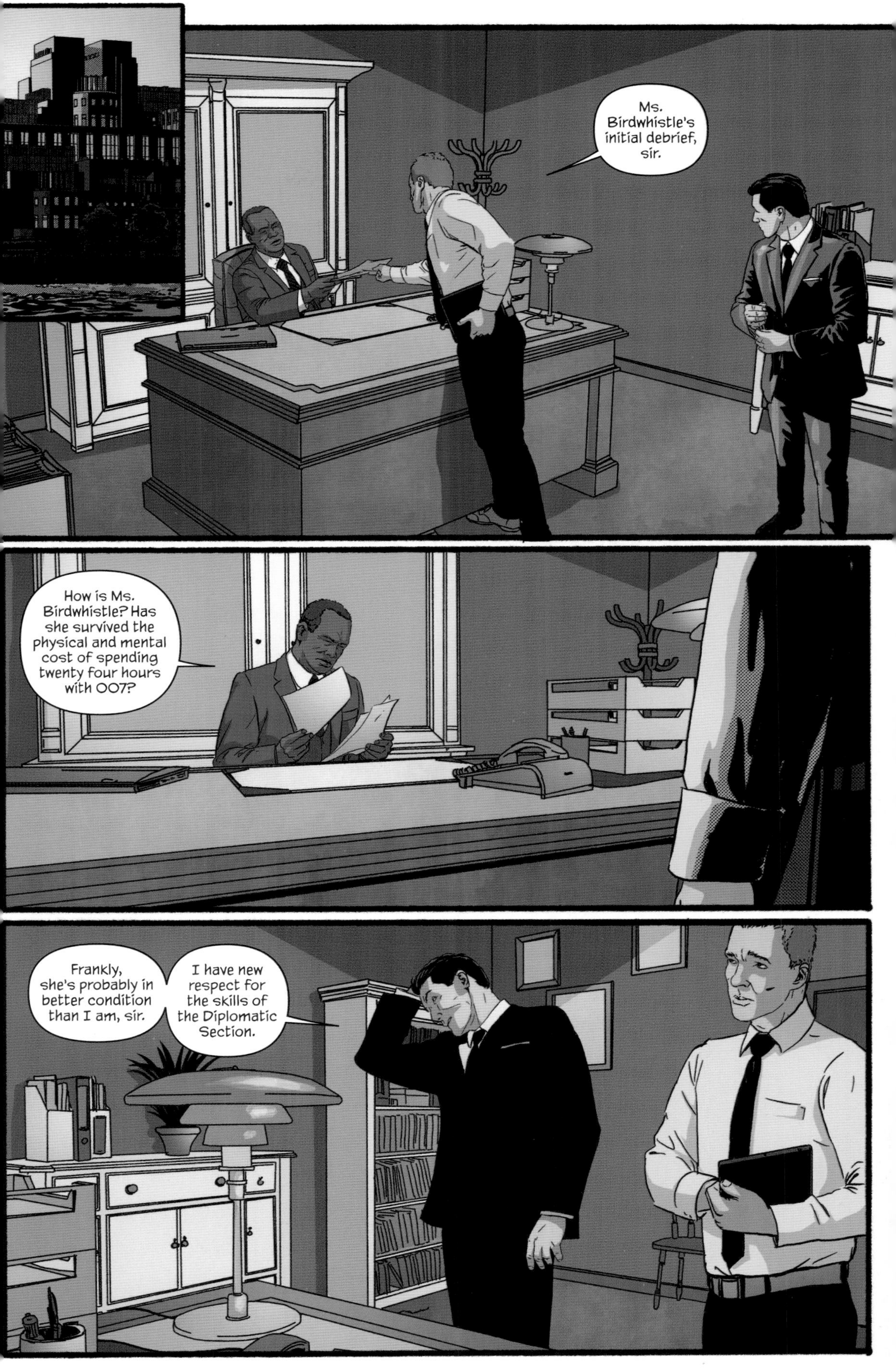
Ms. Birdwhistle's initial debrief, sir.
How is Ms. Birdwhistle? Has she survived the physical and mental cost of spending twenty four hours with 007?
Frankly, she's probably in better condition than I am, sir.
I have new respect for the skills of the Diplomatic Section.

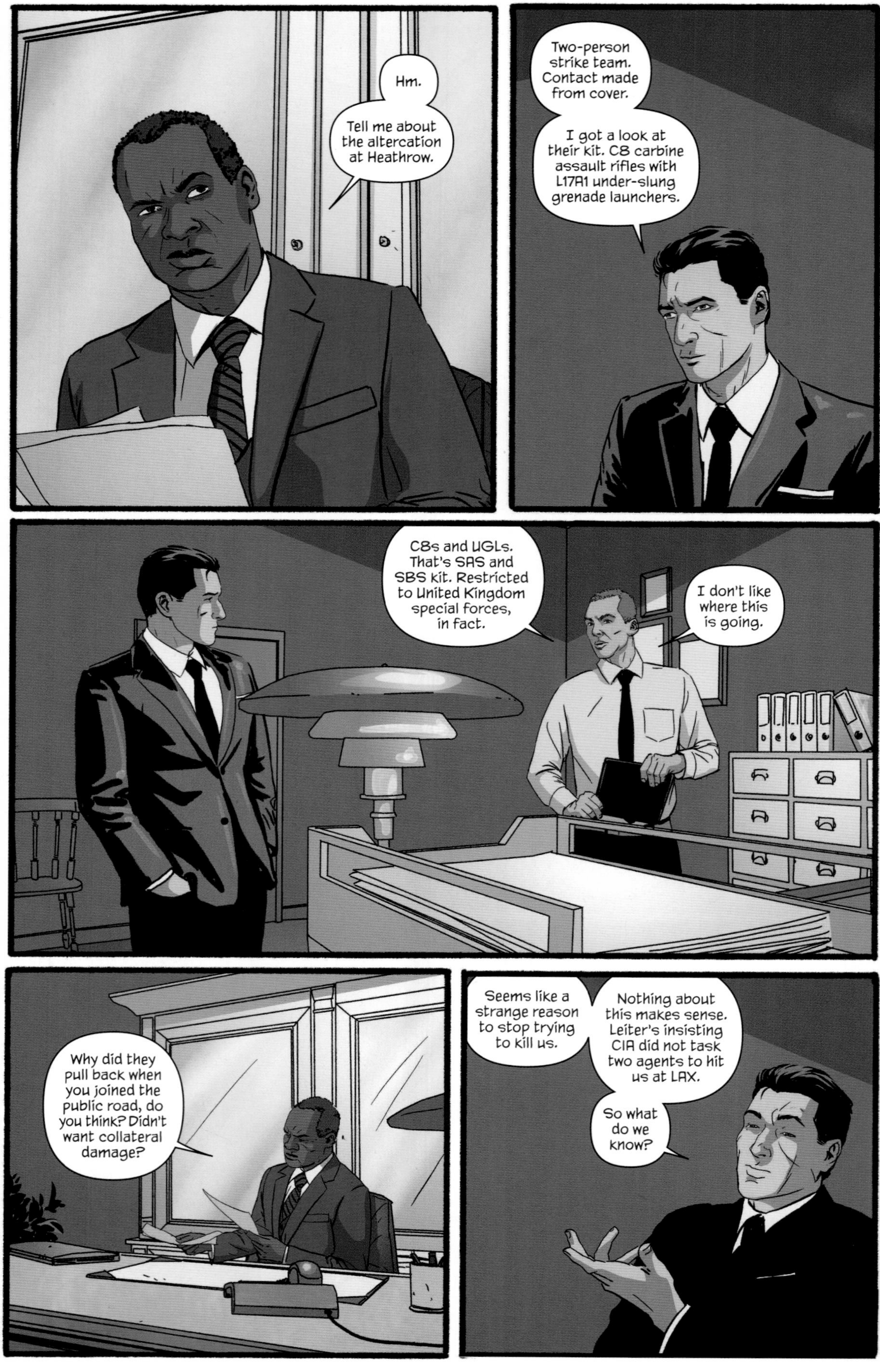
Hm.
Tell me about the altercation at Heathrow.
Two-person strike team. Contact made from cover.
I got a look at their kit. C8 carbine assault rifles with L17A1 under-slung grenade launchers.
C8s and UGLs. That's SAS and SBS kit. Restricted to United Kingdom special forces, in fact.
I don't like where this is going.
Why did they pull back when you joined the public road, do you think? Didn't want collateral damage?
Seems like a strange reason to stop trying to kill us.
Nothing about this makes sense. Leiter's insisting CIA did not task two agents to hit us at LAX.
So what do we know?

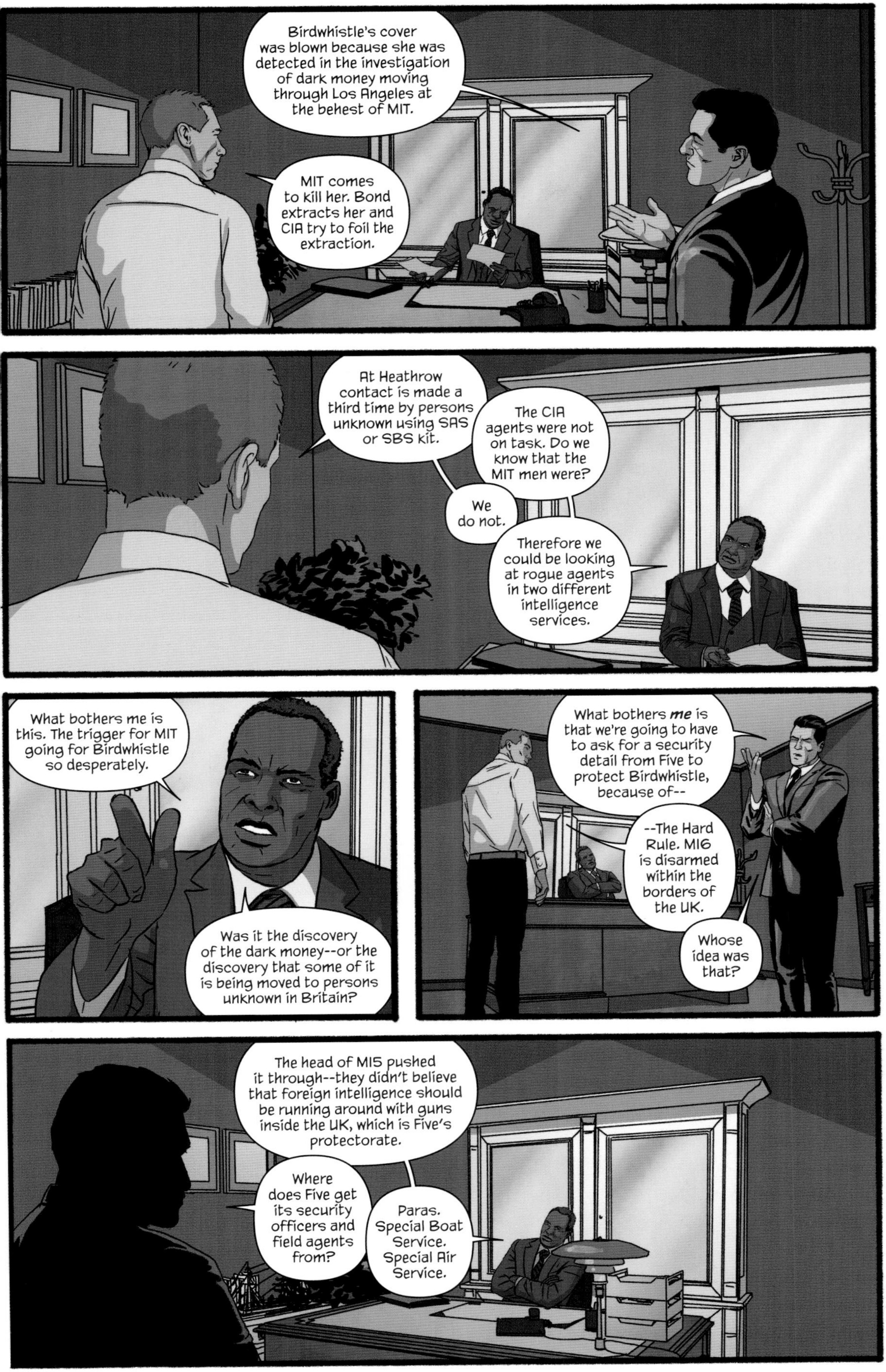
Birdwhistle's cover was blown because she was detected in the investigation of dark money moving through Los Angeles at the behest of MIT.
MIT comes to kill her. Bond extracts her and CIA try to foil the extraction.
At Heathrow contact is made a third time by persons unknown using SAS or SBS kit.
The CIA agents were not on task. Do we know that the MIT men were?
We do not.
Therefore we could be looking at rogue agents in two different intelligence services.
What bothers me is this. The trigger for MIT going for Birdwhistle so desperately.
Was it the discovery of the dark money--or the discovery that some of it is being moved to persons unknown in Britain?
What bothers *me* is that we're going to have to ask for a security detail from Five to protect Birdwhistle, because of--
--The Hard Rule. MI6 is disarmed within the borders of the UK.
Whose idea was that?
The head of MI5 pushed it through--they didn't believe that foreign intelligence should be running around with guns inside the UK, which is Five's protectorate.
Where does Five get its security officers and field agents from?
Paras. Special Boat Service. Special Air Service.

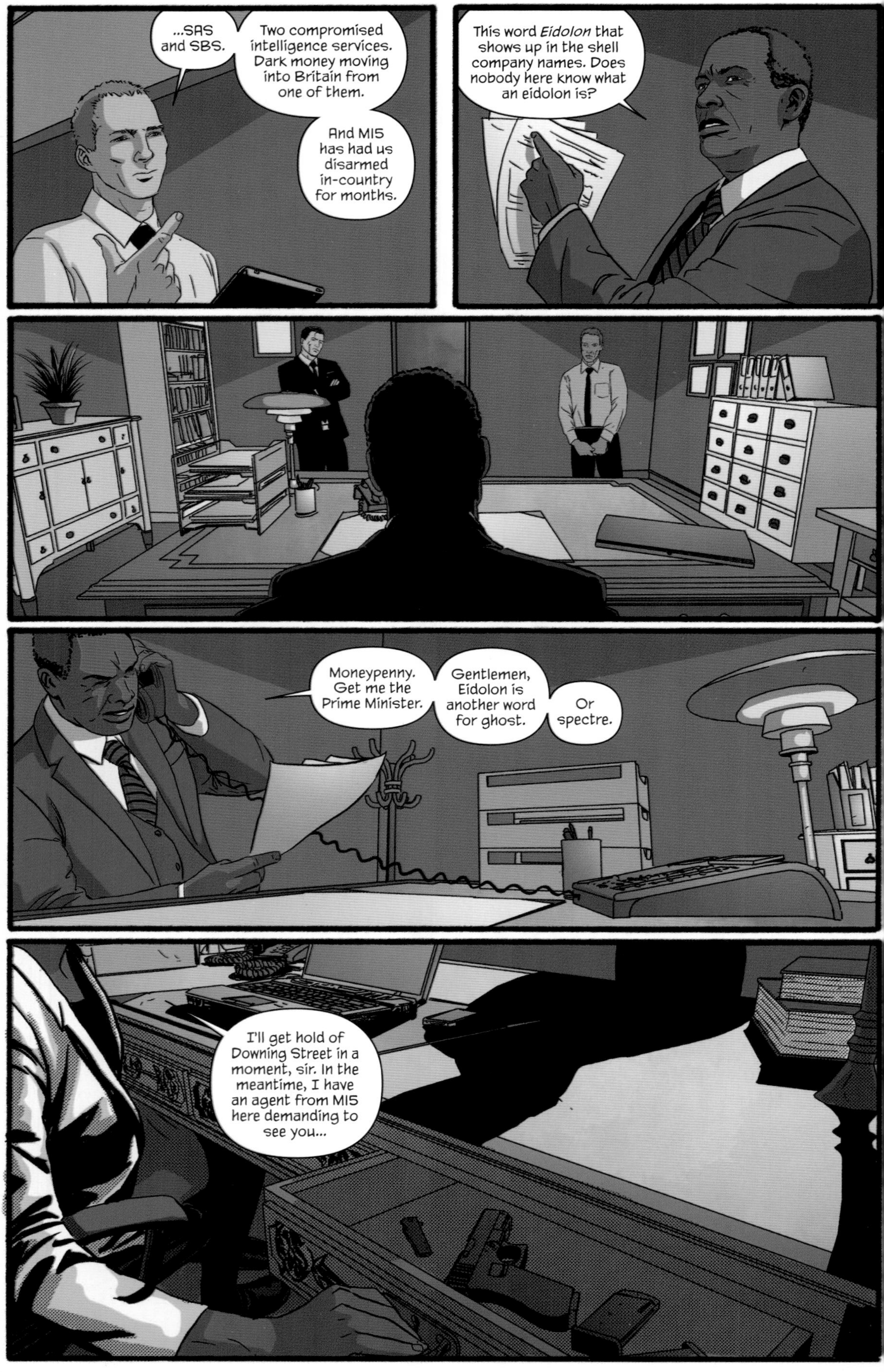
...SAS and SBS.
Two compromised intelligence services. Dark money moving into Britain from one of them.
And MI5 has had us disarmed in-country for months.
This word *Eidolon* that shows up in the shell company names. Does nobody here know what an eidolon is?
Moneypenny. Get me the Prime Minister.
Gentlemen, Eidolon is another word for ghost.
Or spectre.
I'll get hold of Downing Street in a moment, sir. In the meantime, I have an agent from MI5 here demanding to see you...

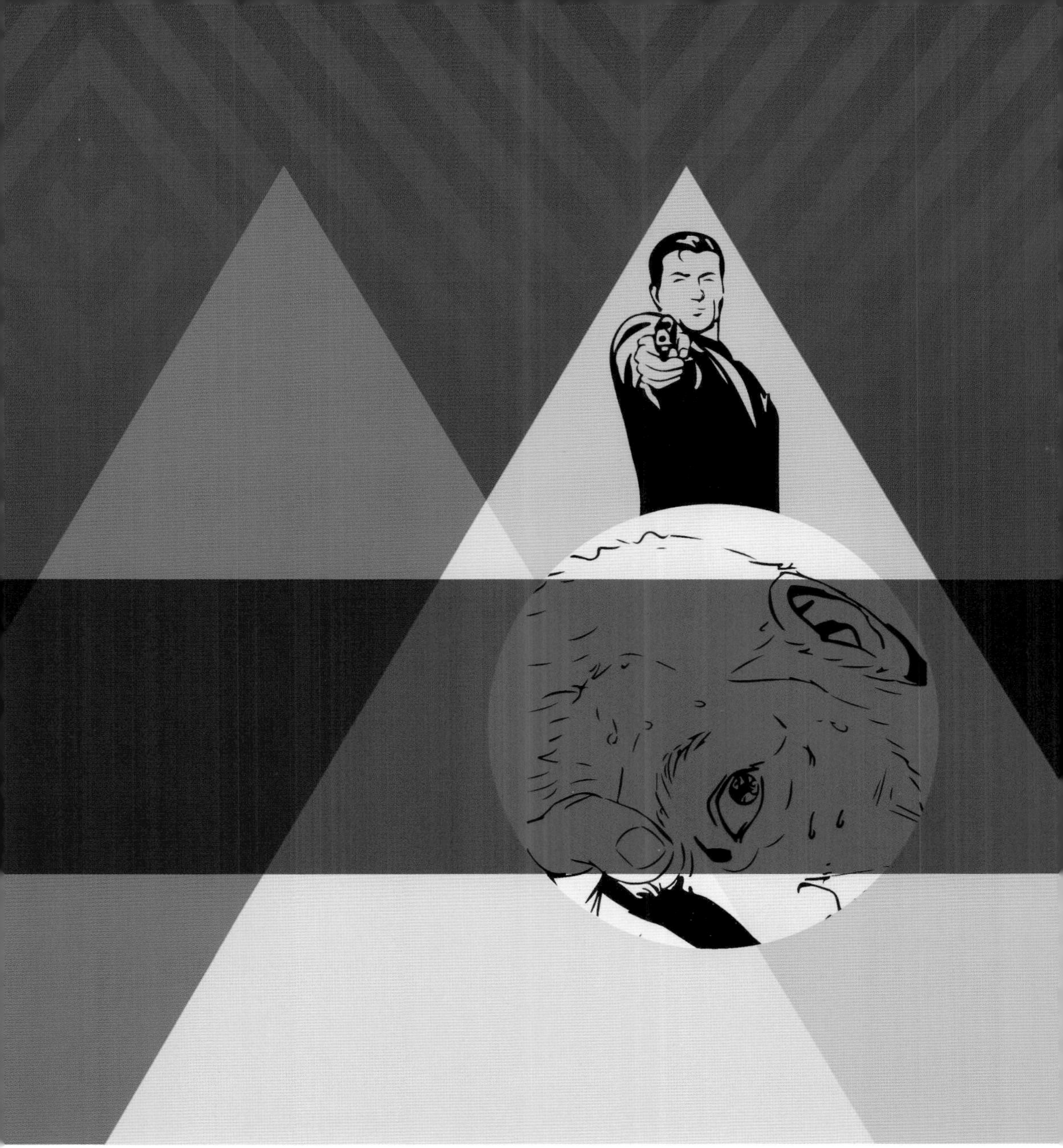

issue nine

issue #9 main cover by **DOM REARDON**

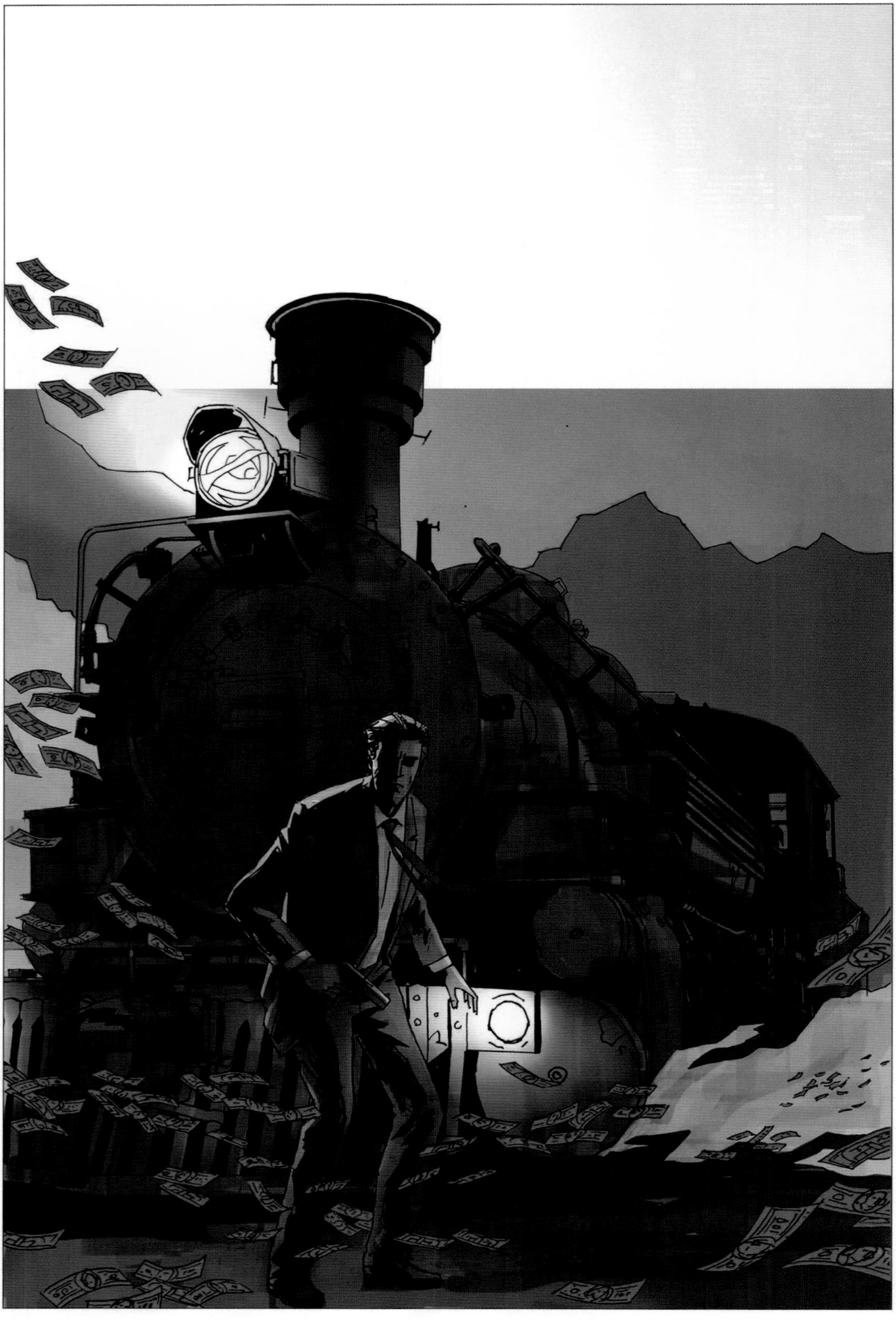

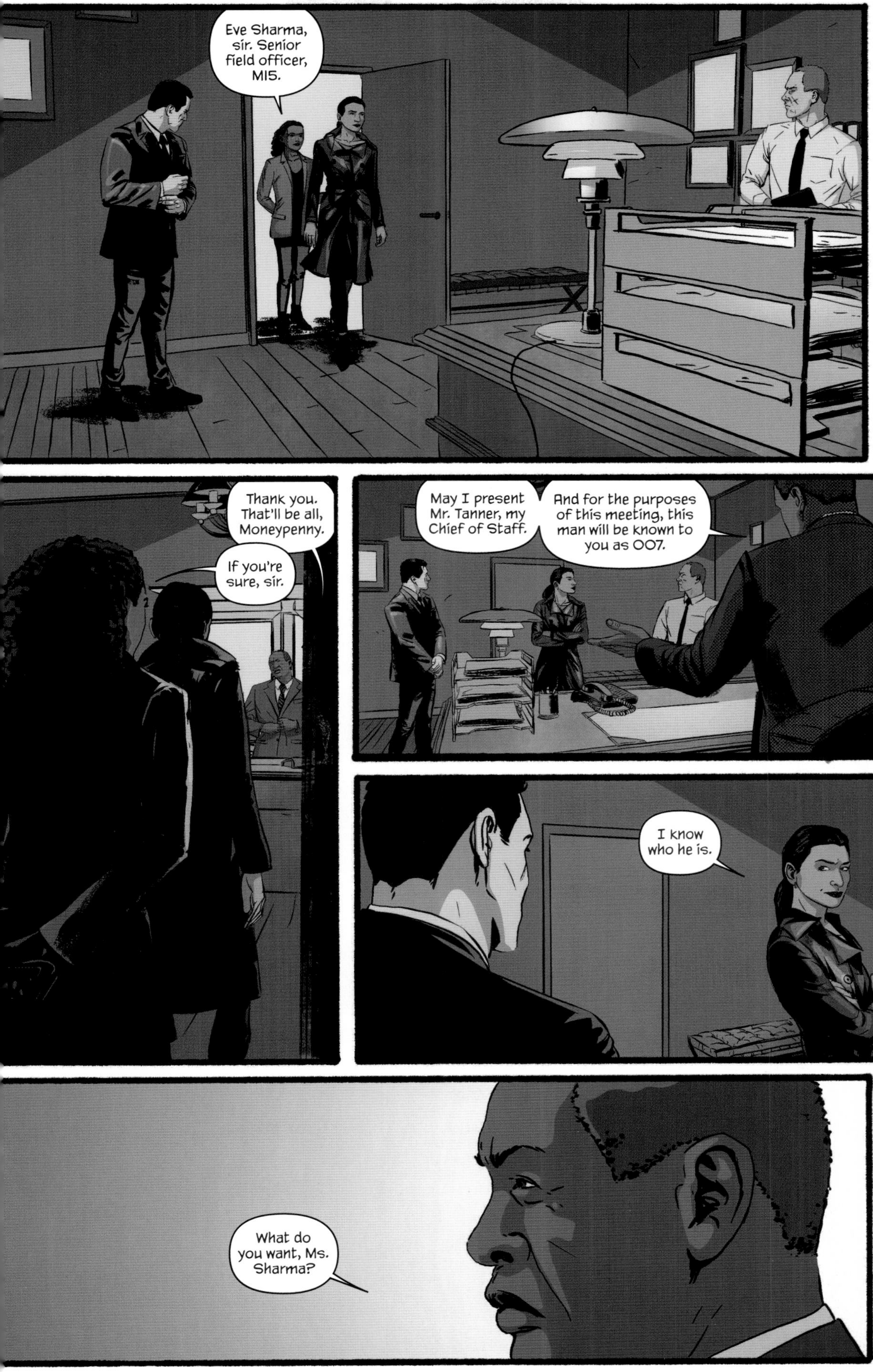
Eve Sharma, sir. Senior field officer, MI5.
Thank you. That'll be all, Moneypenny.
If you're sure, sir.
May I present Mr. Tanner, my Chief of Staff.
And for the purposes of this meeting, this man will be known to you as 007.
I know who he is.
What do you want, Ms. Sharma?

It's really very simple, sir.

A violent, explosive attempt to kill two MI6 agents at Heathrow Airport qualifies as a domestic security issue.

Which makes it an MI5 case, not an MI6 case.

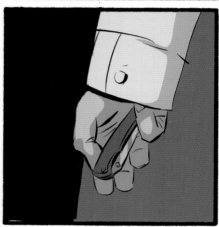

We can and will be handling it, Ms. Sharma.

With all due respect, sir.

The initial inspection of the scene suggests Mr. Bond's vehicle was assaulted with a UGL fitting on a special forces weapon.

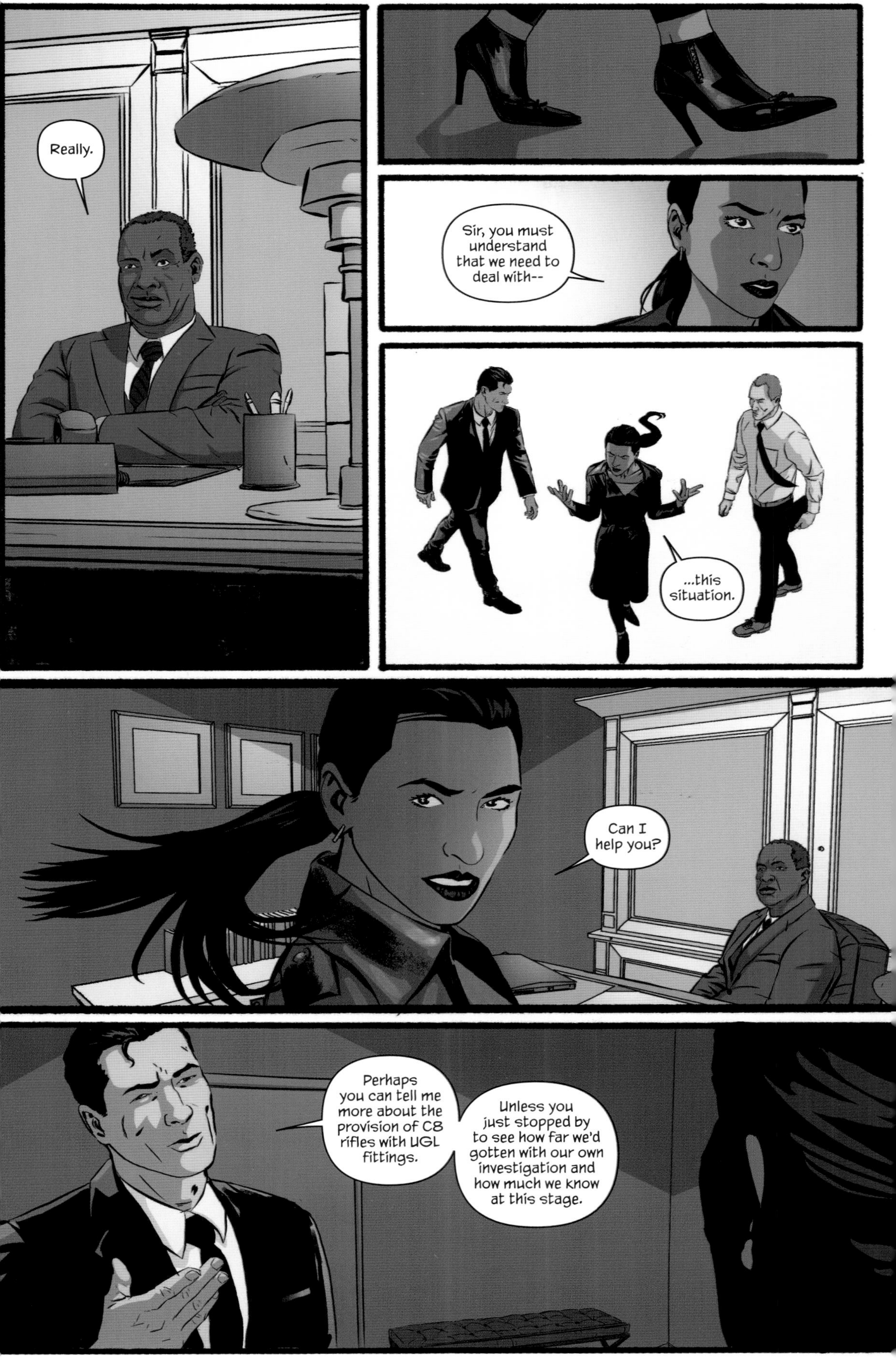
Really.
Sir, you must understand that we need to deal with--
...this situation.
Can I help you?
Perhaps you can tell me more about the provision of C8 rifles with UGL fittings.
Unless you just stopped by to see how far we'd gotten with our own investigation and how much we know at this stage.

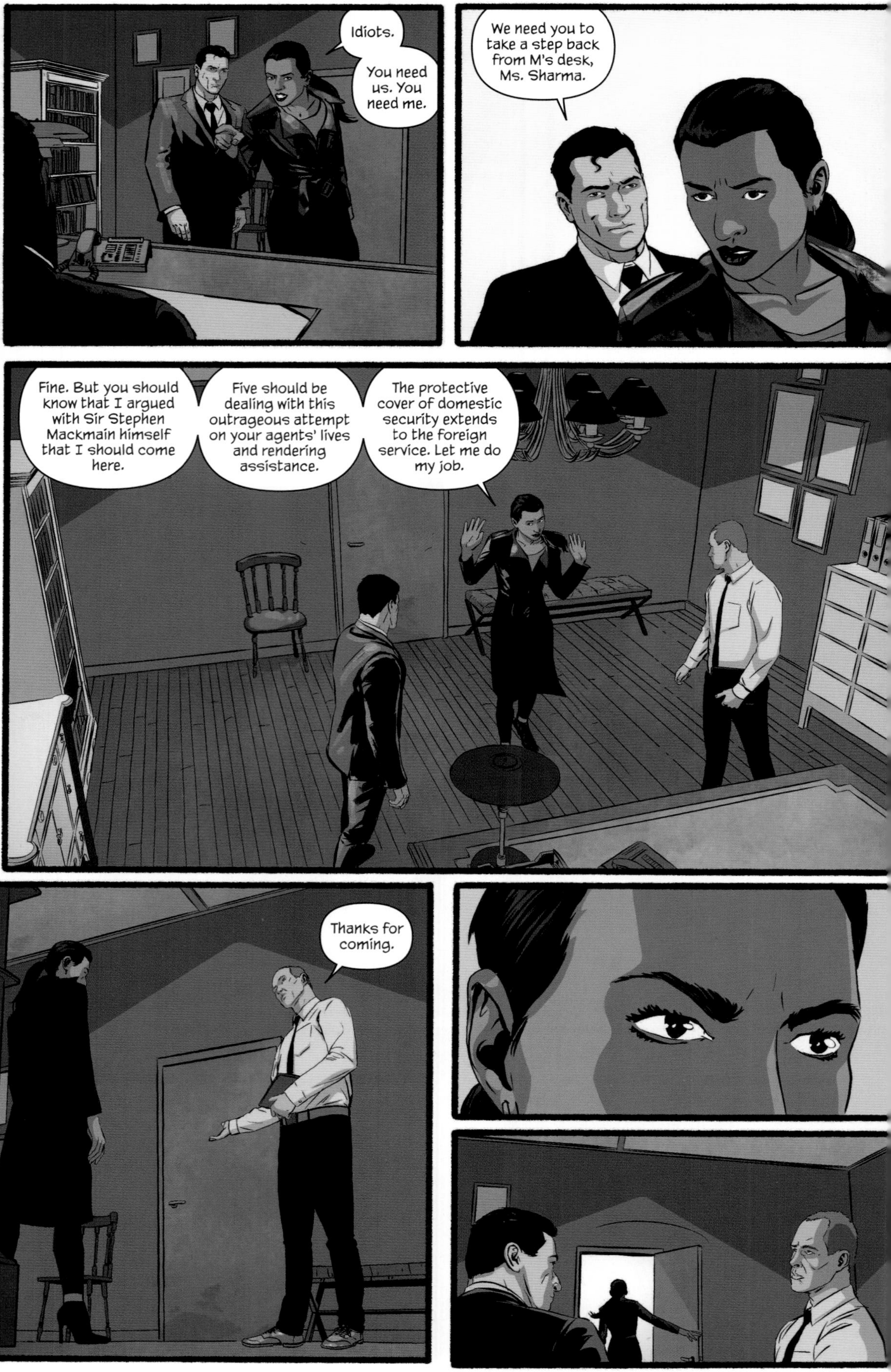
Idiots.
You need us. You need me.
We need you to take a step back from M's desk, Ms. Sharma.
Fine. But you should know that I argued with Sir Stephen Mackmain himself that I should come here.
Five should be dealing with this outrageous attempt on your agents' lives and rendering assistance.
The protective cover of domestic security extends to the foreign service. Let me do my job.
Thanks for coming.

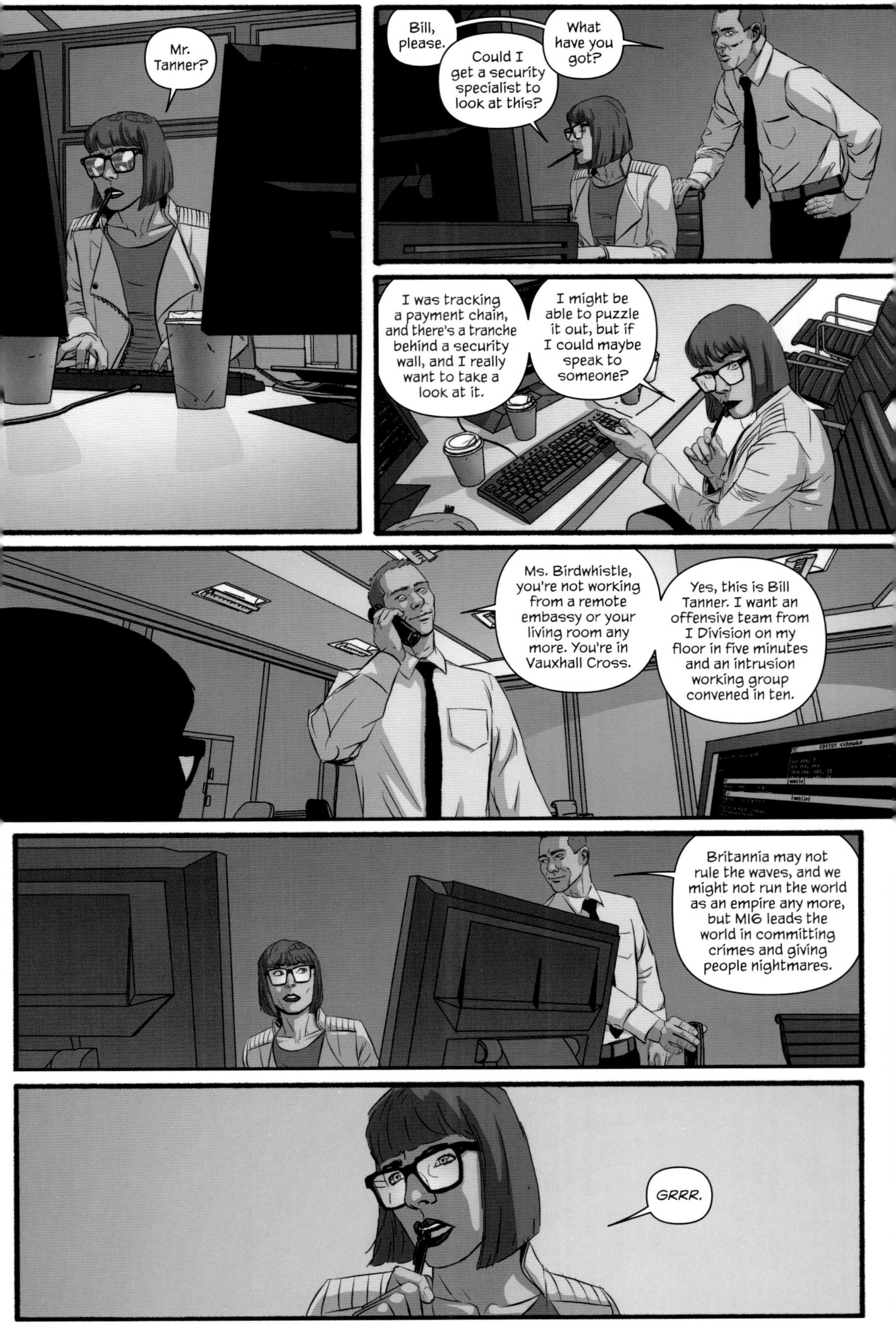
Mr. Tanner?
Bill, please.
What have you got?
Could I get a security specialist to look at this?
I was tracking a payment chain, and there's a tranche behind a security wall, and I really want to take a look at it.
I might be able to puzzle it out, but if I could maybe speak to someone?
Ms. Birdwhistle, you're not working from a remote embassy or your living room any more. You're in Vauxhall Cross.
Yes, this is Bill Tanner. I want an offensive team from I Division on my floor in five minutes and an intrusion working group convened in ten.
Britannia may not rule the waves, and we might not run the world as an empire any more, but MI6 leads the world in committing crimes and giving people nightmares.
GRRR.

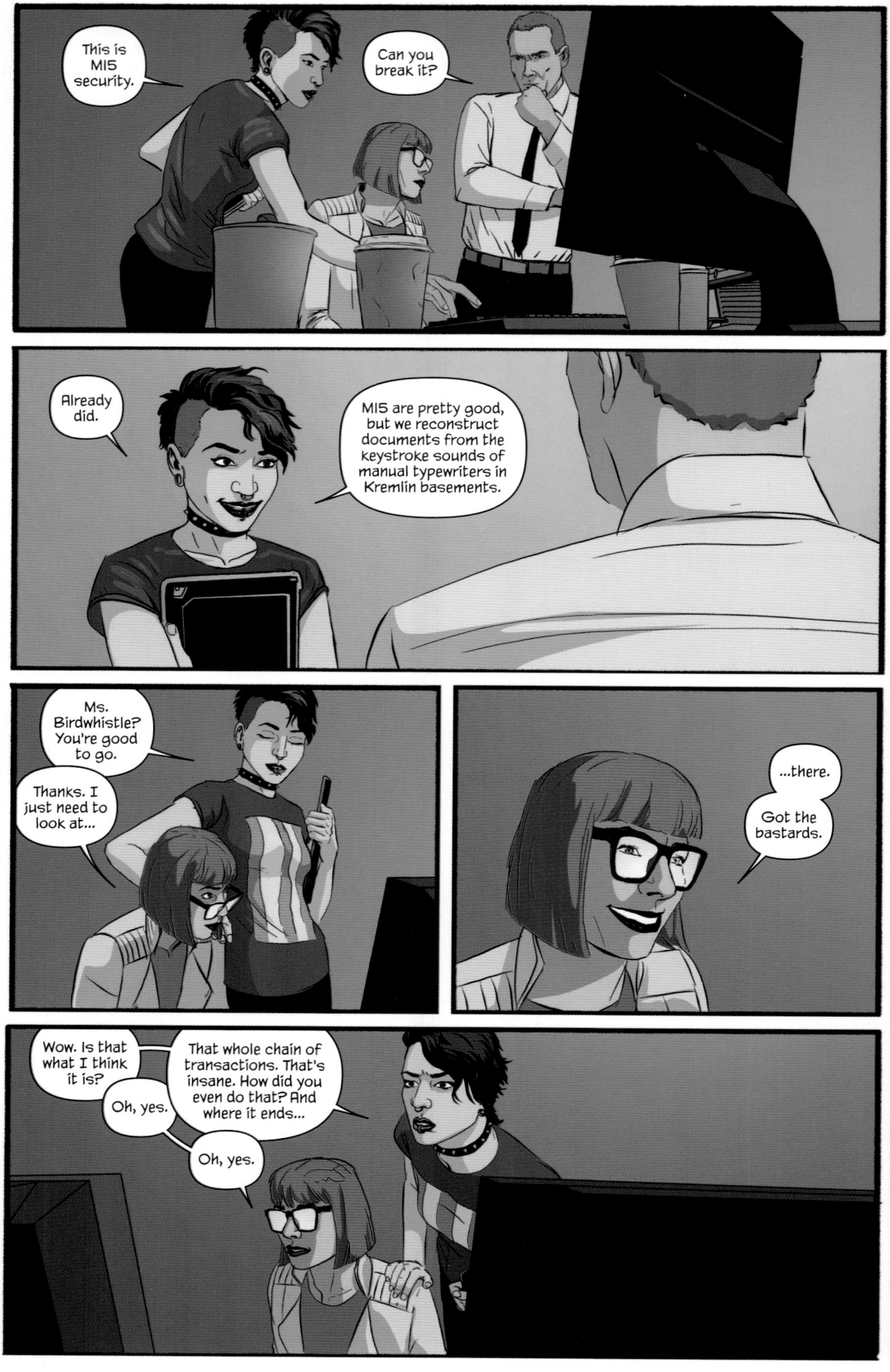
This is MI5 security.
Can you break it?
Already did.
MI5 are pretty good, but we reconstruct documents from the keystroke sounds of manual typewriters in Kremlin basements.
Ms. Birdwhistle? You're good to go.
Thanks. I just need to look at...
...there.
Got the bastards.
Wow. Is that what I think it is?
Oh, yes.
That whole chain of transactions. That's insane. How did you even do that? And where it ends...
Oh, yes.

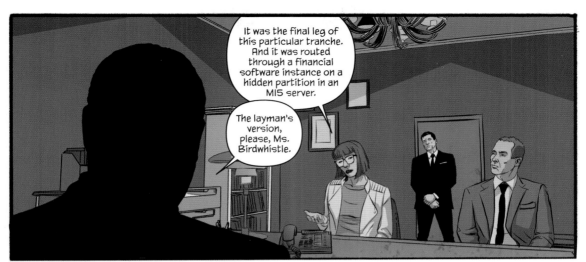

It was the final leg of this particular tranche. And it was routed through a financial software instance on a hidden partition in an MI5 server.

The layman's version, please, Ms. Birdwhistle.

From there, money is...disguised, let's say, and moved through MI5 channels to something called Strategic Reserve Fleet.

The Strategic Reserve Fleet? That's a myth.

On the contrary, Mr. Tanner. You should never underestimate the essential strangeness of this country.

What's he talking about?

He's talking about Box Tunnel. A secret underground town.

A maze of tunnels under a hill and a quarry, administrated by MI5, containing records, computing installations, and the Strategic Reserve Fleet.

A fleet of steam locomotives, placed underground against a nuclear attack on Britain.

The electromagnetic pulses from nuclear explosions, you see, would cripple our electrified railway system.

Very good.

So, post-World War Three, the steam engine would be essential technology again.

That said, it was my understanding that Box Tunnel had been sealed up and abandoned years ago.

Just past Chippenham, 007. Two hours by car from here, if the M4 isn't a complete disaster.

I think you should see what's being kept in Box Tunnel these days.

You want me to break into an MI5 installation. Should I buy a water pistol on the way? A spud gun?

No. You'll go and see Major Boothroyd first.

You will not have back-up, nor will you be allowed to carry any identification. This is a deniable operation.

I am still in negotiations with No. 10 about the Hard Rule, and I will not flagrantly flout the law of the land.

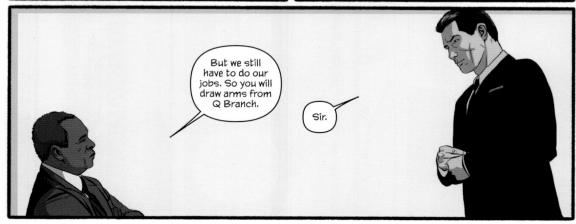

But we still have to do our jobs. So you will draw arms from Q Branch.

Sir.

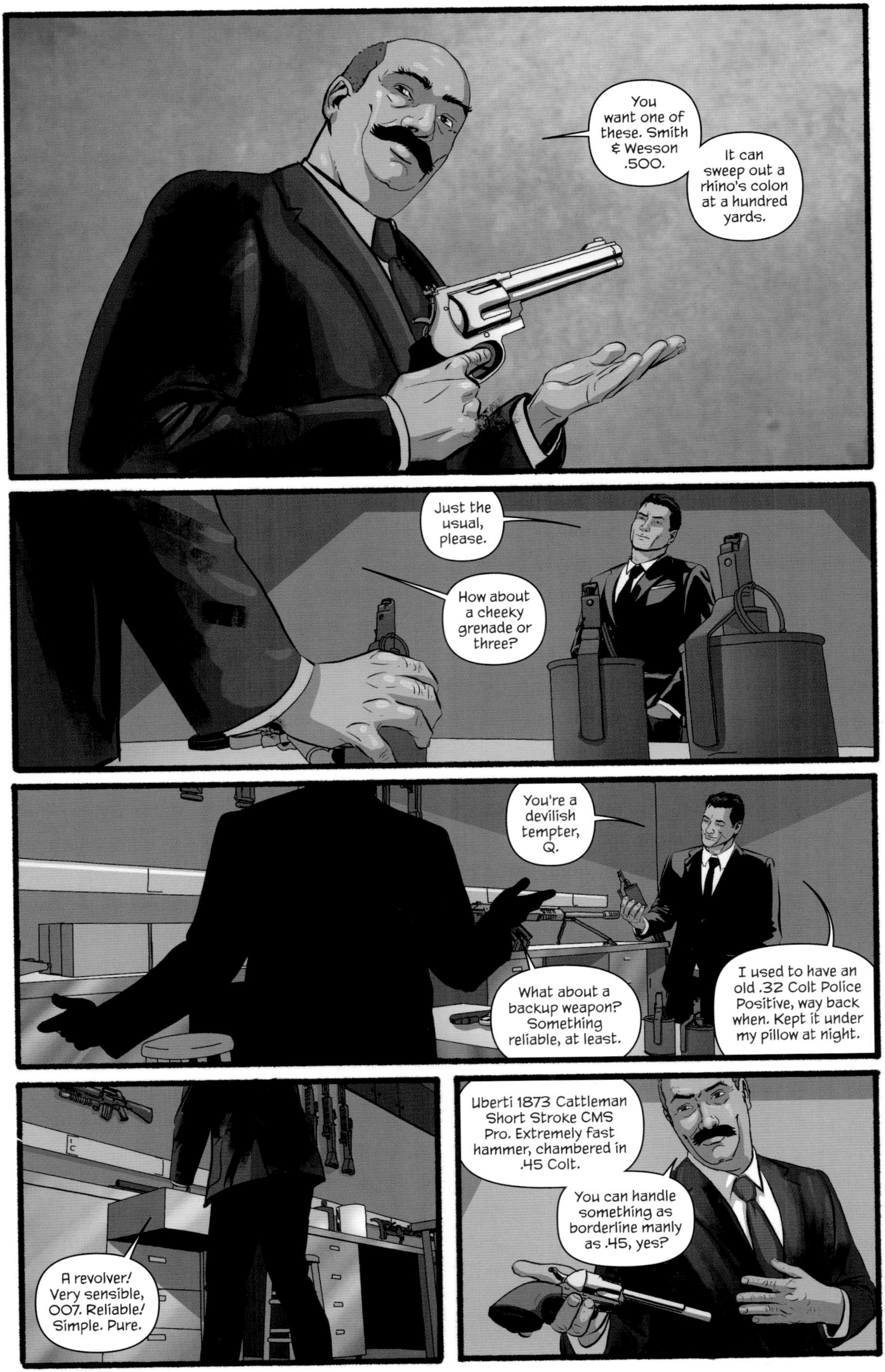
You want one of these. Smith & Wesson .500.
It can sweep out a rhino's colon at a hundred yards.
Just the usual, please.
How about a cheeky grenade or three?
You're a devilish tempter, Q.
What about a backup weapon? Something reliable, at least.
I used to have an old .32 Colt Police Positive, way back when. Kept it under my pillow at night.
A revolver! Very sensible, 007. Reliable! Simple. Pure.
Uberti 1873 Cattleman Short Stroke CMS Pro. Extremely fast hammer, chambered in .45 Colt.
You can handle something as borderline manly as .45, yes?

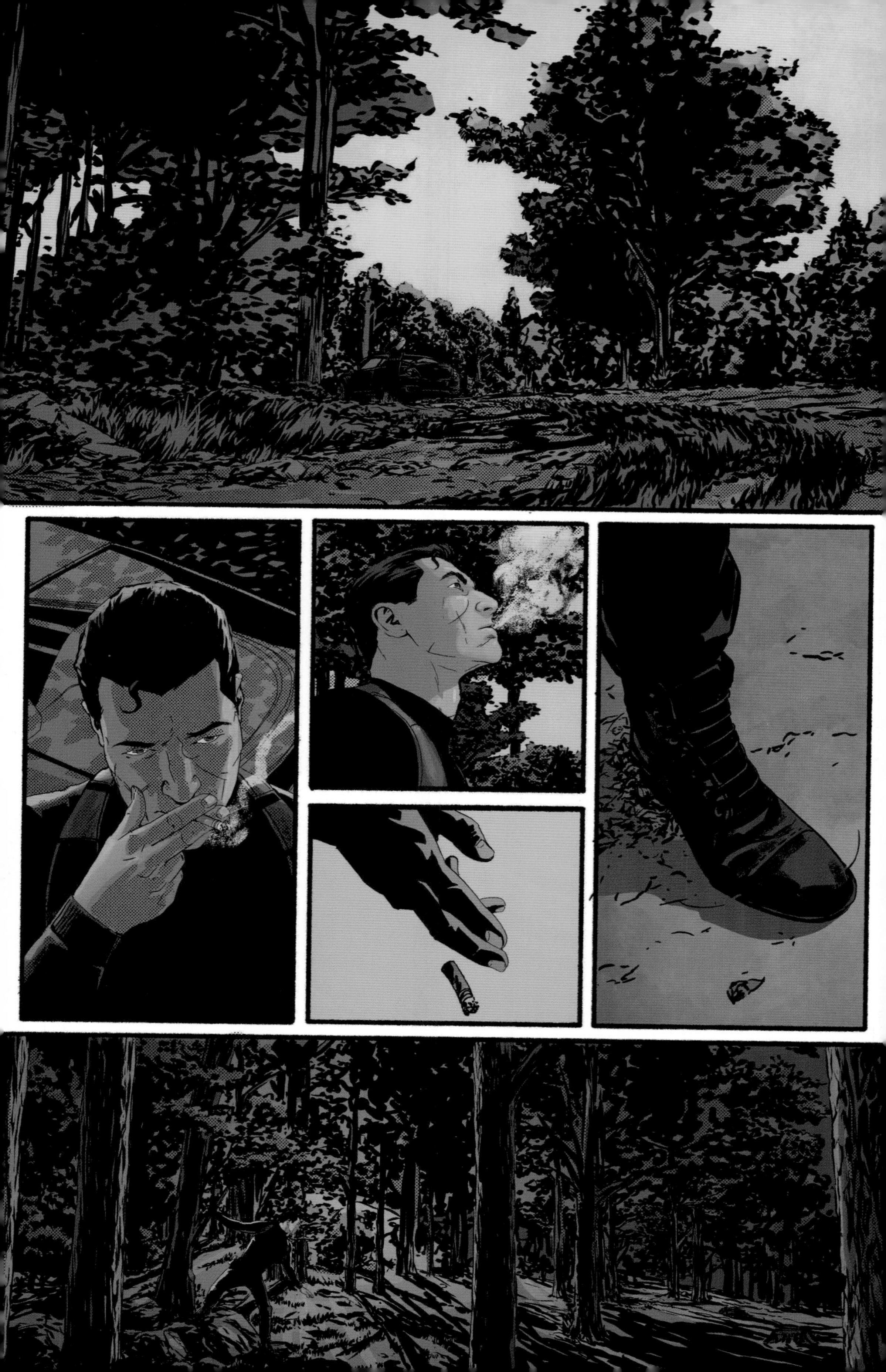

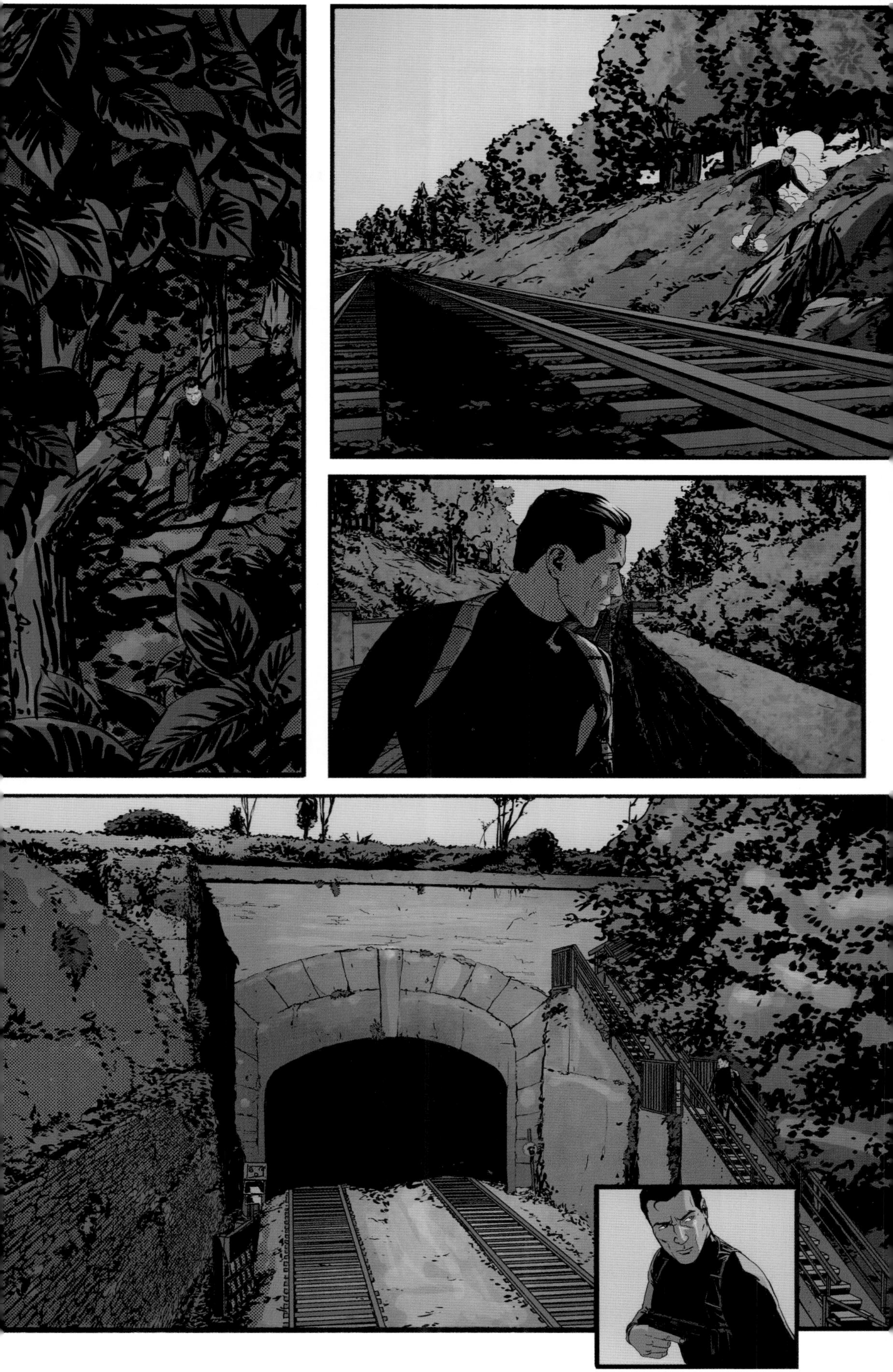

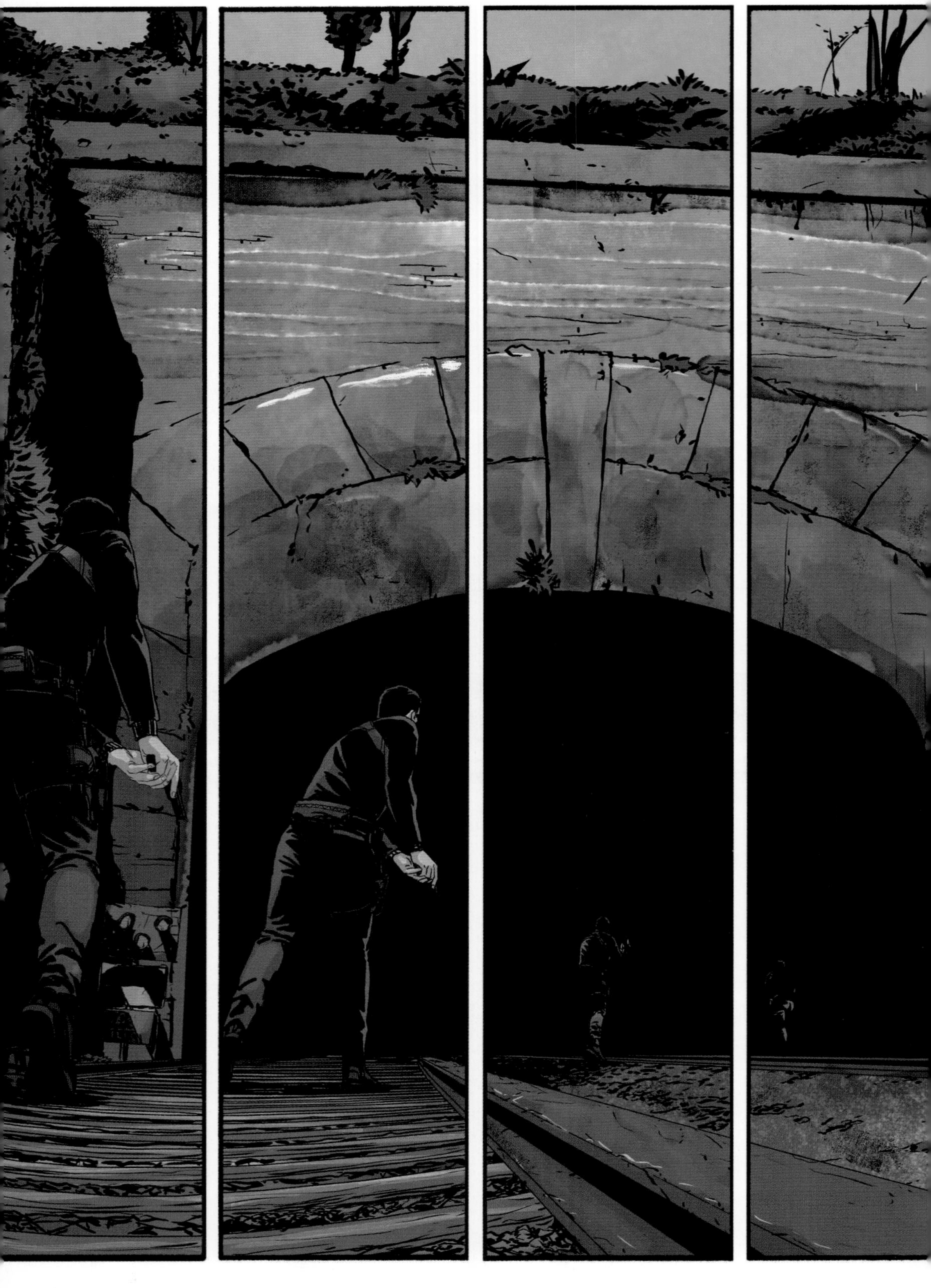

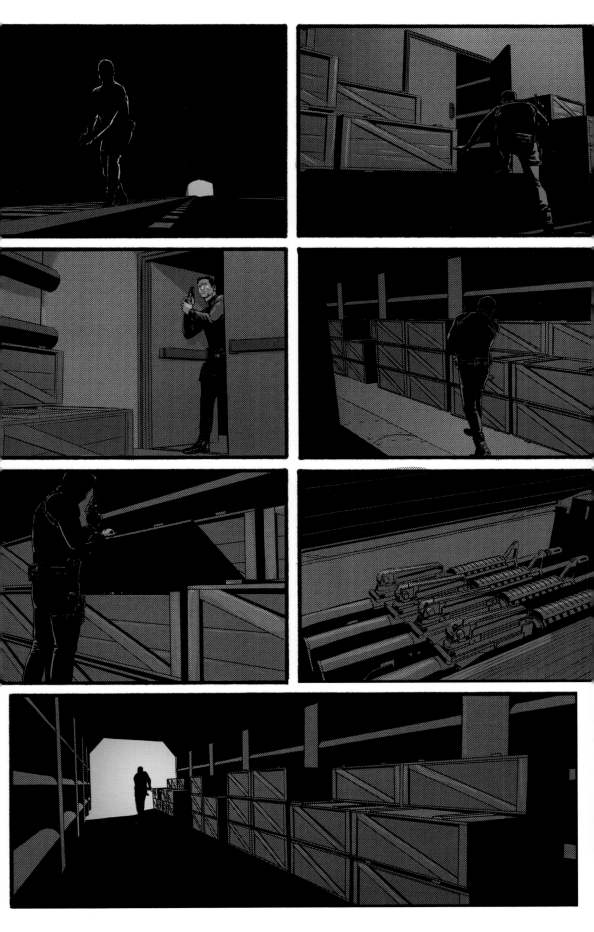

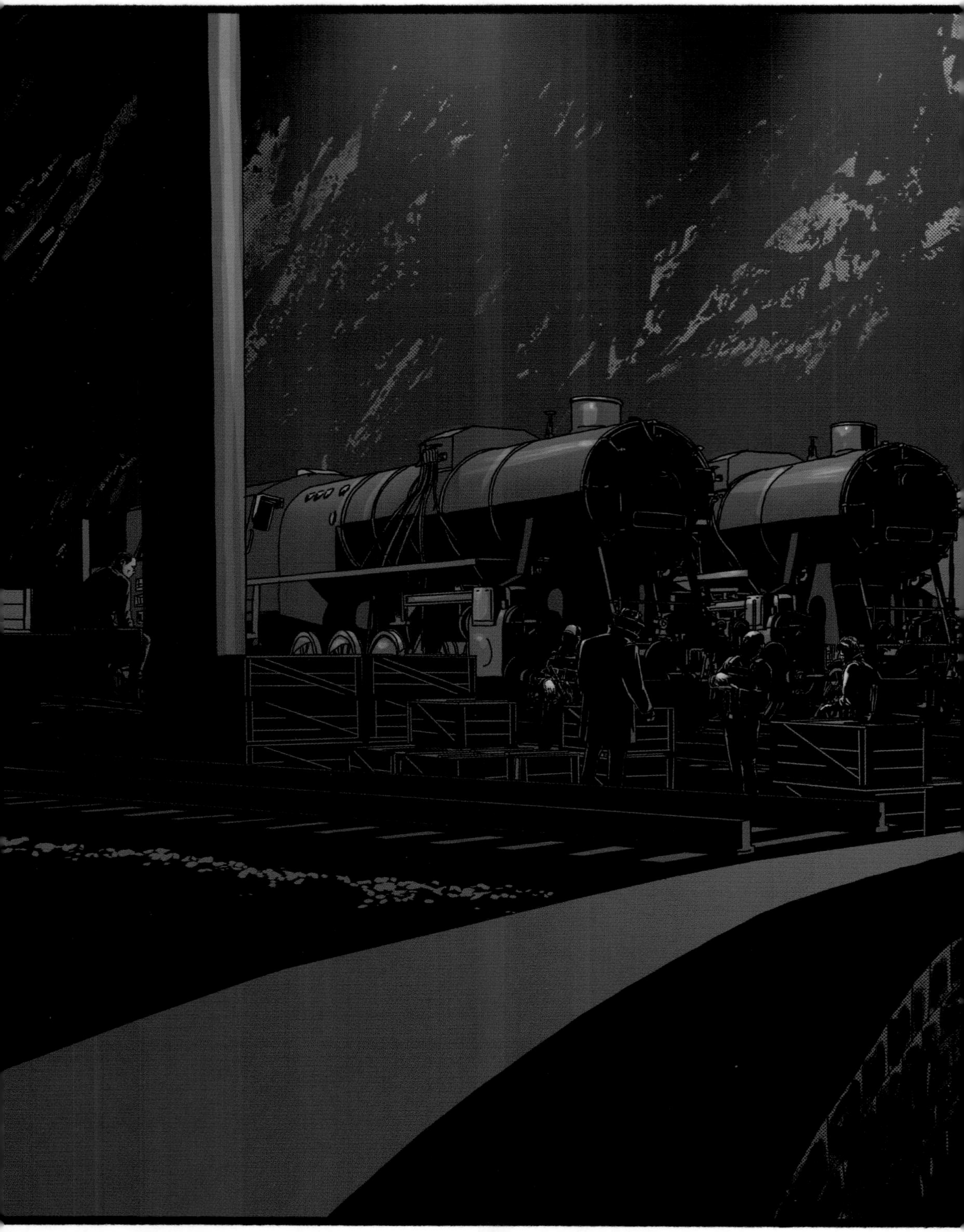

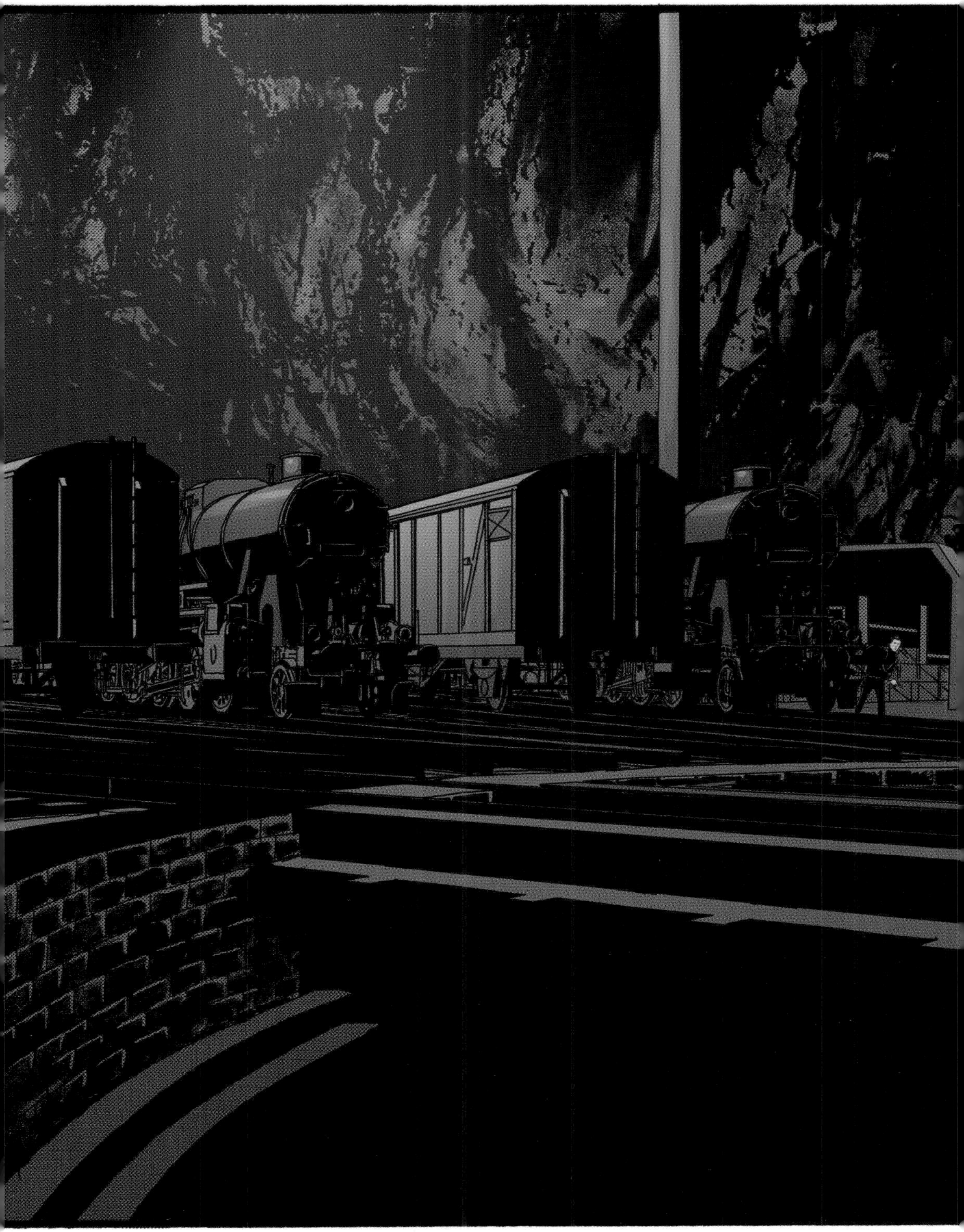

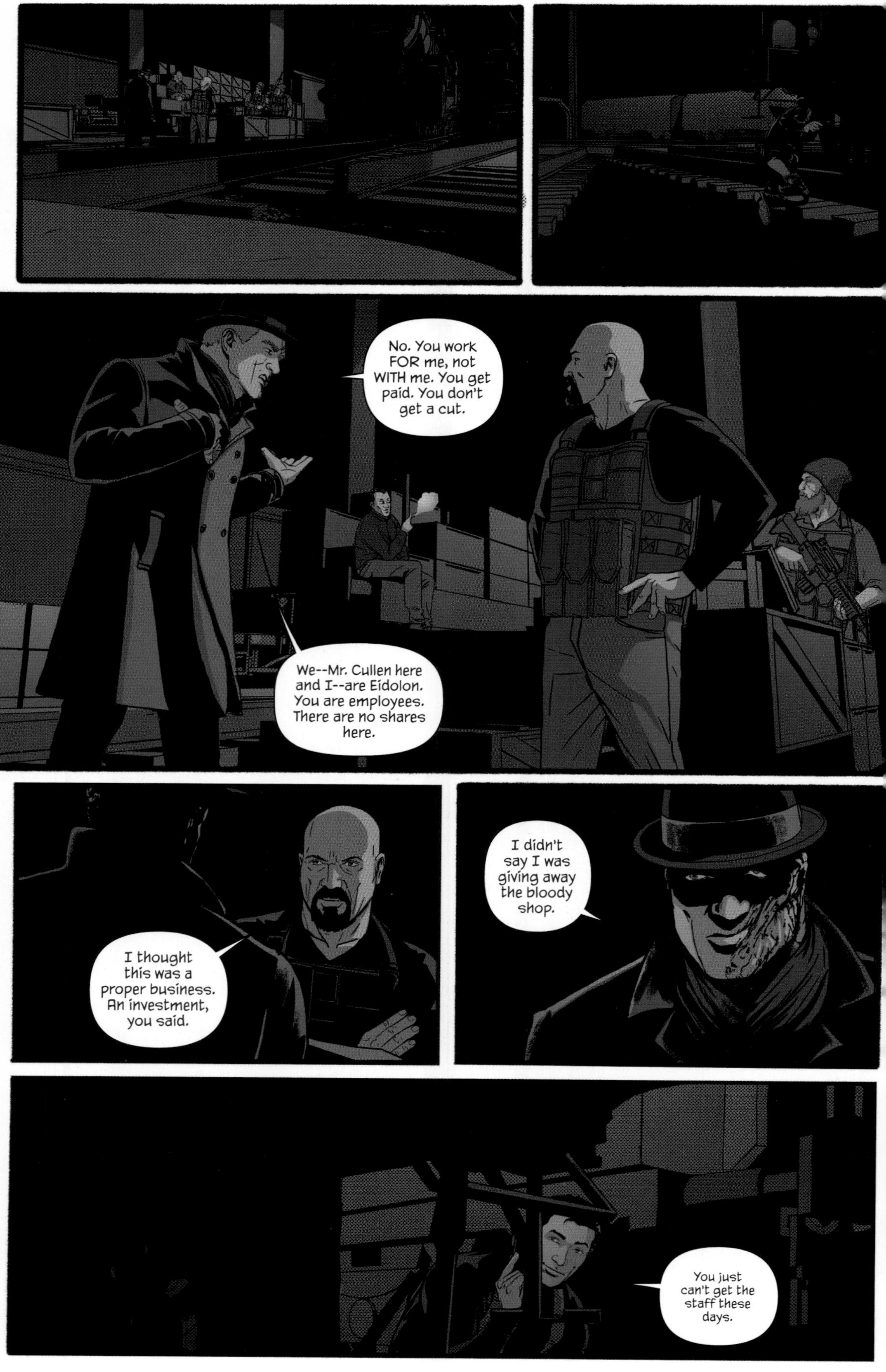
No. You work FOR me, not WITH me. You get paid. You don't get a cut.
We--Mr. Cullen here and I--are Eidolon. You are employees. There are no shares here.
I thought this was a proper business. An investment, you said.
I didn't say I was giving away the bloody shop.
You just can't get the staff these days.

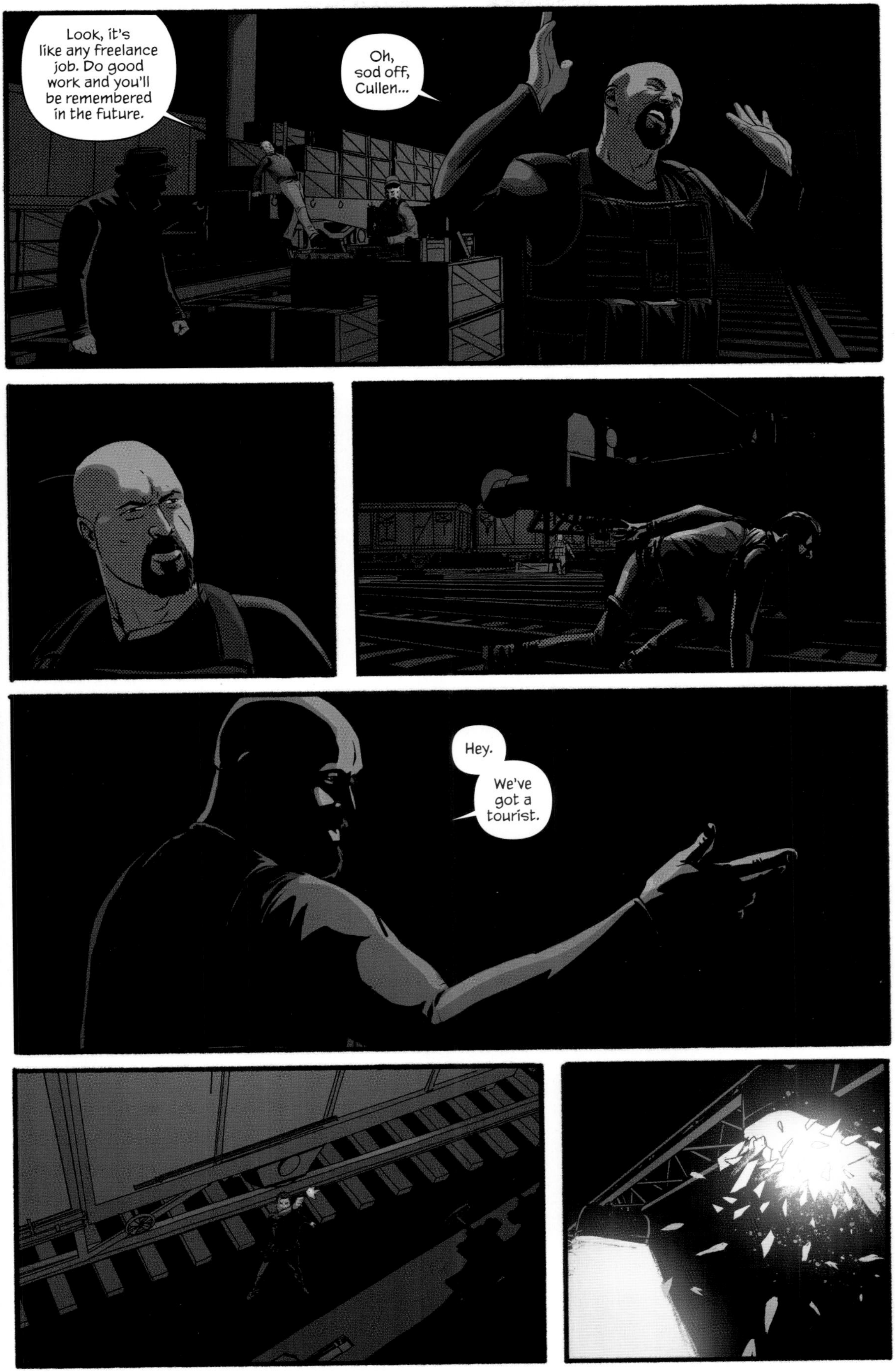
Look, it's like any freelance job. Do good work and you'll be remembered in the future.
Oh, sod off, Cullen...
Hey.
We've got a tourist.

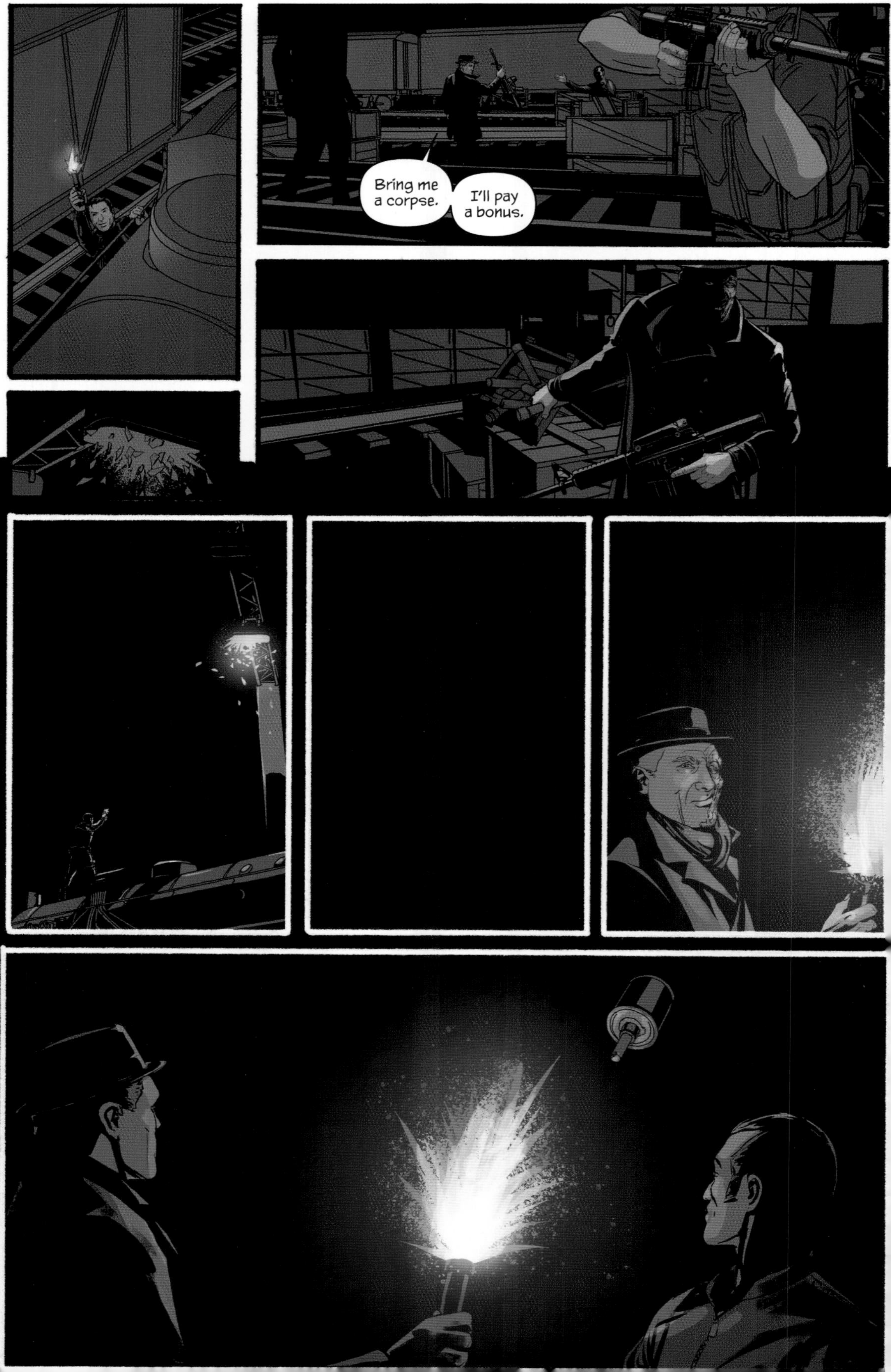
Bring me a corpse.
I'll pay a bonus.

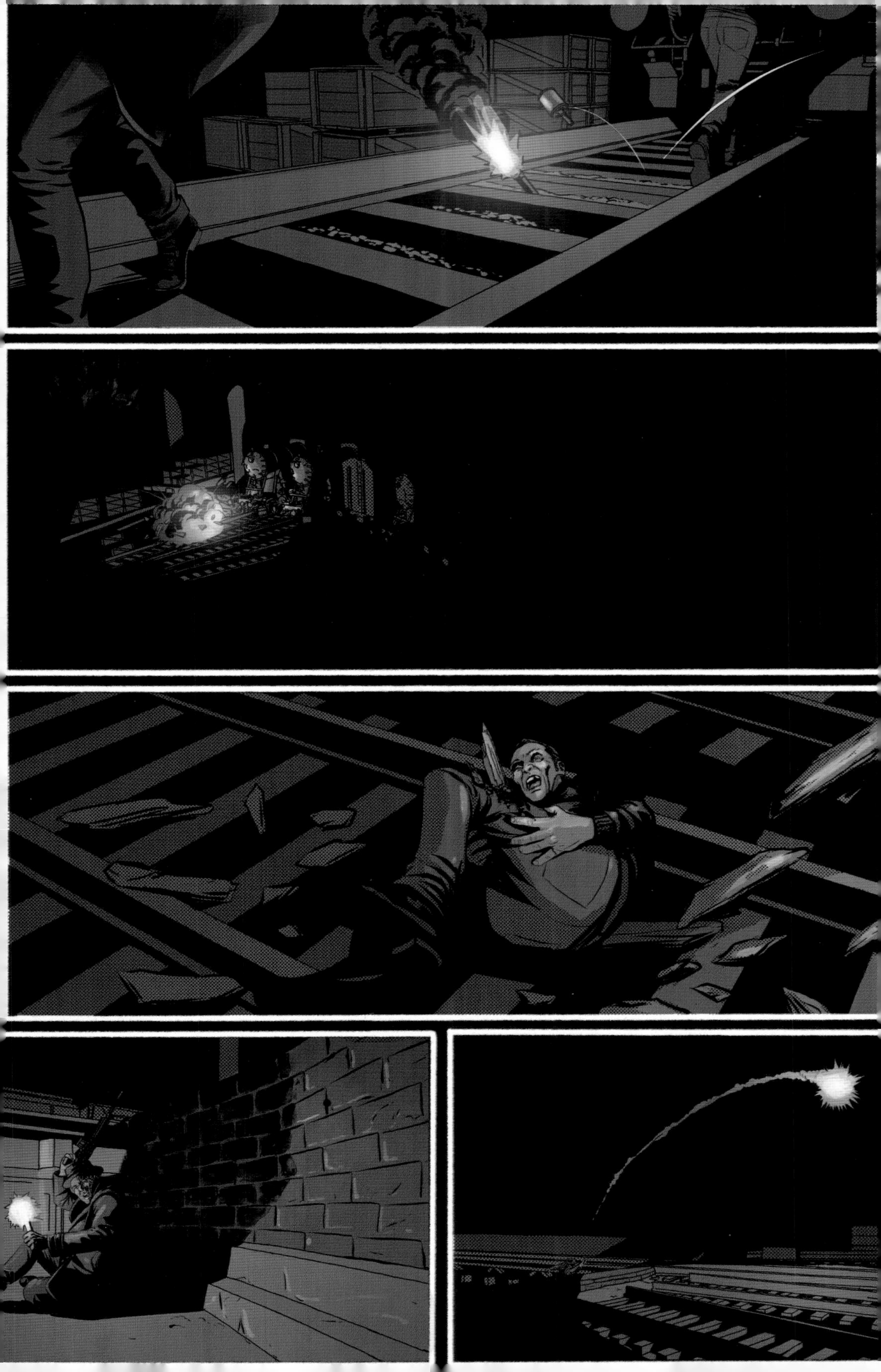

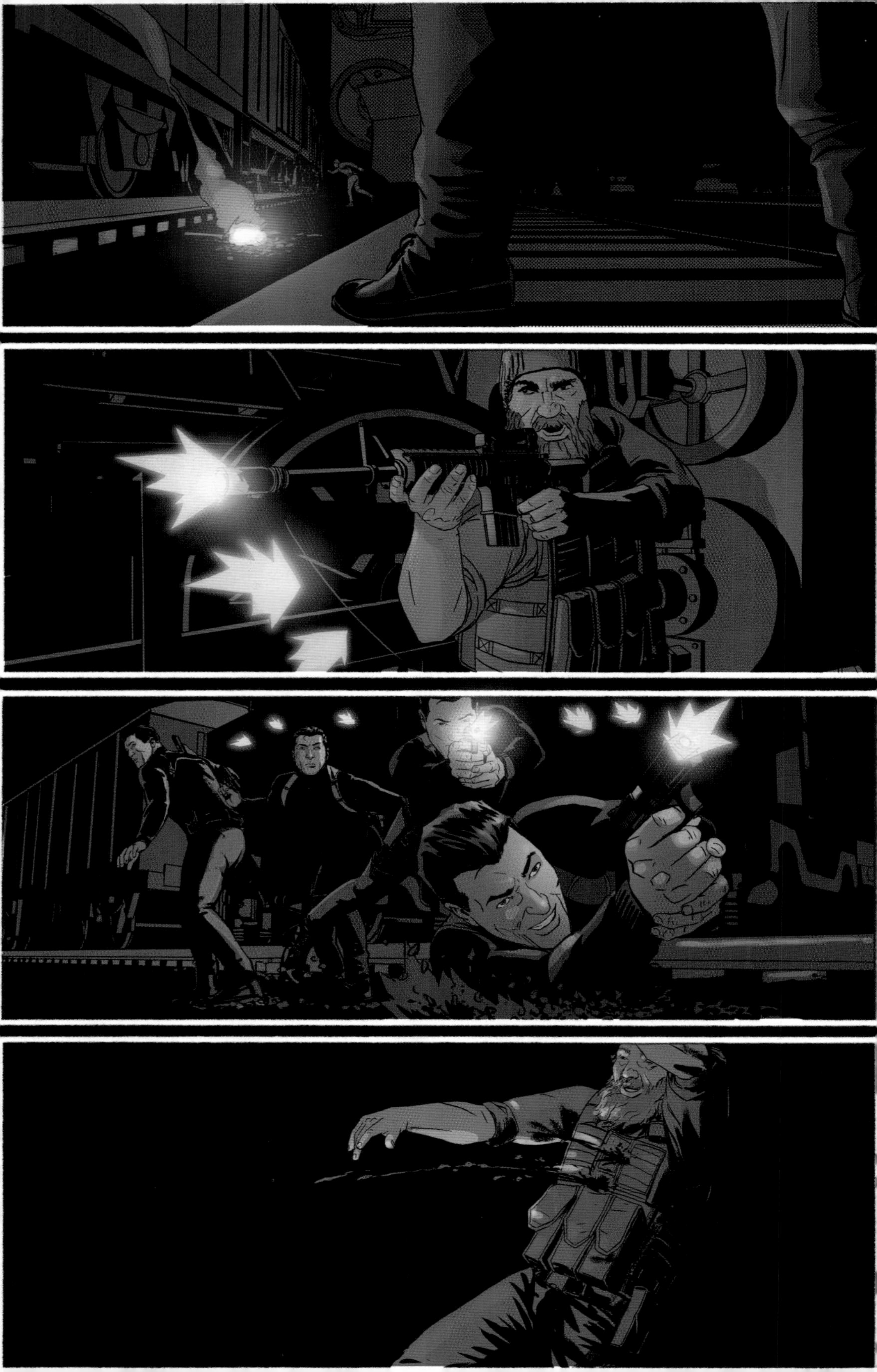

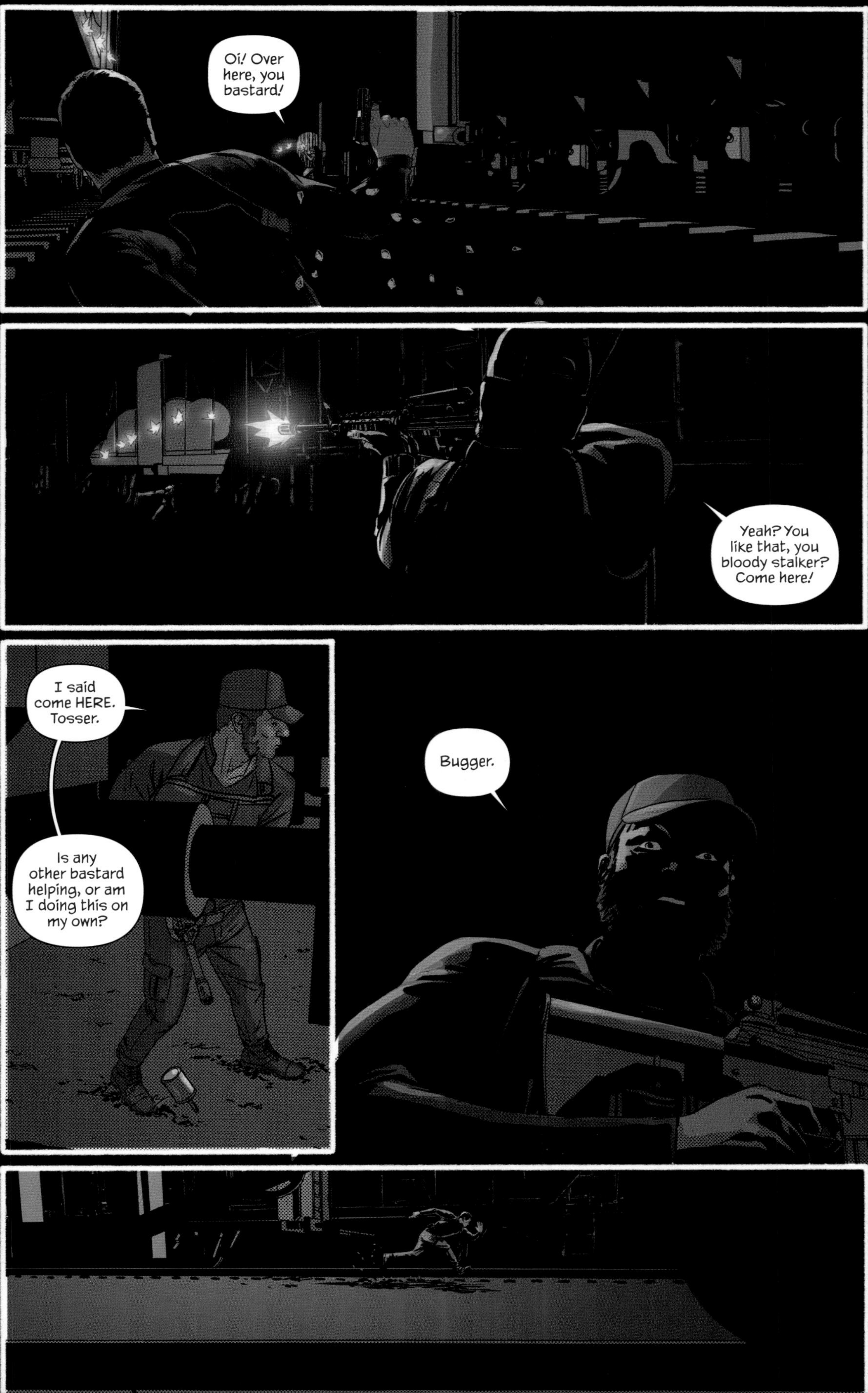
Oi! Over here, you bastard!
Yeah? You like that, you bloody stalker? Come here!
I said come HERE. Tosser.
Is any other bastard helping, or am I doing this on my own?
Bugger.

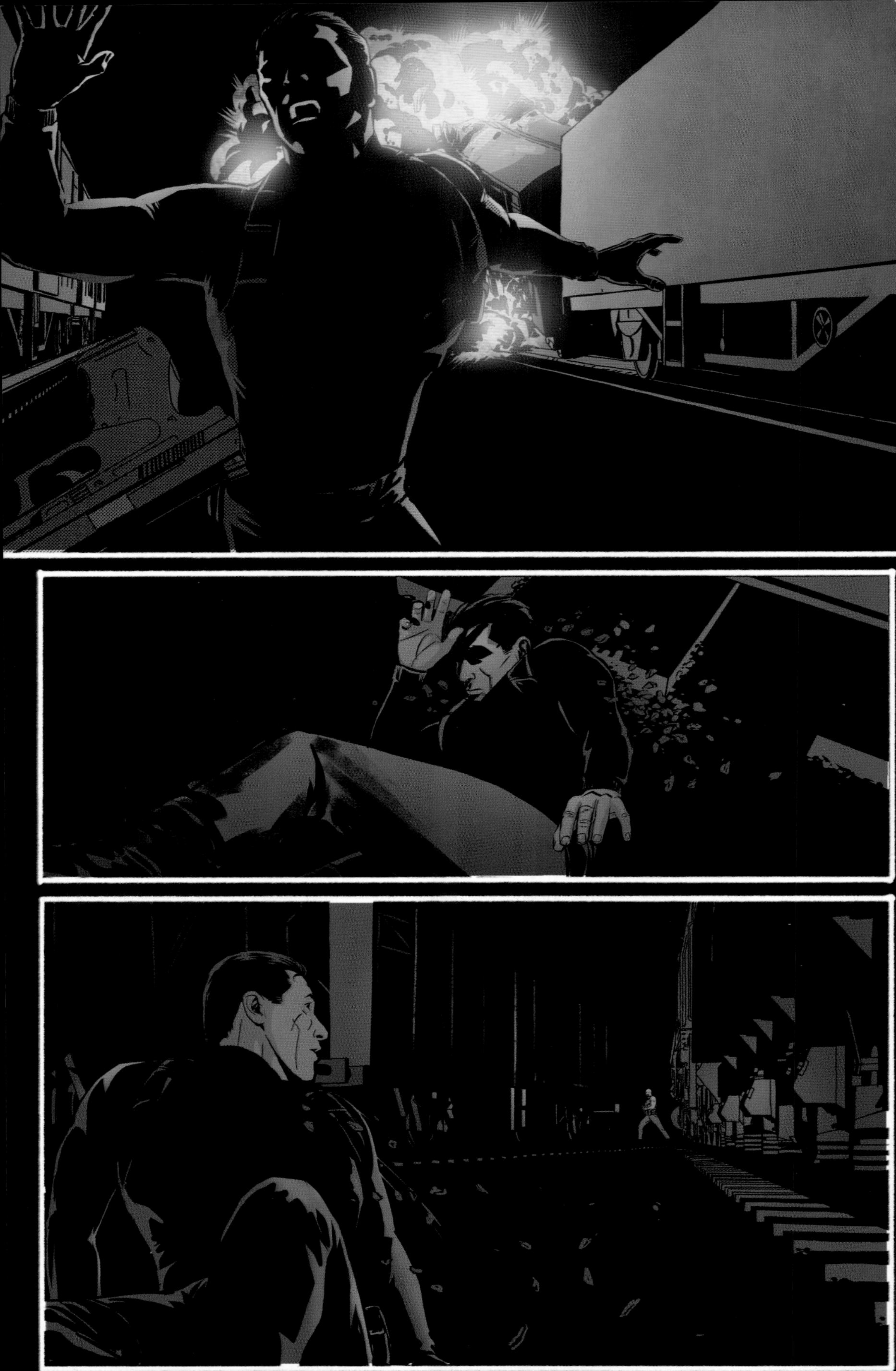

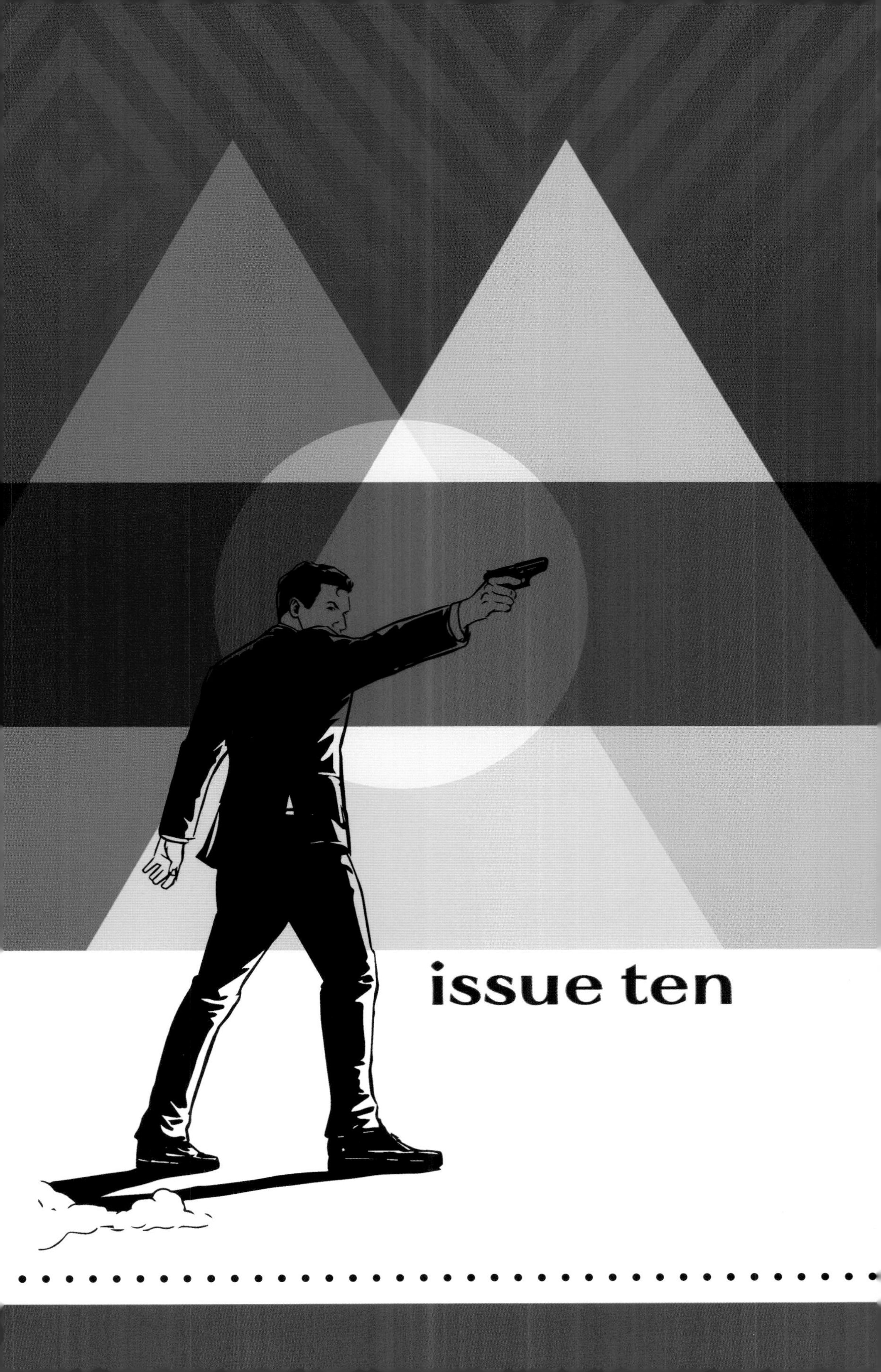
issue ten

issue #10 main cover by **DOM REARDON**

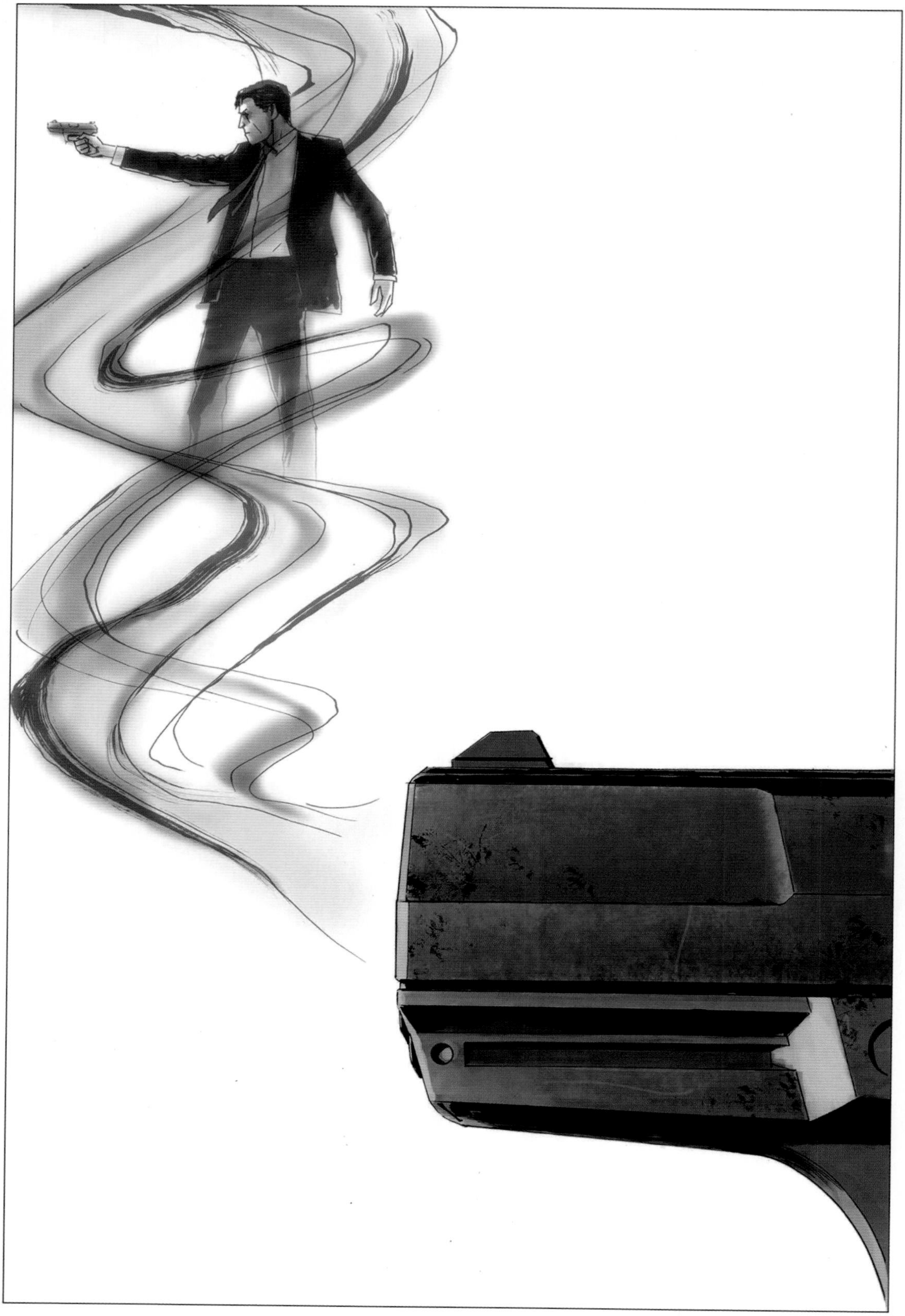

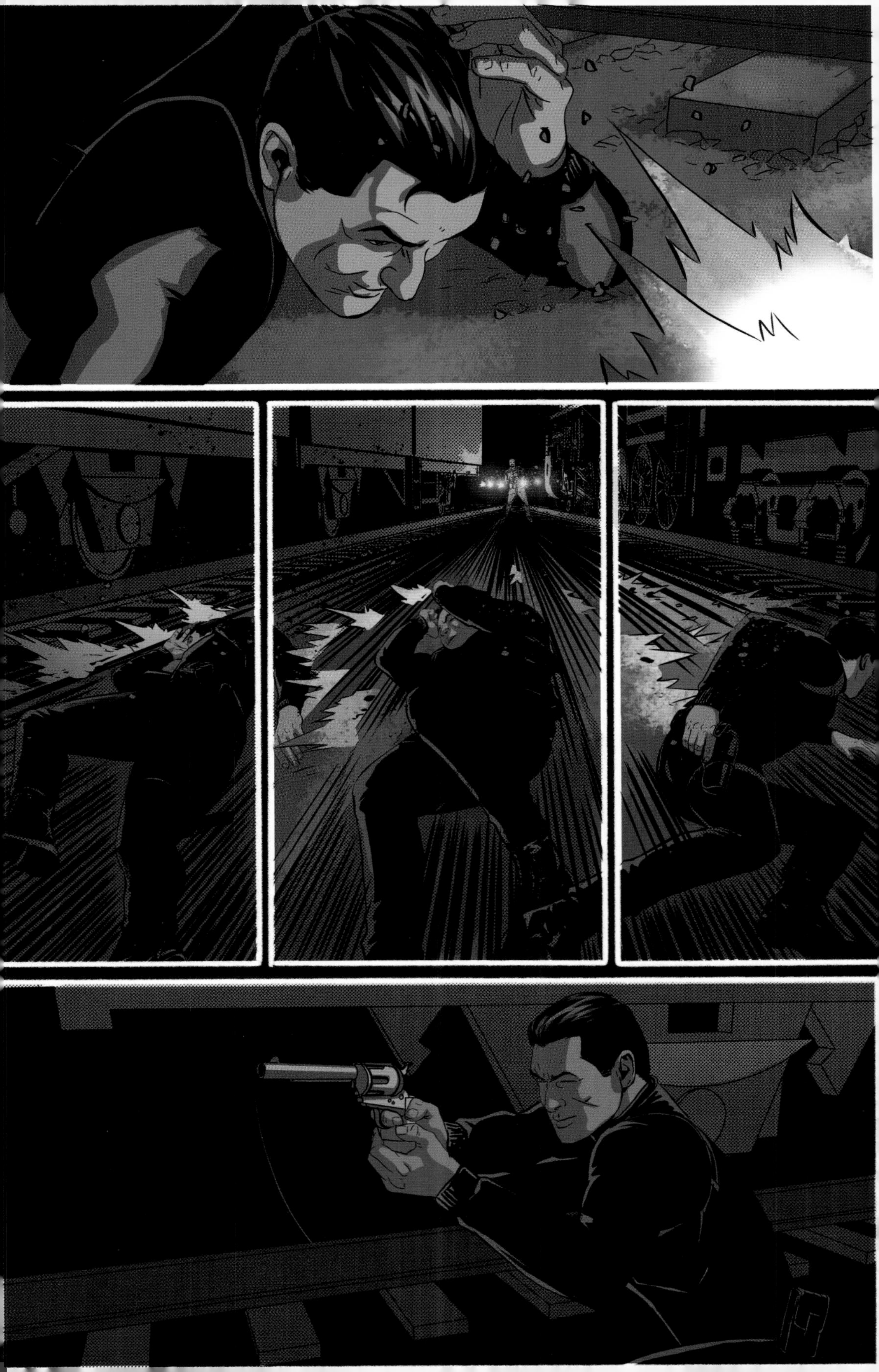

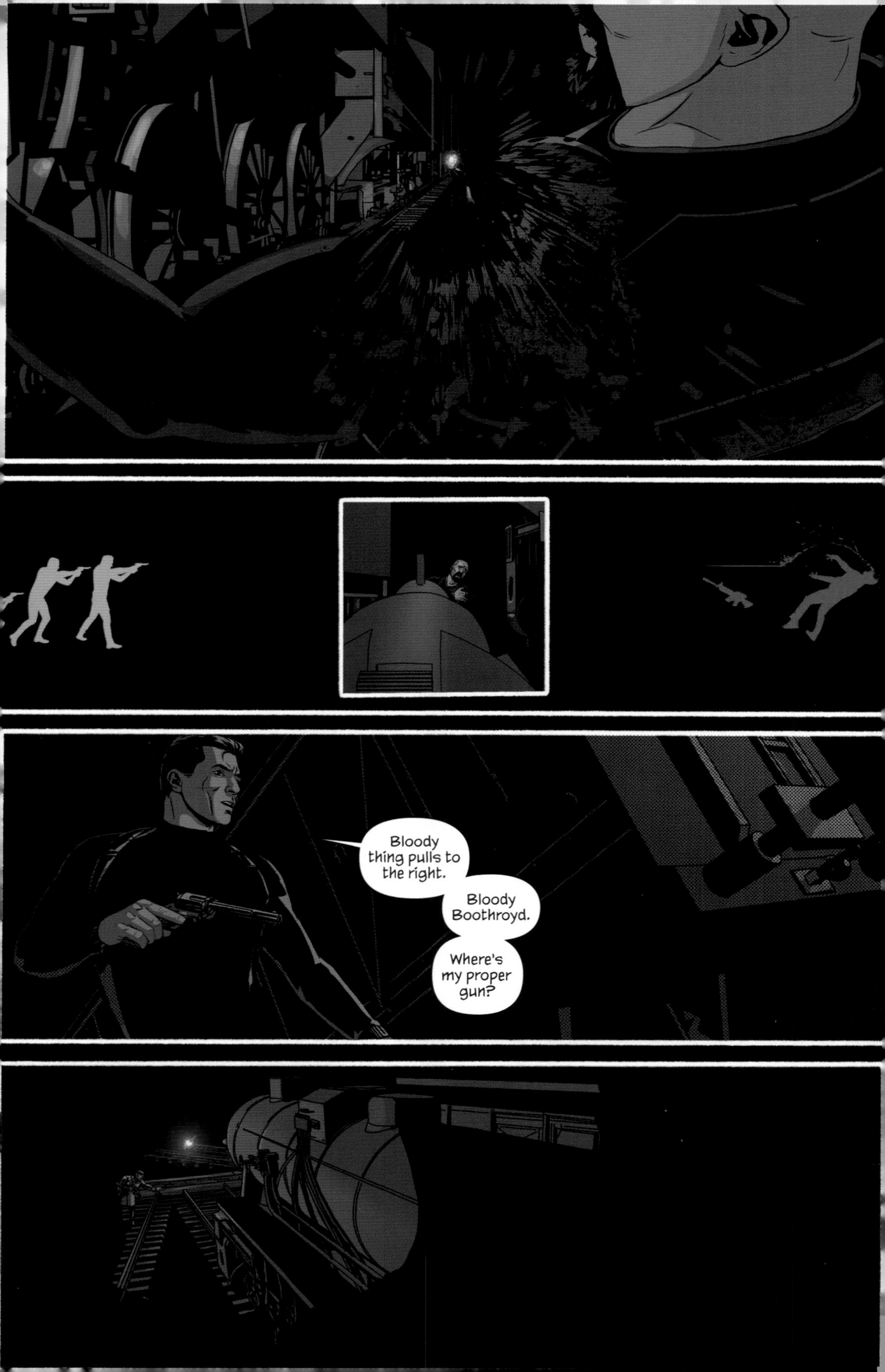
Bloody thing pulls to the right.
Bloody Boothroyd.
Where's my proper gun?

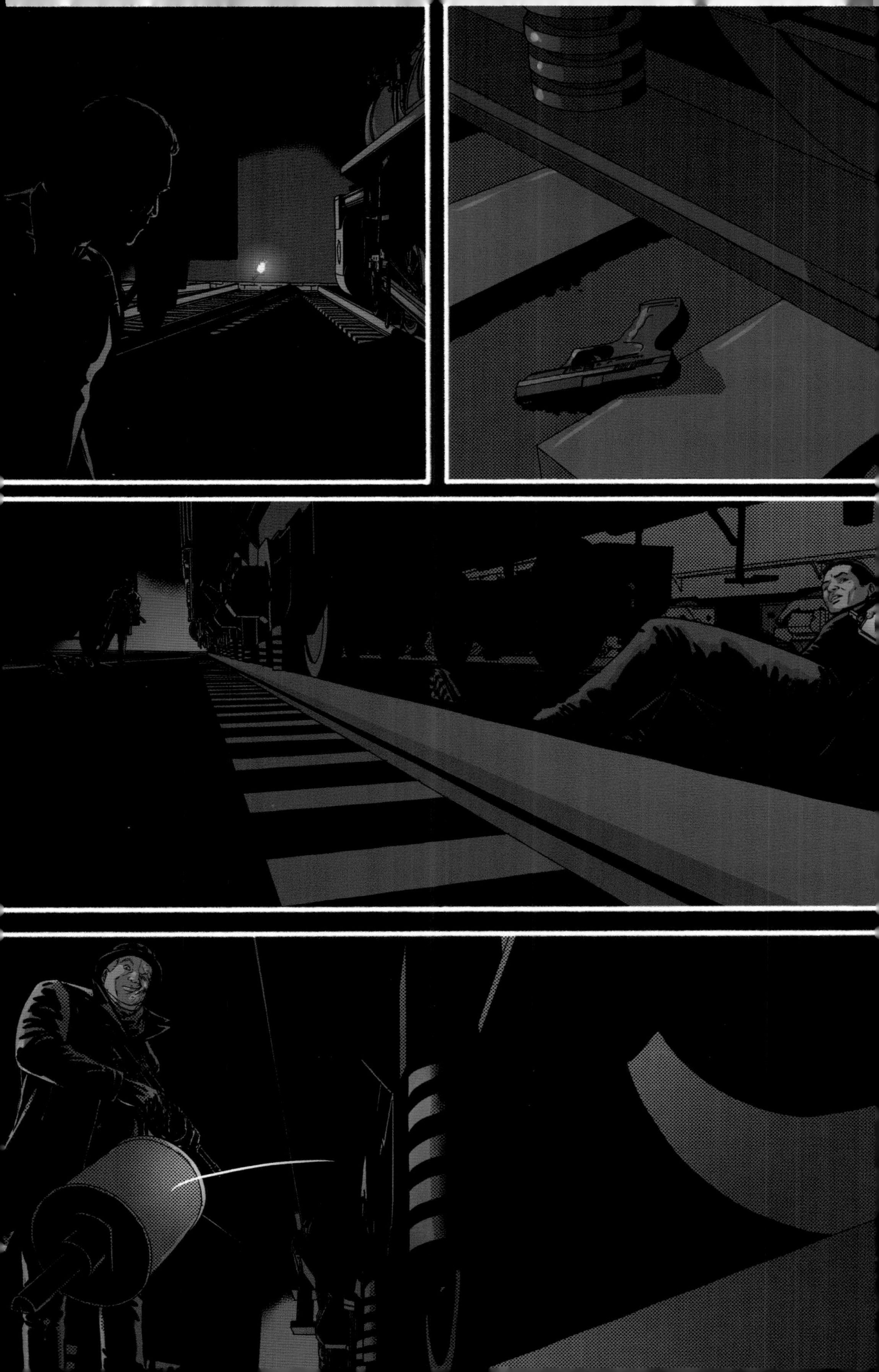

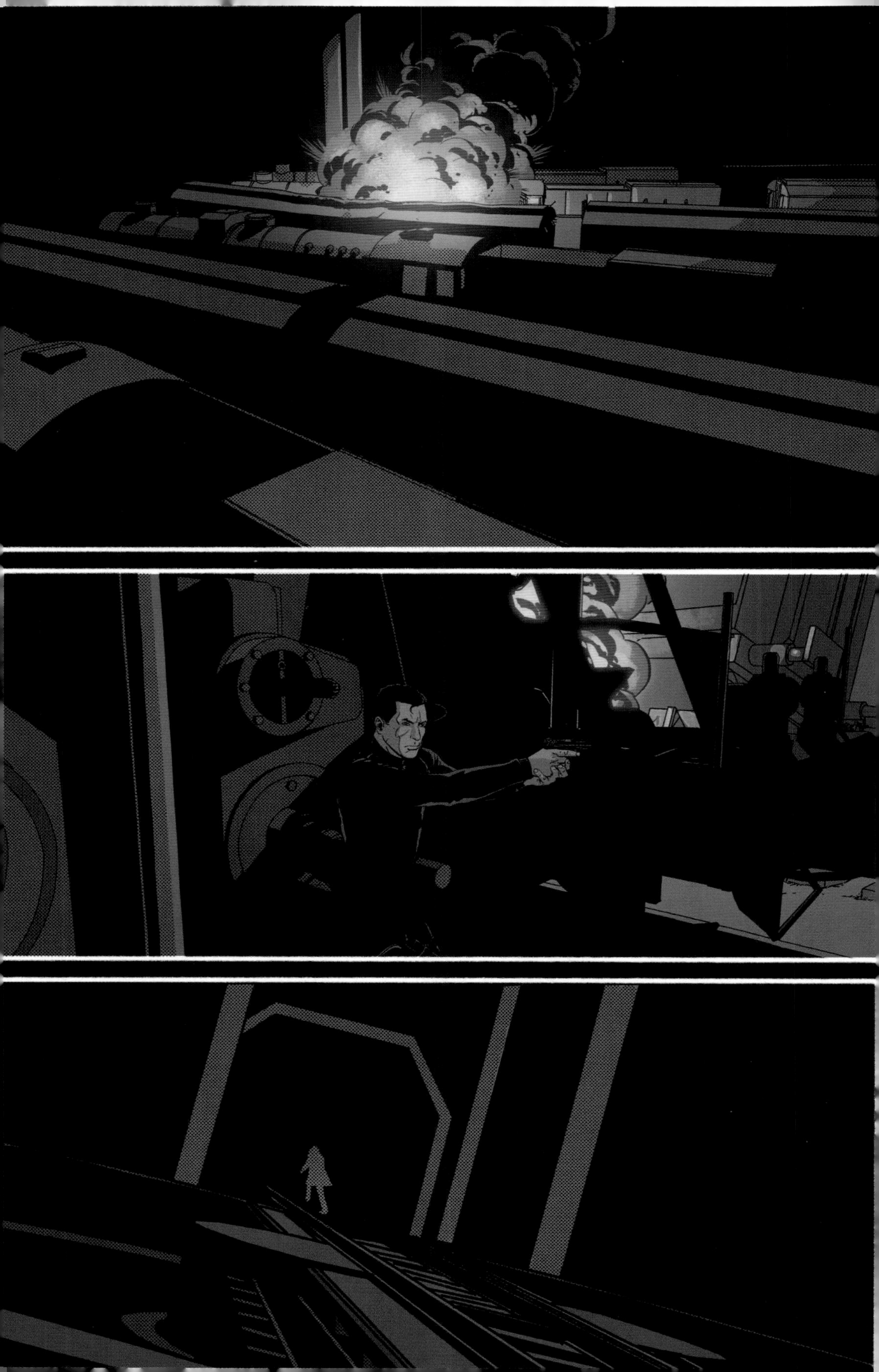

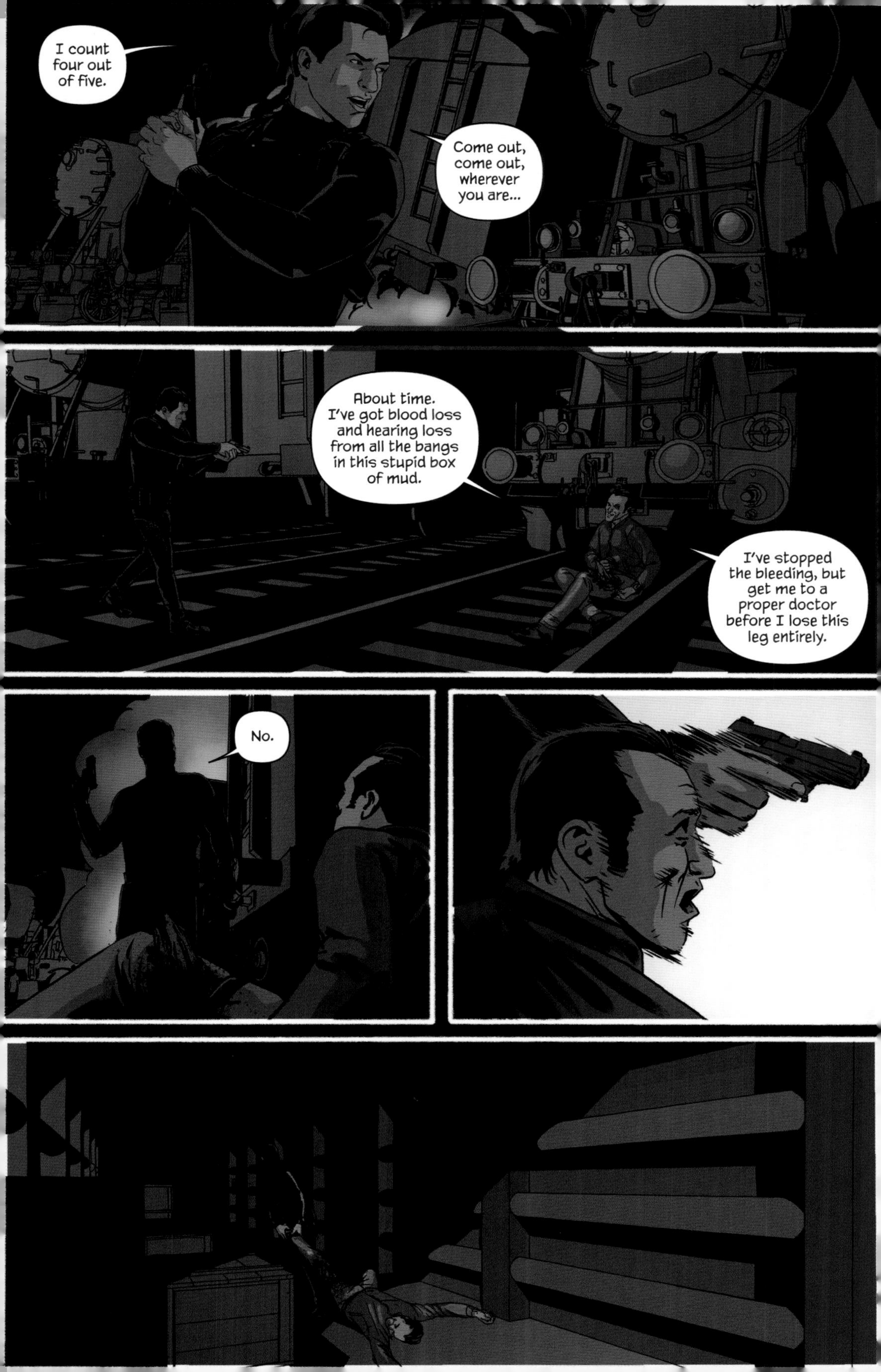
I count four out of five.
Come out, come out, wherever you are...
About time. I've got blood loss and hearing loss from all the bangs in this stupid box of mud.
I've stopped the bleeding, but get me to a proper doctor before I lose this leg entirely.
No.

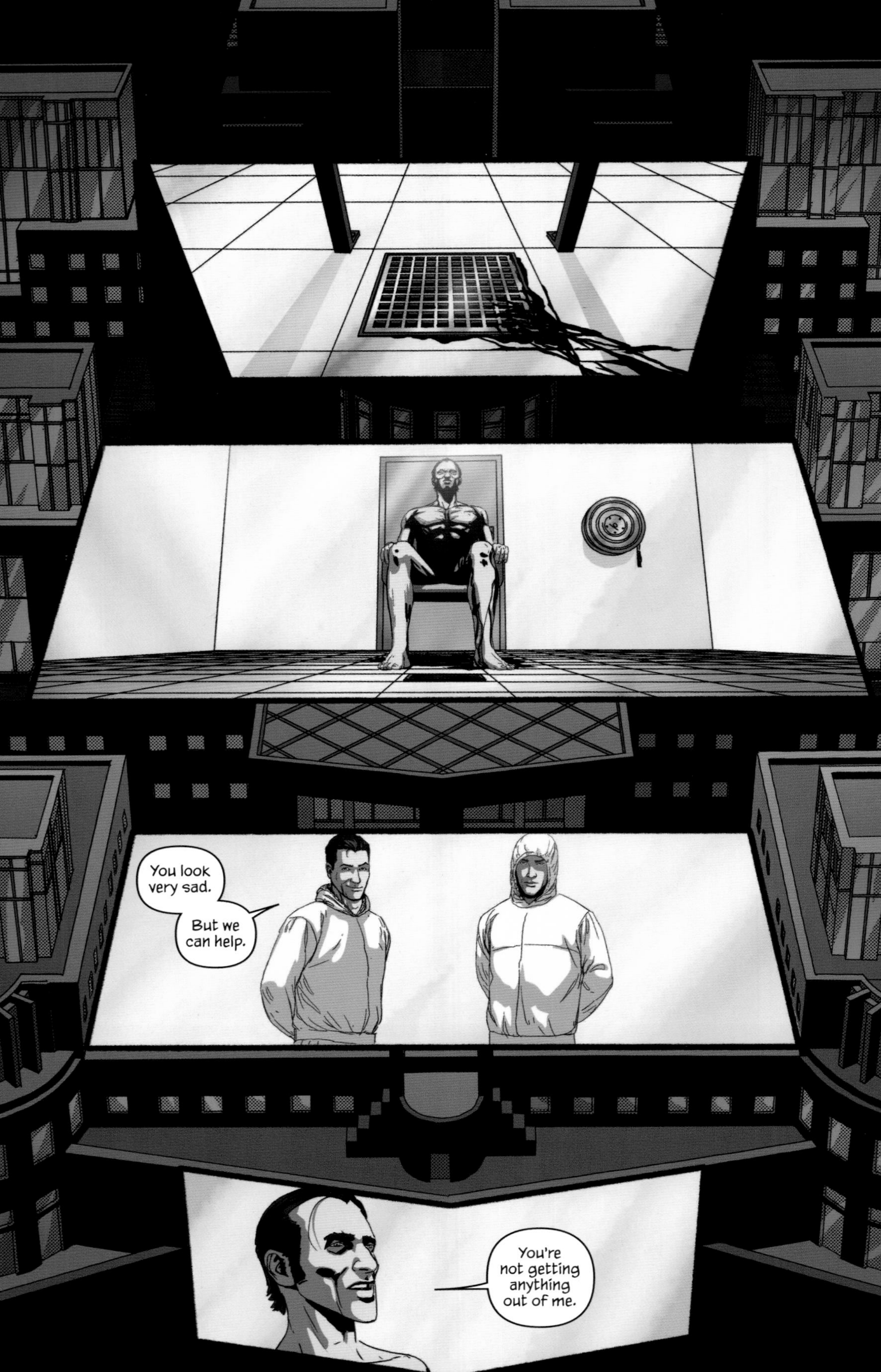
You look very sad.
But we can help.
You're not getting anything out of me.

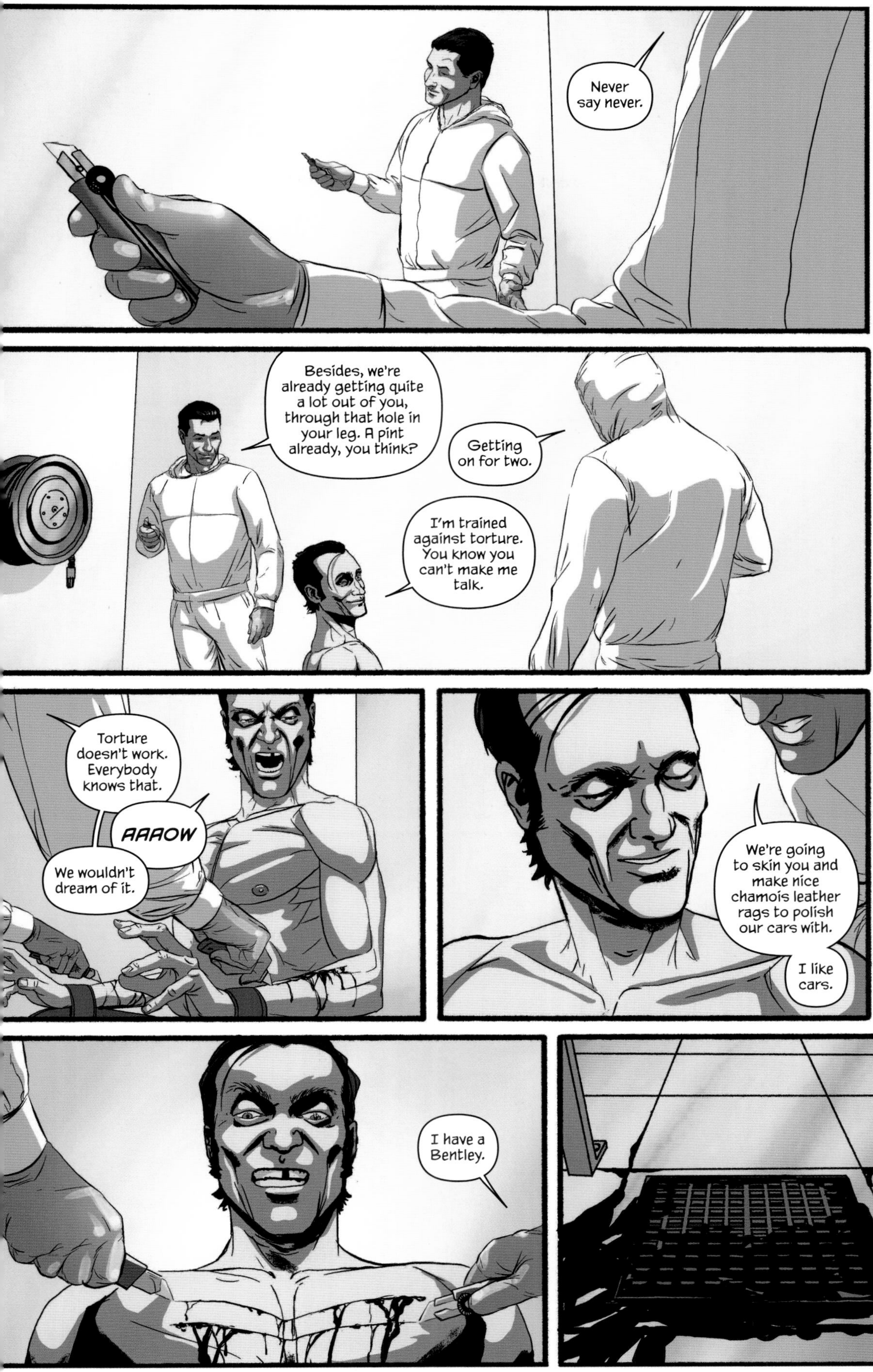
Never say never.
Besides, we're already getting quite a lot out of you, through that hole in your leg. A pint already, you think?
Getting on for two.
I'm trained against torture. You know you can't make me talk.
Torture doesn't work. Everybody knows that.
AAAOW
We wouldn't dream of it.
We're going to skin you and make nice chamois leather rags to polish our cars with.
I like cars.
I have a Bentley.

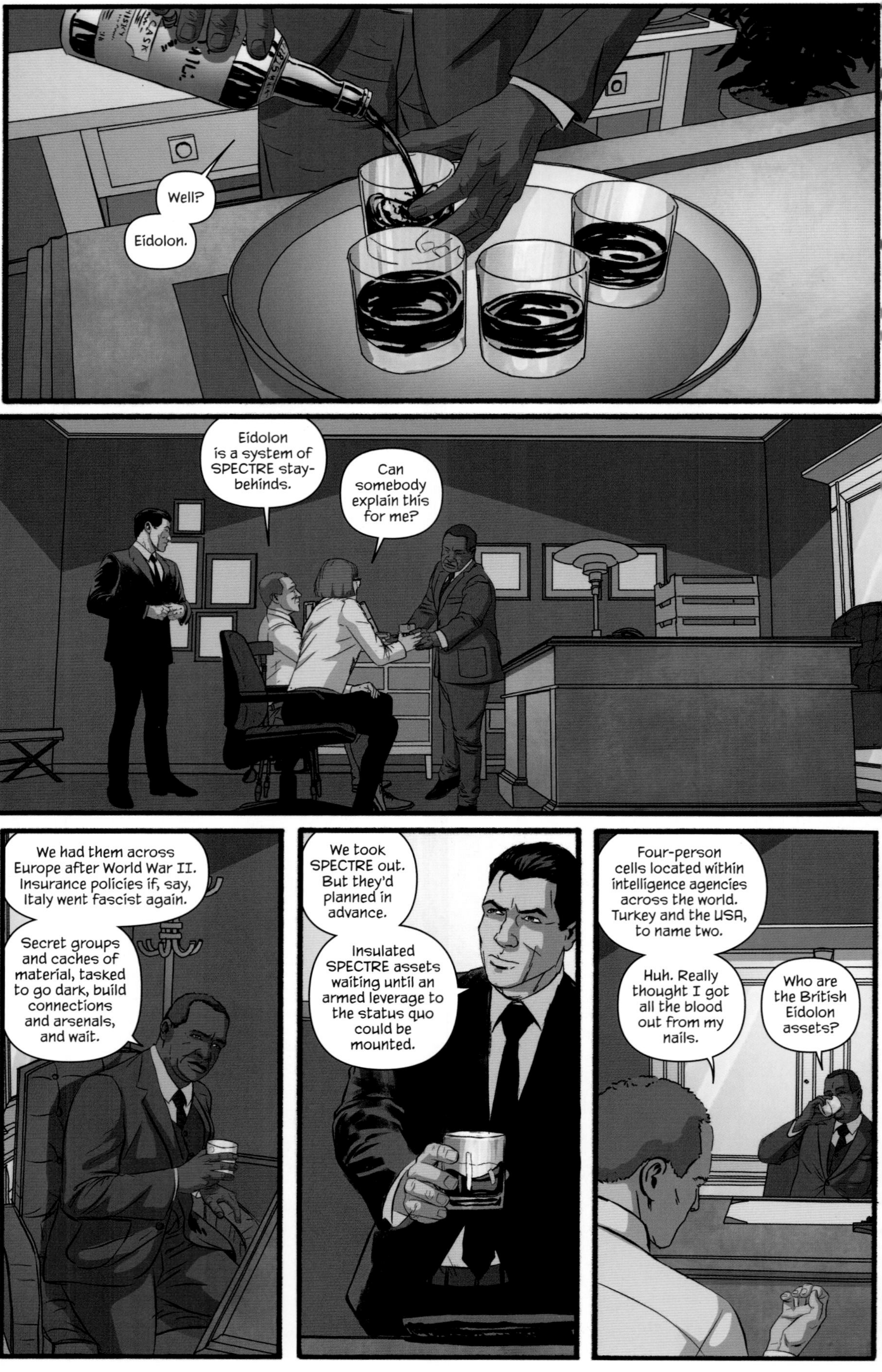
Well?
Eidolon.
Eidolon is a system of SPECTRE stay-behinds.
Can somebody explain this for me?
We had them across Europe after World War II. Insurance policies if, say, Italy went fascist again.
Secret groups and caches of material, tasked to go dark, build connections and arsenals, and wait.
We took SPECTRE out. But they'd planned in advance.
Insulated SPECTRE assets waiting until an armed leverage to the status quo could be mounted.
Four-person cells located within intelligence agencies across the world. Turkey and the USA, to name two.
Huh. Really thought I got all the blood out from my nails.
Who are the British Eidolon assets?

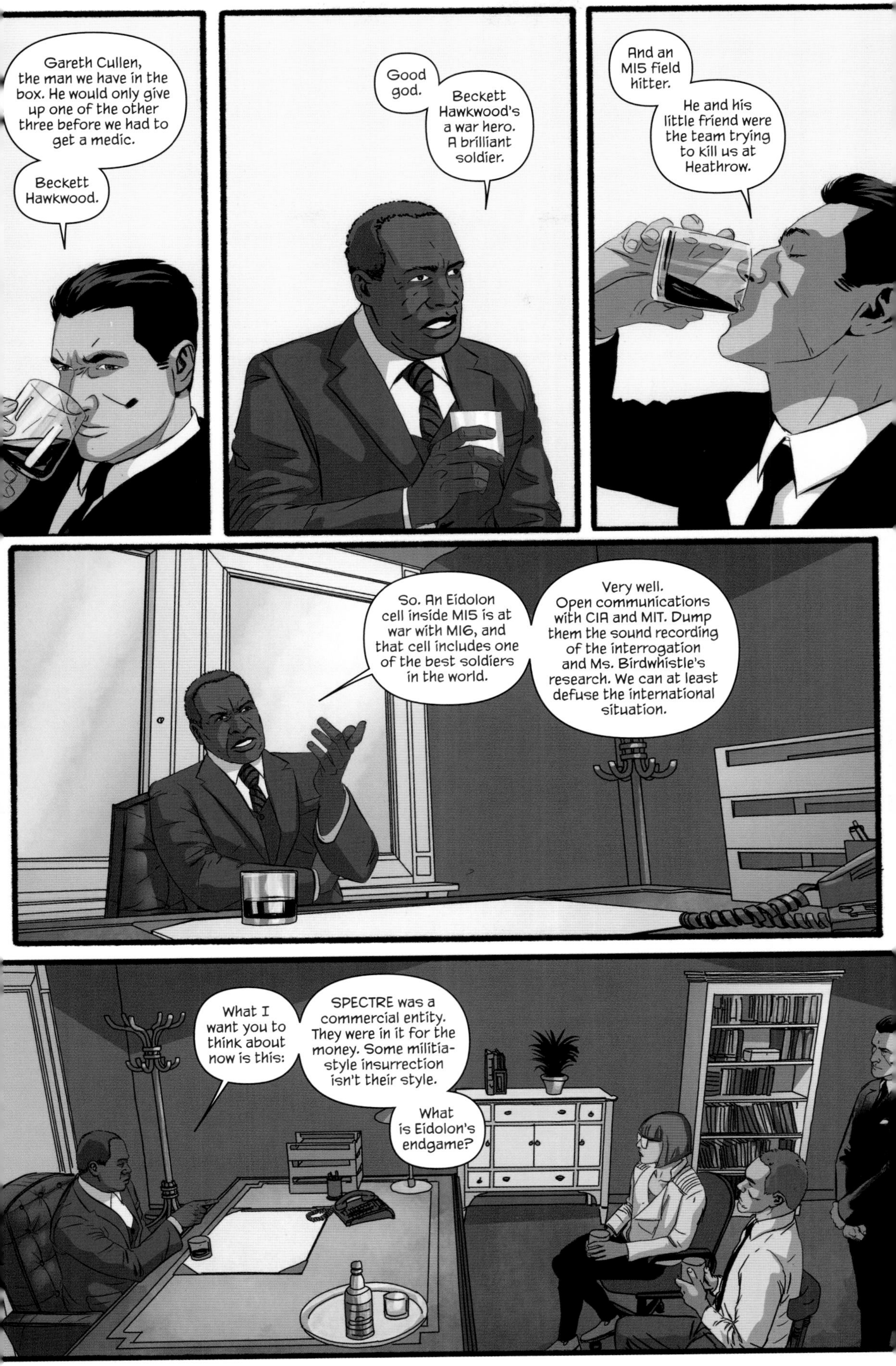
Gareth Cullen, the man we have in the box. He would only give up one of the other three before we had to get a medic.
Beckett Hawkwood.
Good god.
Beckett Hawkwood's a war hero. A brilliant soldier.
And an MI5 field hitter.
He and his little friend were the team trying to kill us at Heathrow.
So. An Eidolon cell inside MI5 is at war with MI6, and that cell includes one of the best soldiers in the world.
Very well. Open communications with CIA and MIT. Dump them the sound recording of the interrogation and Ms. Birdwhistle's research. We can at least defuse the international situation.
What I want you to think about now is this:
SPECTRE was a commercial entity. They were in it for the money. Some militia-style insurrection isn't their style.
What is Eidolon's endgame?

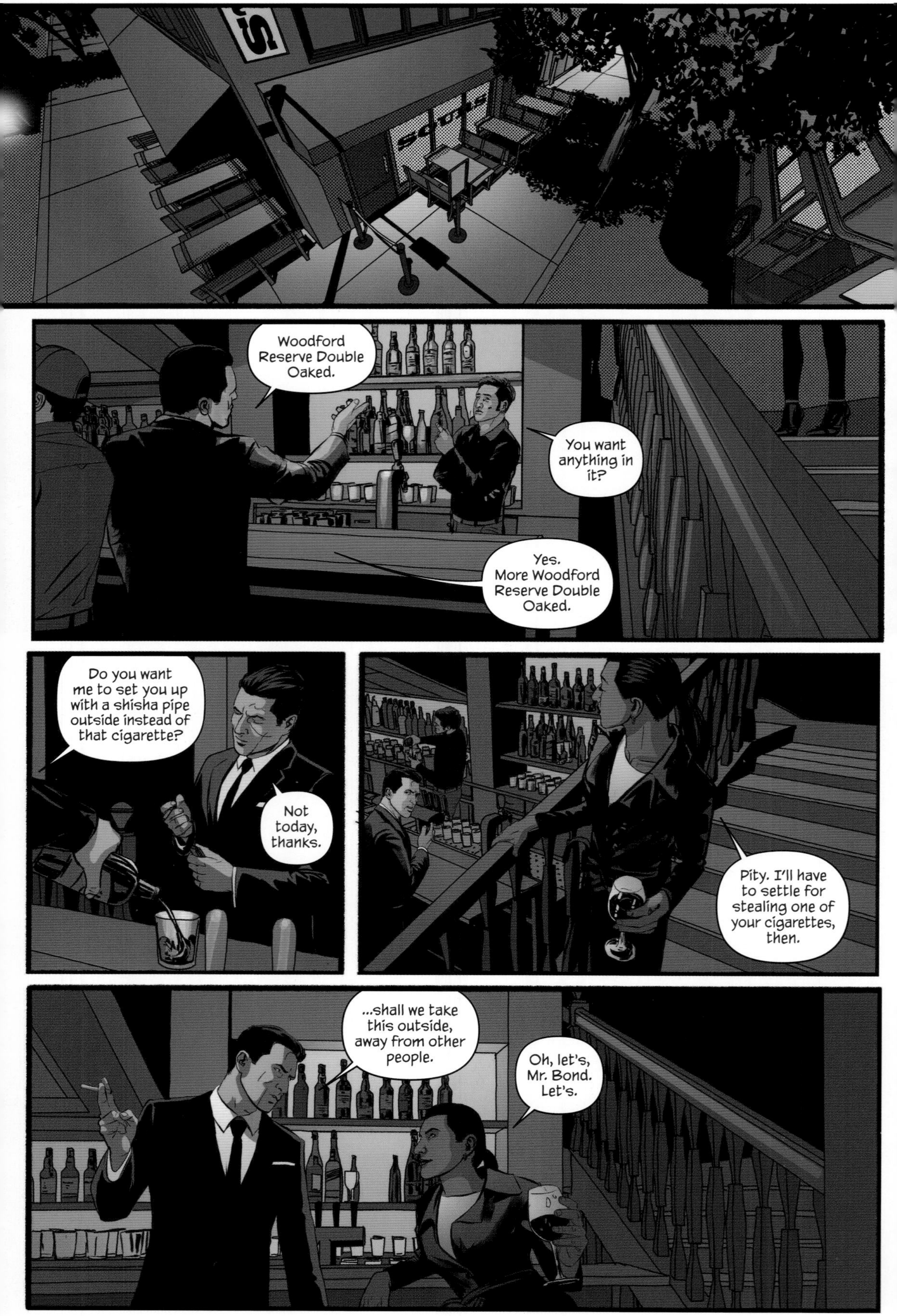
Woodford Reserve Double Oaked.
You want anything in it?
Yes. More Woodford Reserve Double Oaked.
Do you want me to set you up with a shisha pipe outside instead of that cigarette?
Not today, thanks.
Pity. I'll have to settle for stealing one of your cigarettes, then.
...shall we take this outside, away from other people.
Oh, let's, Mr. Bond. Let's.

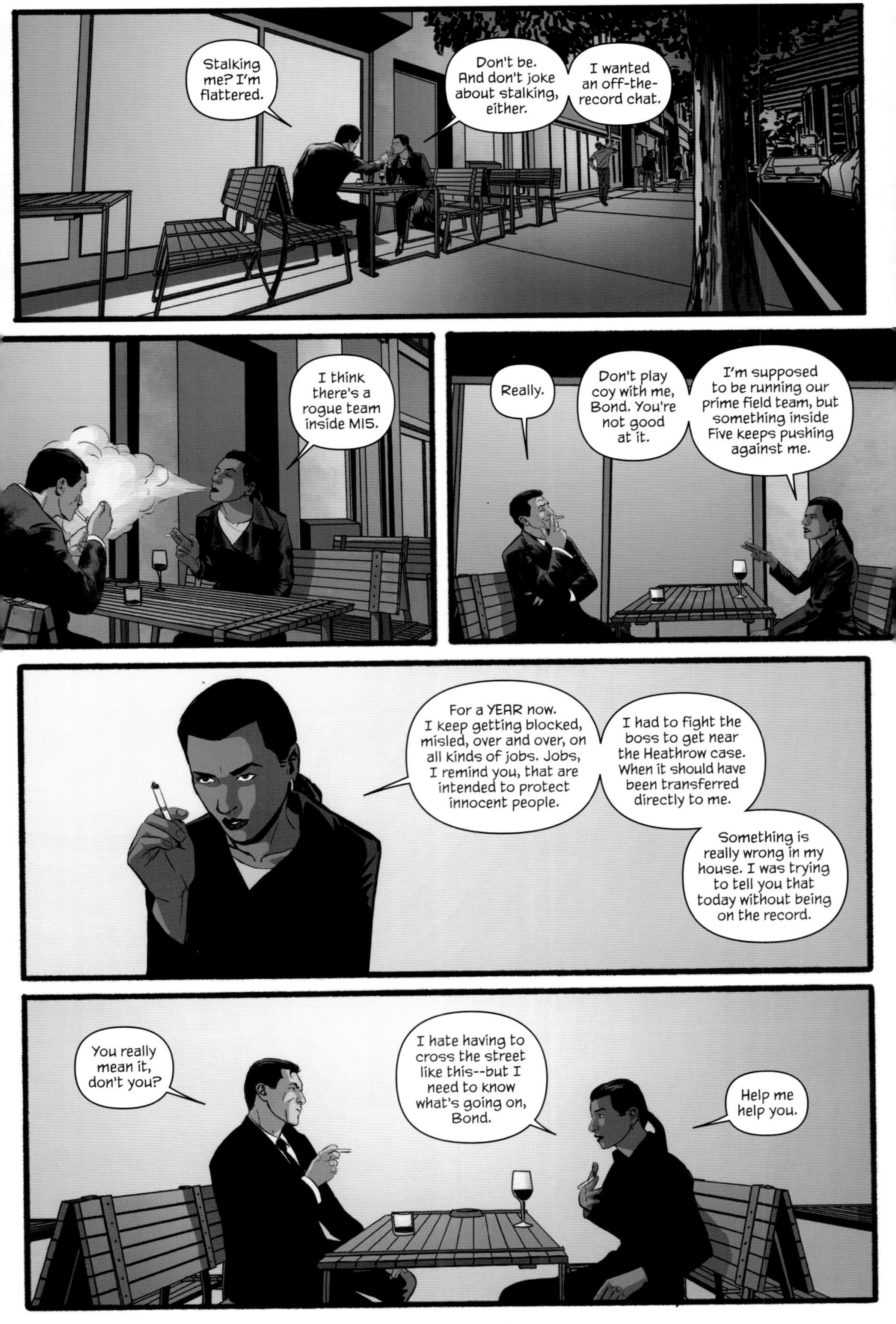
Stalking me? I'm flattered.
Don't be. And don't joke about stalking, either.
I wanted an off-the-record chat.
I think there's a rogue team inside MI5.
Really.
Don't play coy with me, Bond. You're not good at it.
I'm supposed to be running our prime field team, but something inside Five keeps pushing against me.
For a YEAR now. I keep getting blocked, misled, over and over, on all kinds of jobs. Jobs, I remind you, that are intended to protect innocent people.
I had to fight the boss to get near the Heathrow case. When it should have been transferred directly to me.
Something is really wrong in my house. I was trying to tell you that today without being on the record.
You really mean it, don't you?
I hate having to cross the street like this--but I need to know what's going on, Bond.
Help me help you.

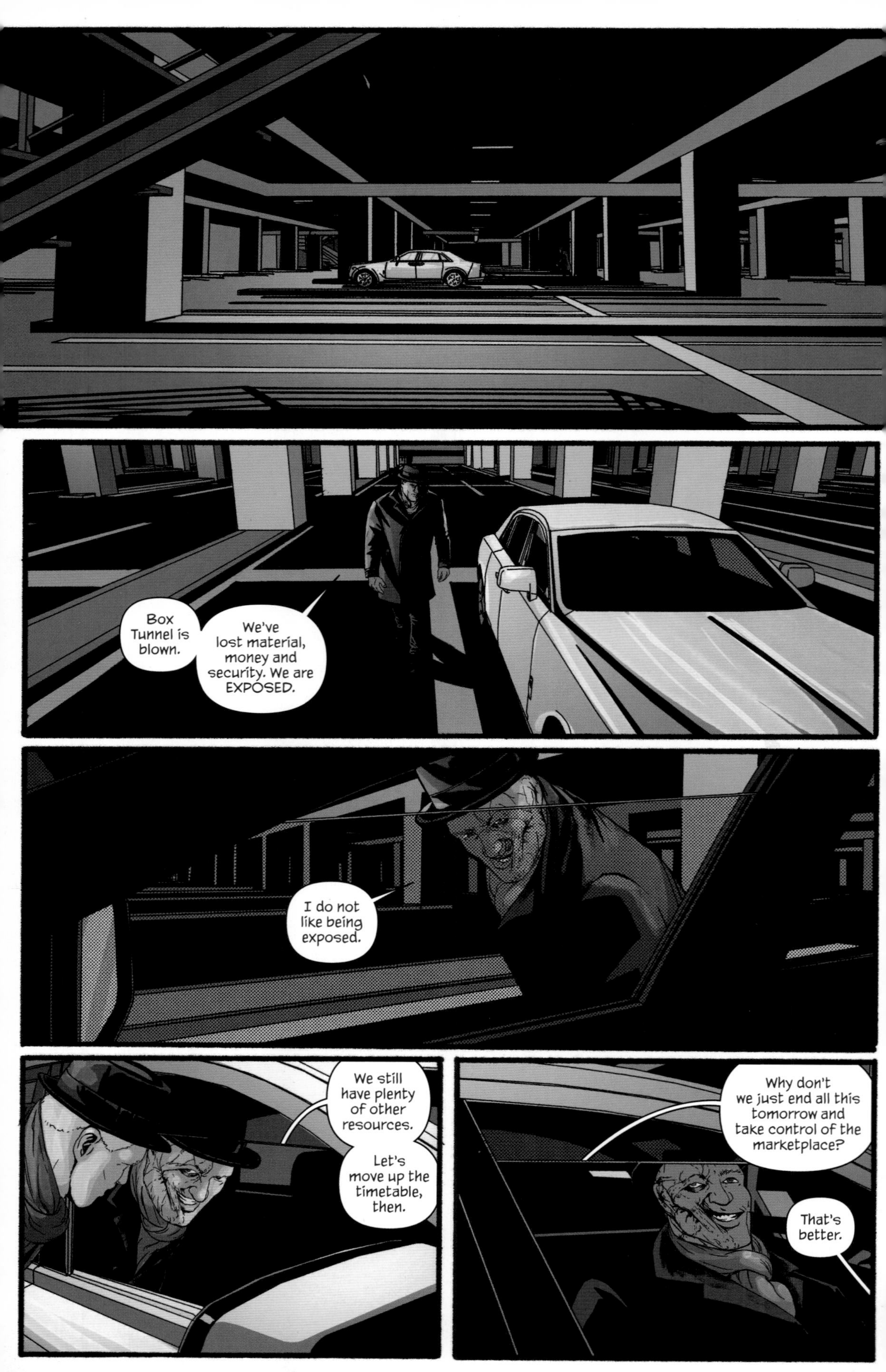
Box Tunnel is blown.
We've lost material, money and security. We are EXPOSED.
I do not like being exposed.
We still have plenty of other resources.
Let's move up the timetable, then.
Why don't we just end all this tomorrow and take control of the marketplace?
That's better.

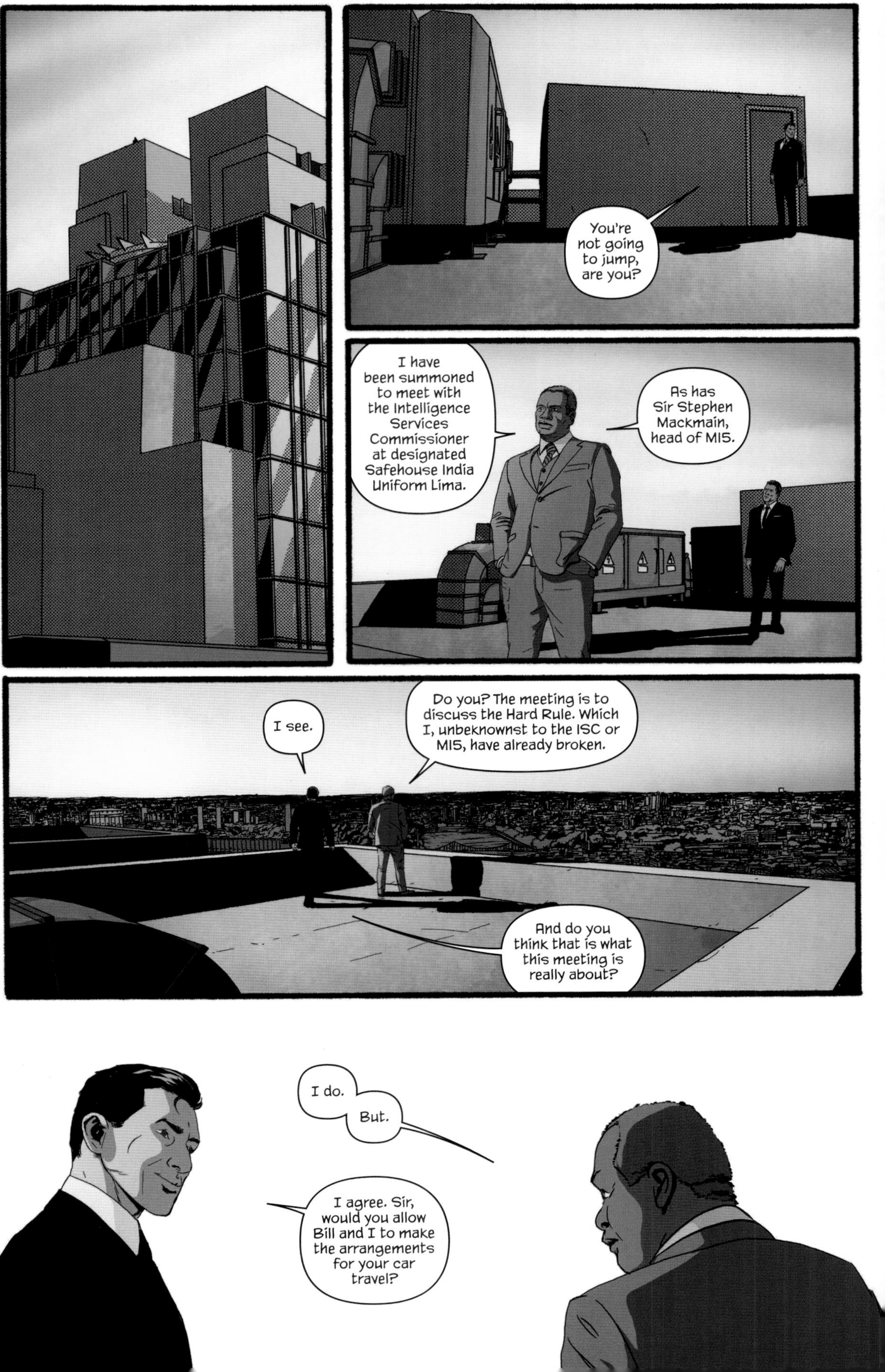
You're not going to jump, are you?
I have been summoned to meet with the Intelligence Services Commissioner at designated Safehouse India Uniform Lima.
As has Sir Stephen Mackmain, head of MI5.
I see.
Do you? The meeting is to discuss the Hard Rule. Which I, unbeknownst to the ISC or MI5, have already broken.
And do you think that is what this meeting is really about?
I do.
But.
I agree. Sir, would you allow Bill and I to make the arrangements for your car travel?

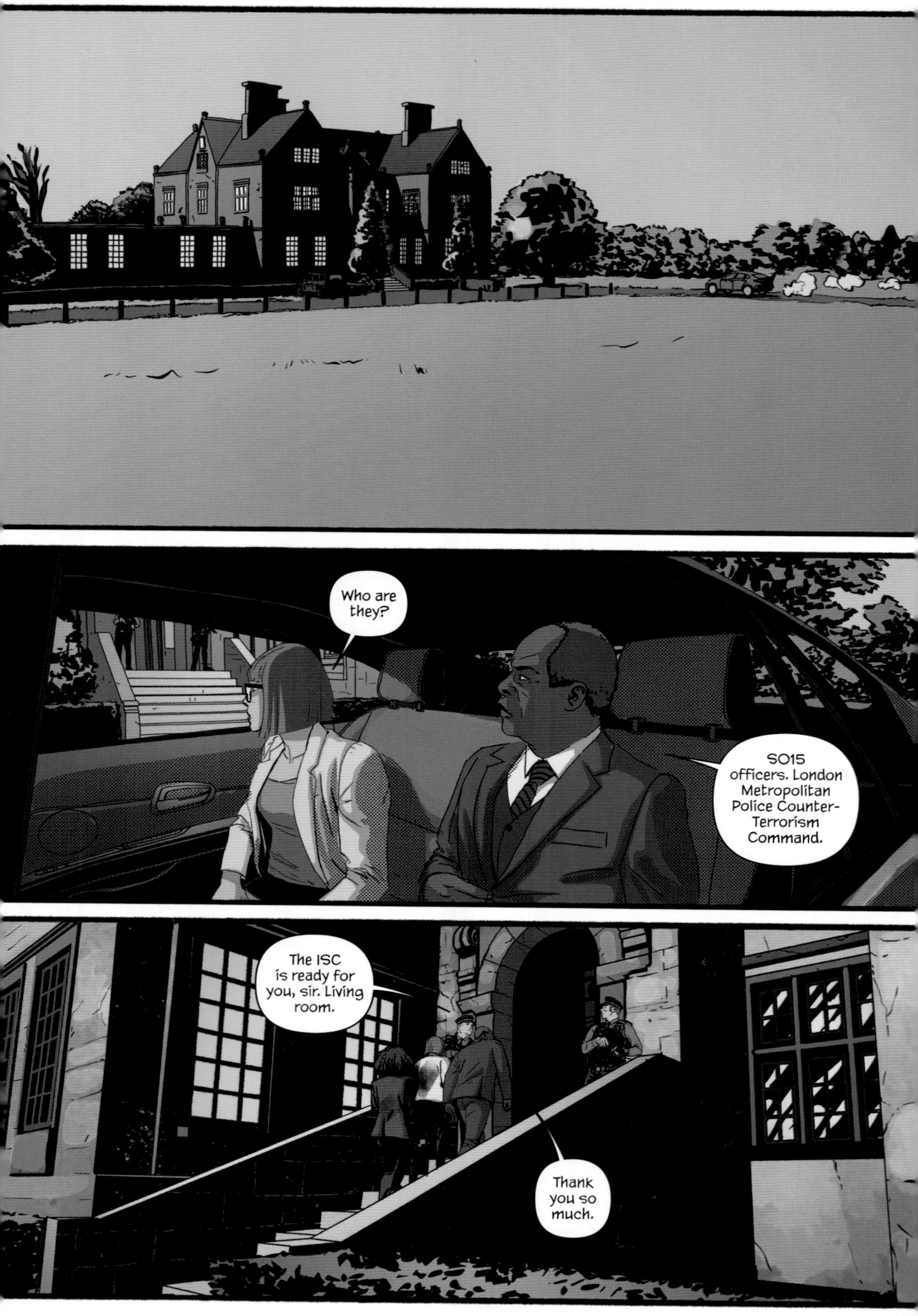
Who are they?
SO15 officers. London Metropolitan Police Counter-Terrorism Command.
The ISC is ready for you, sir. Living room.
Thank you so much.

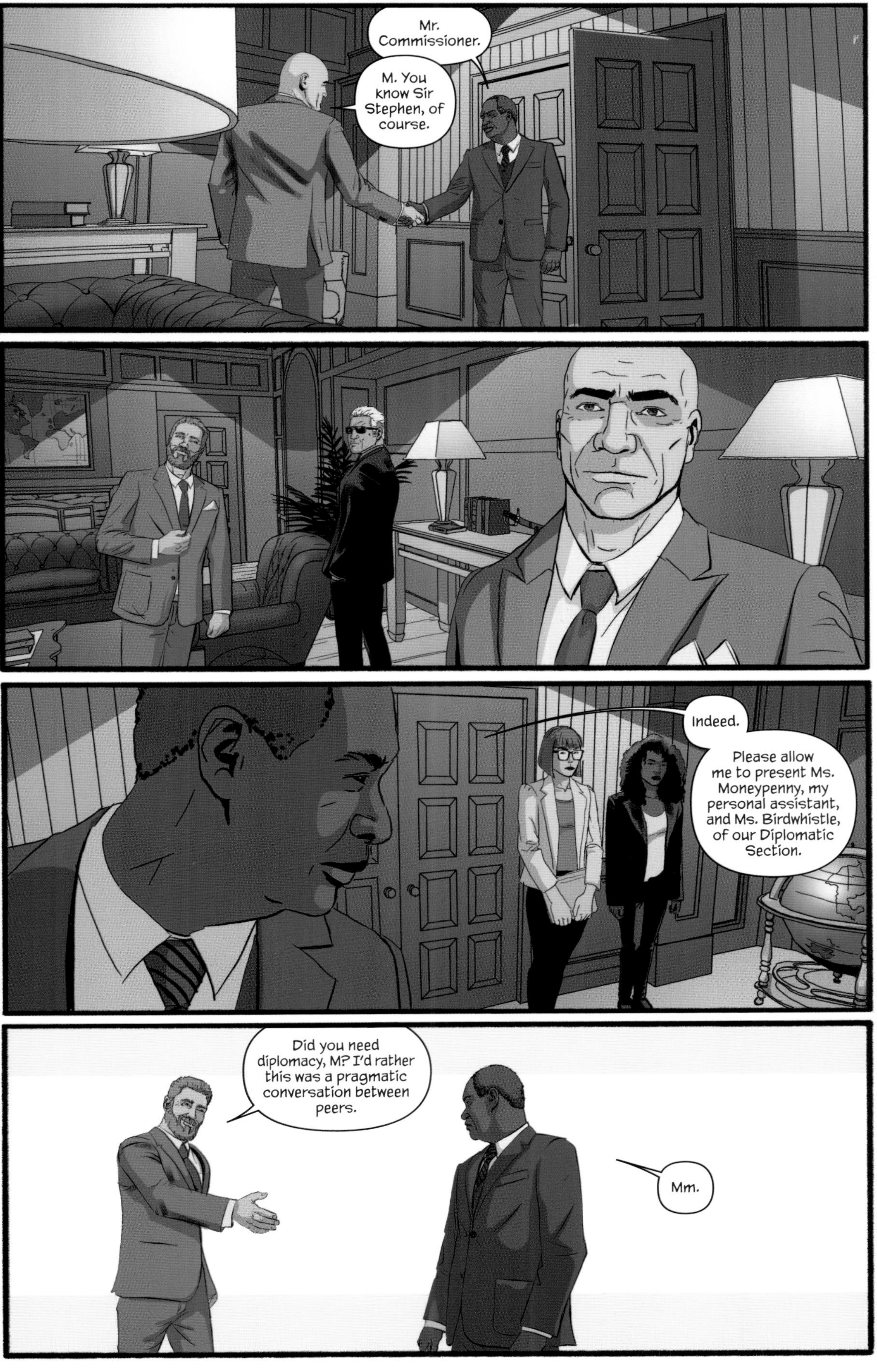
Mr. Commissioner.
M. You know Sir Stephen, of course.
Indeed.
Please allow me to present Ms. Moneypenny, my personal assistant, and Ms. Birdwhistle, of our Diplomatic Section.
Did you need diplomacy, M? I'd rather this was a pragmatic conversation between peers.
Mm.

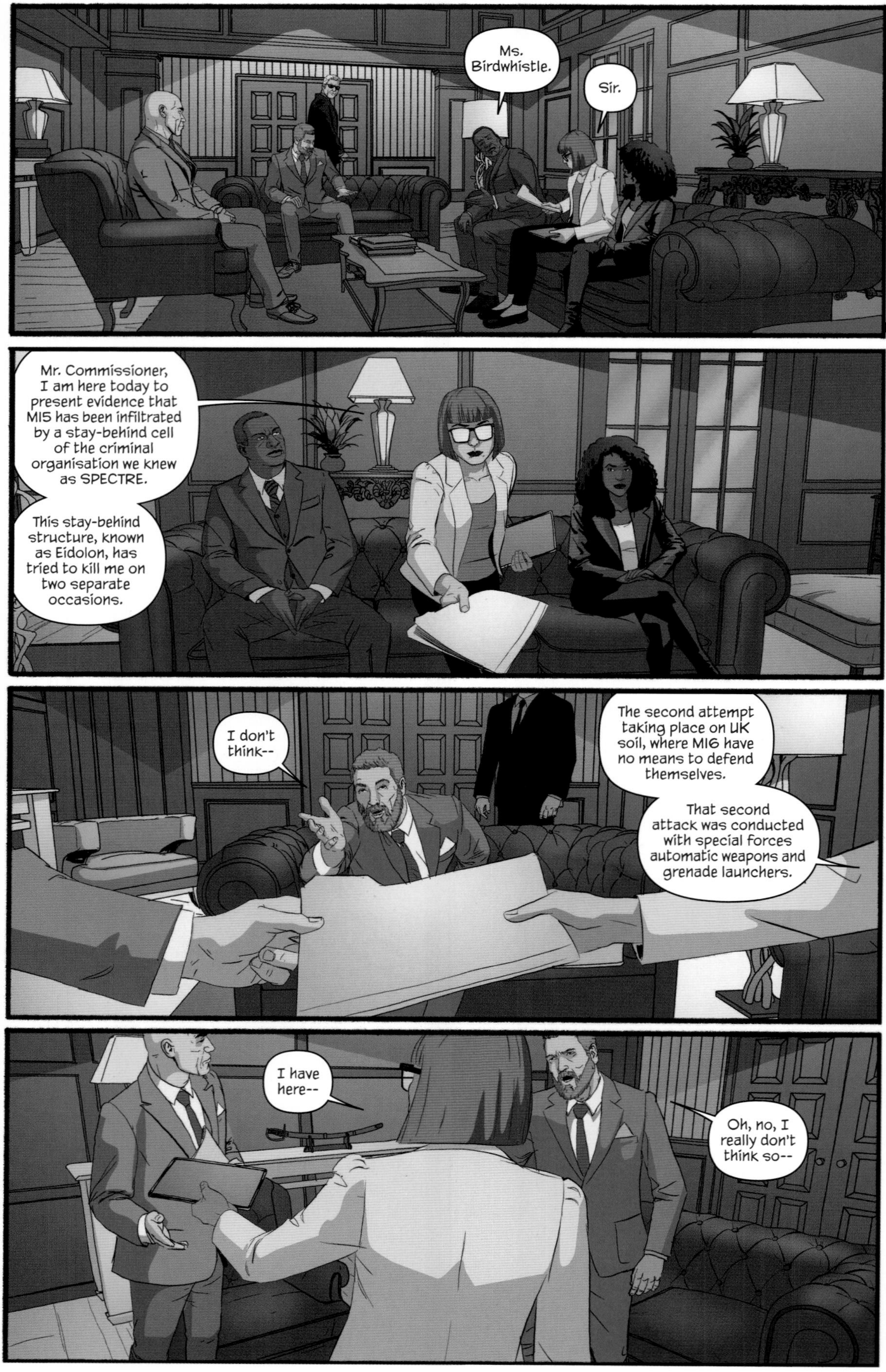
Ms. Birdwhistle.
Sir.
Mr. Commissioner, I am here today to present evidence that MI5 has been infiltrated by a stay-behind cell of the criminal organisation we knew as SPECTRE.
This stay-behind structure, known as Eidolon, has tried to kill me on two separate occasions.
I don't think--
The second attempt taking place on UK soil, where MI6 have no means to defend themselves.
That second attack was conducted with special forces automatic weapons and grenade launchers.
I have here--
Oh, no, I really don't think so--

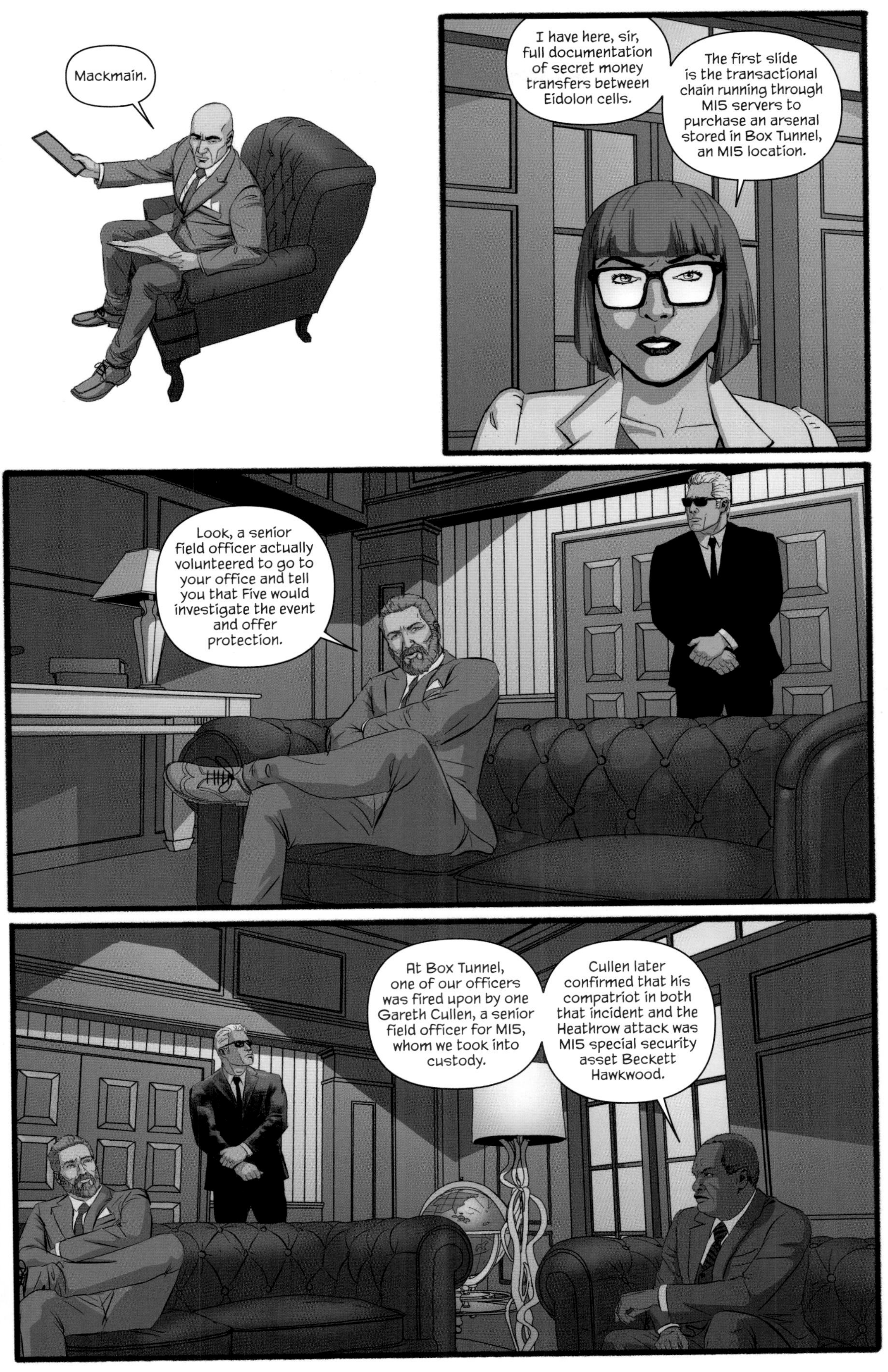
Mackmain.
I have here, sir, full documentation of secret money transfers between Eidolon cells.
The first slide is the transactional chain running through MI5 servers to purchase an arsenal stored in Box Tunnel, an MI5 location.
Look, a senior field officer actually volunteered to go to your office and tell you that Five would investigate the event and offer protection.
At Box Tunnel, one of our officers was fired upon by one Gareth Cullen, a senior field officer for MI5, whom we took into custody.
Cullen later confirmed that his compatriot in both that incident and the Heathrow attack was MI5 special security asset Beckett Hawkwood.

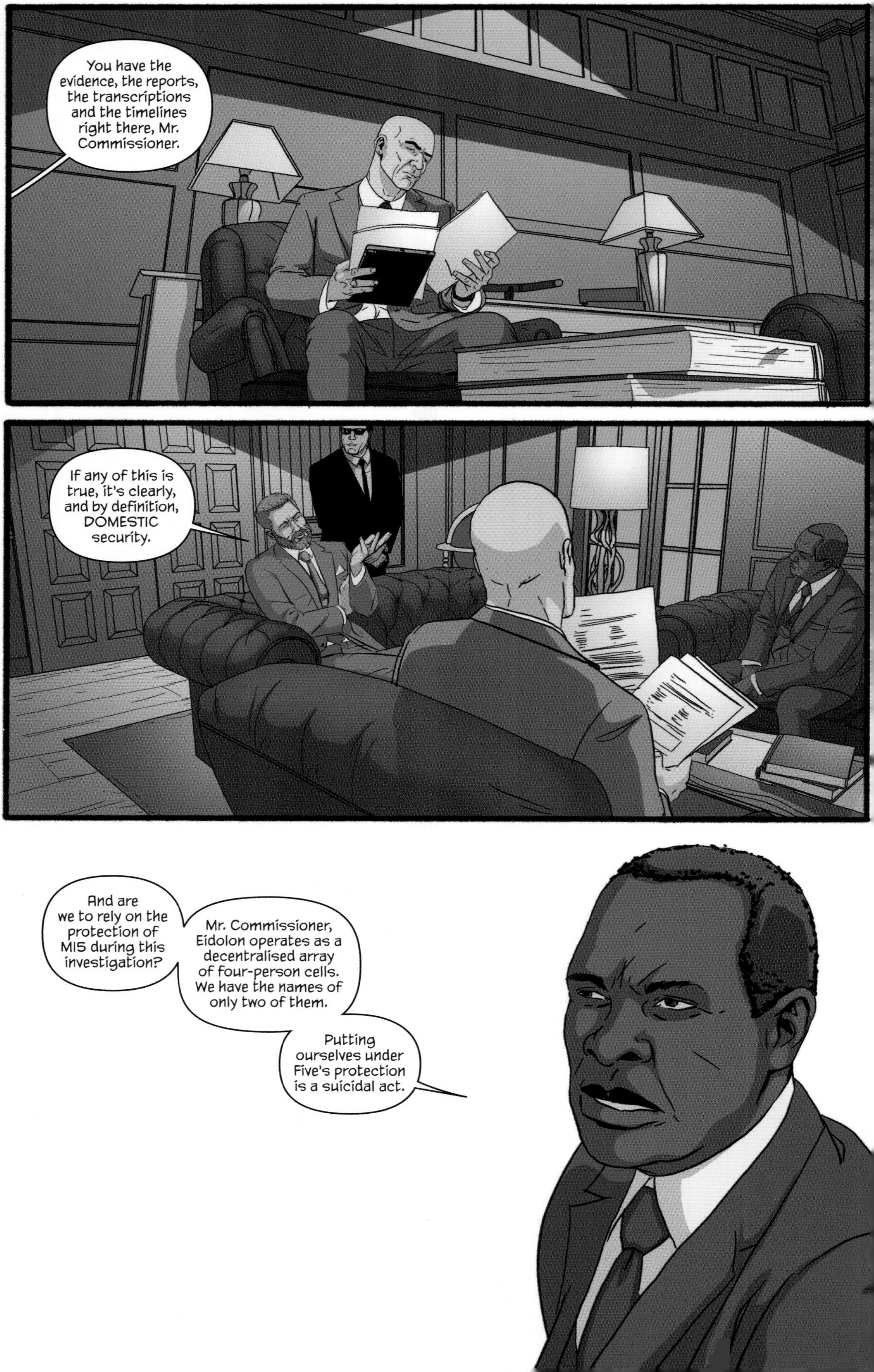
You have the evidence, the reports, the transcriptions and the timelines right there, Mr. Commissioner.
If any of this is true, it's clearly, and by definition, DOMESTIC security.
And are we to rely on the protection of MI5 during this investigation?
Mr. Commissioner, Eidolon operates as a decentralised array of four-person cells. We have the names of only two of them.
Putting ourselves under Five's protection is a suicidal act.

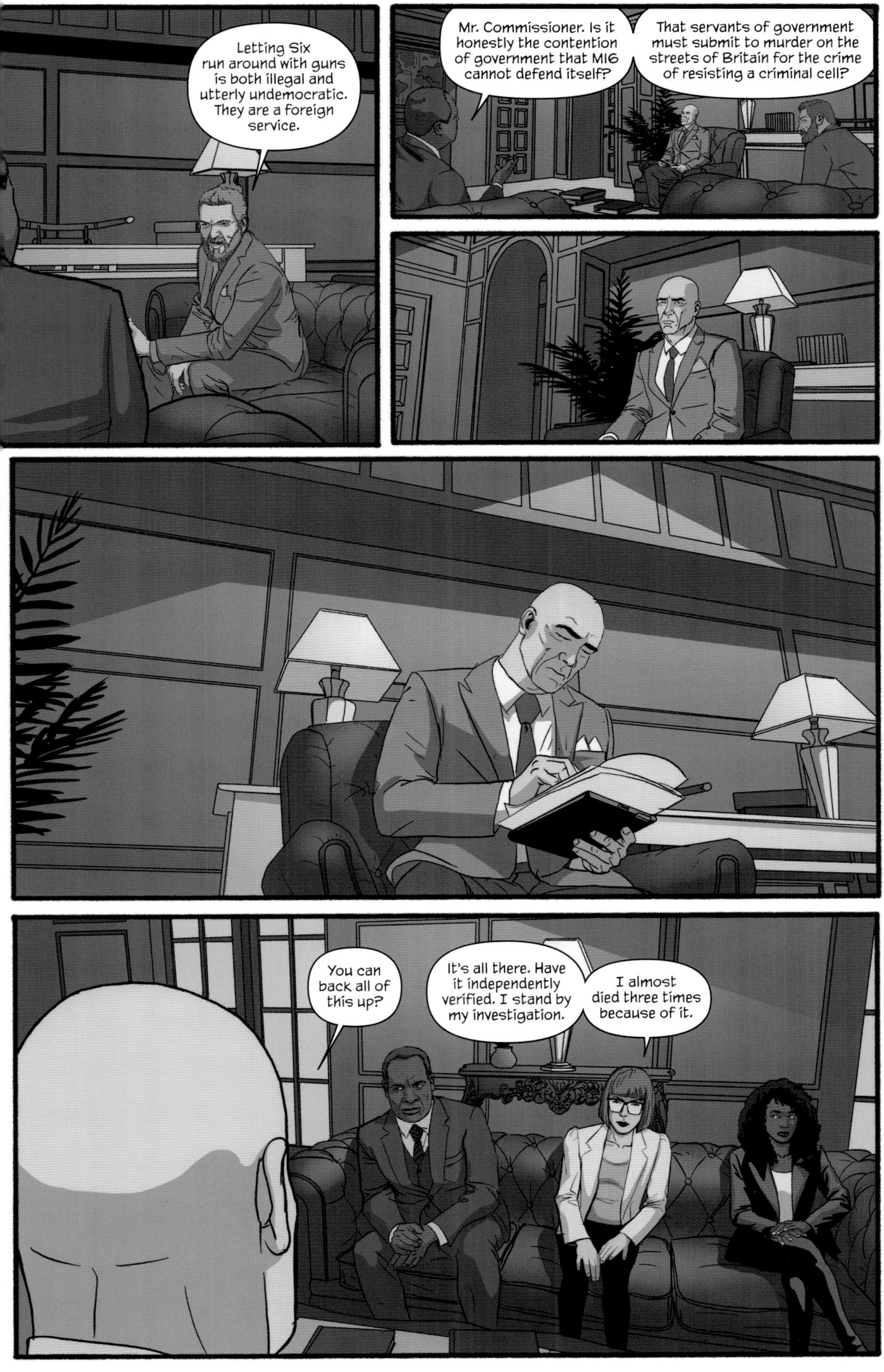
Letting Six run around with guns is both illegal and utterly undemocratic. They are a foreign service.
Mr. Commissioner. Is it honestly the contention of government that MI6 cannot defend itself?
That servants of government must submit to murder on the streets of Britain for the crime of resisting a criminal cell?
You can back all of this up?
It's all there. Have it independently verified. I stand by my investigation.
I almost died three times because of it.

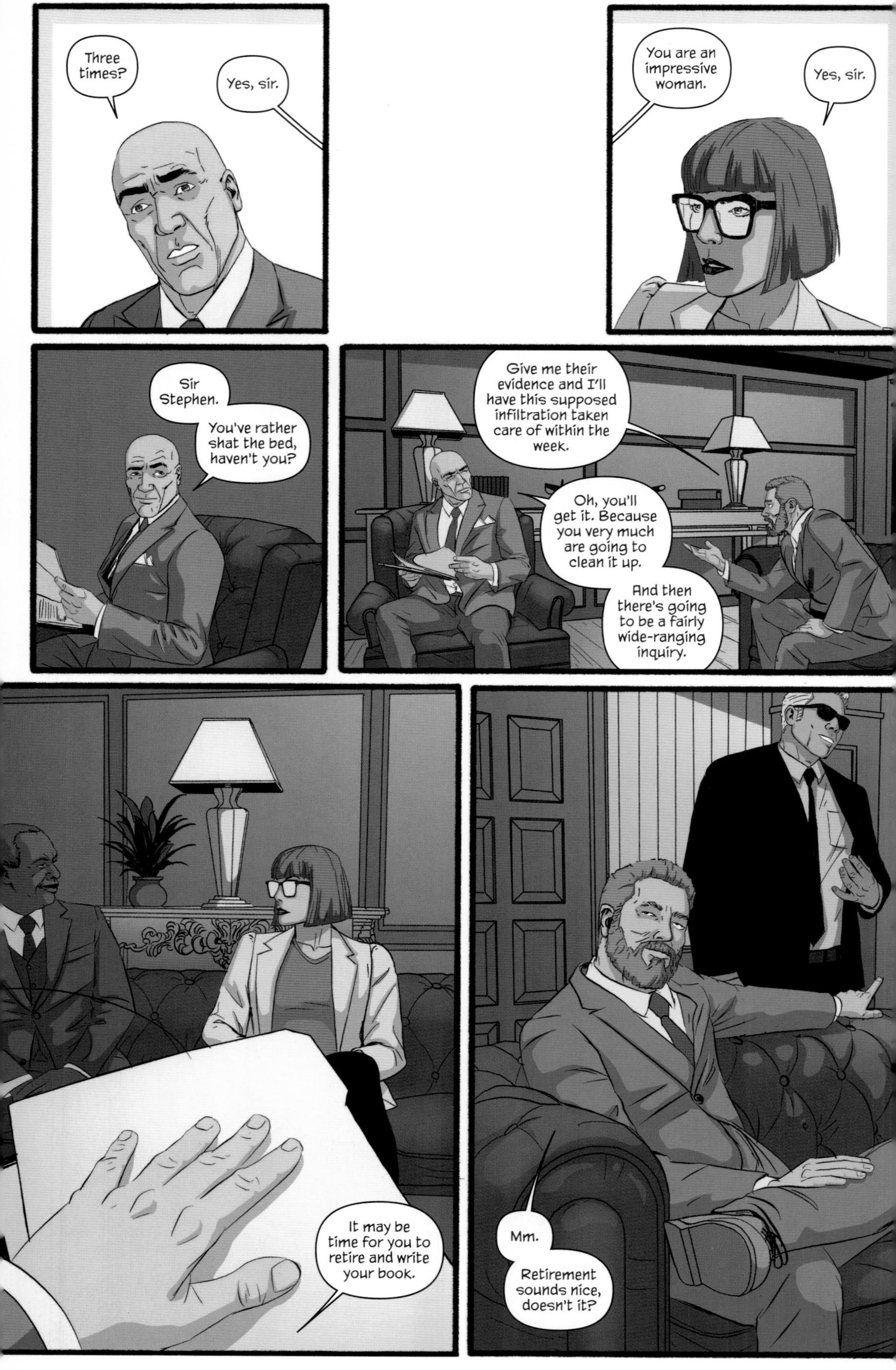
Three times?
Yes, sir.
You are an impressive woman.
Yes, sir.
Sir Stephen.
You've rather shat the bed, haven't you?
Give me their evidence and I'll have this supposed infiltration taken care of within the week.
Oh, you'll get it. Because you very much are going to clean it up.
And then there's going to be a fairly wide-ranging inquiry.
It may be time for you to retire and write your book.
Mm.
Retirement sounds nice, doesn't it?

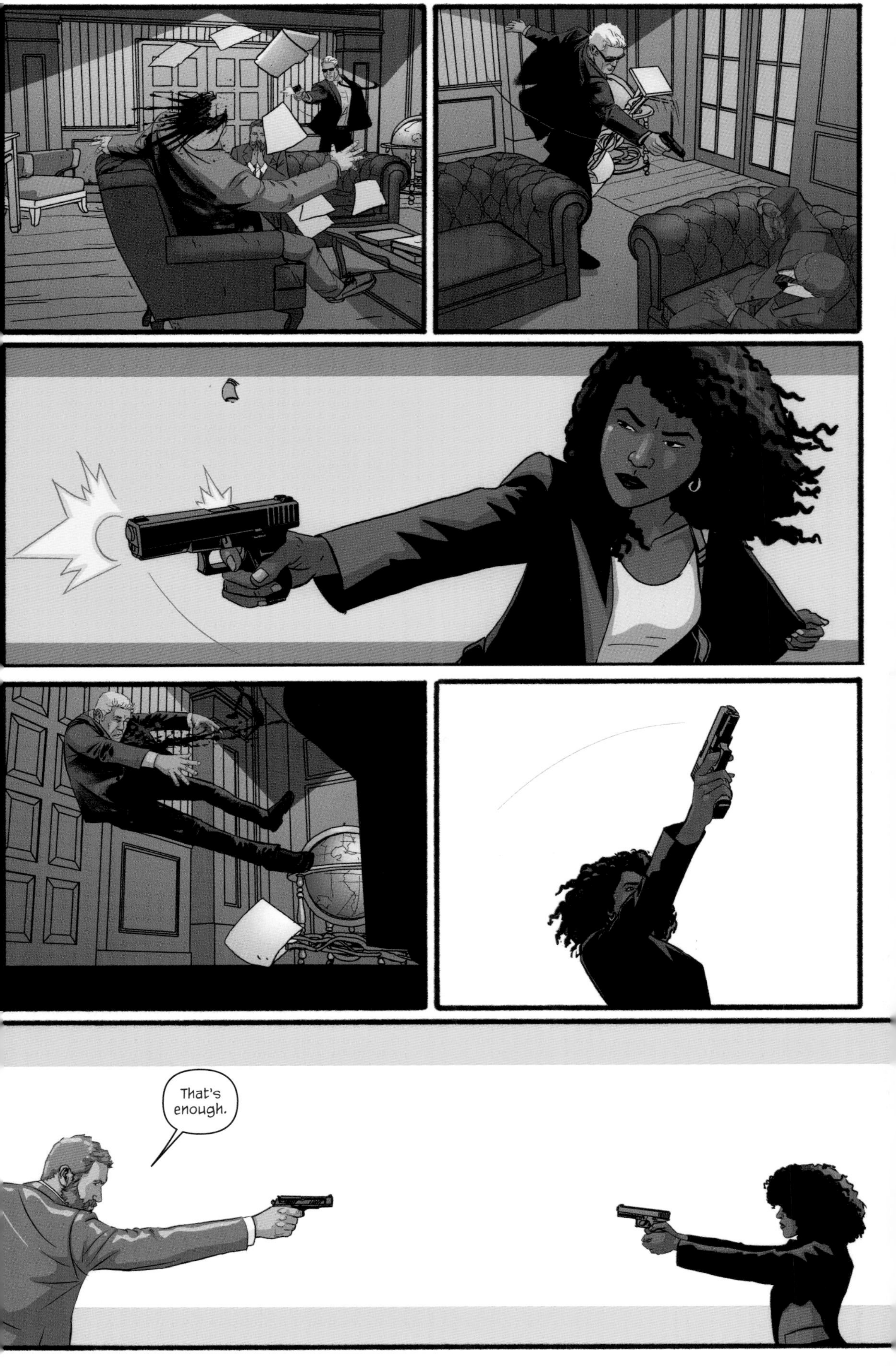
That's enough.

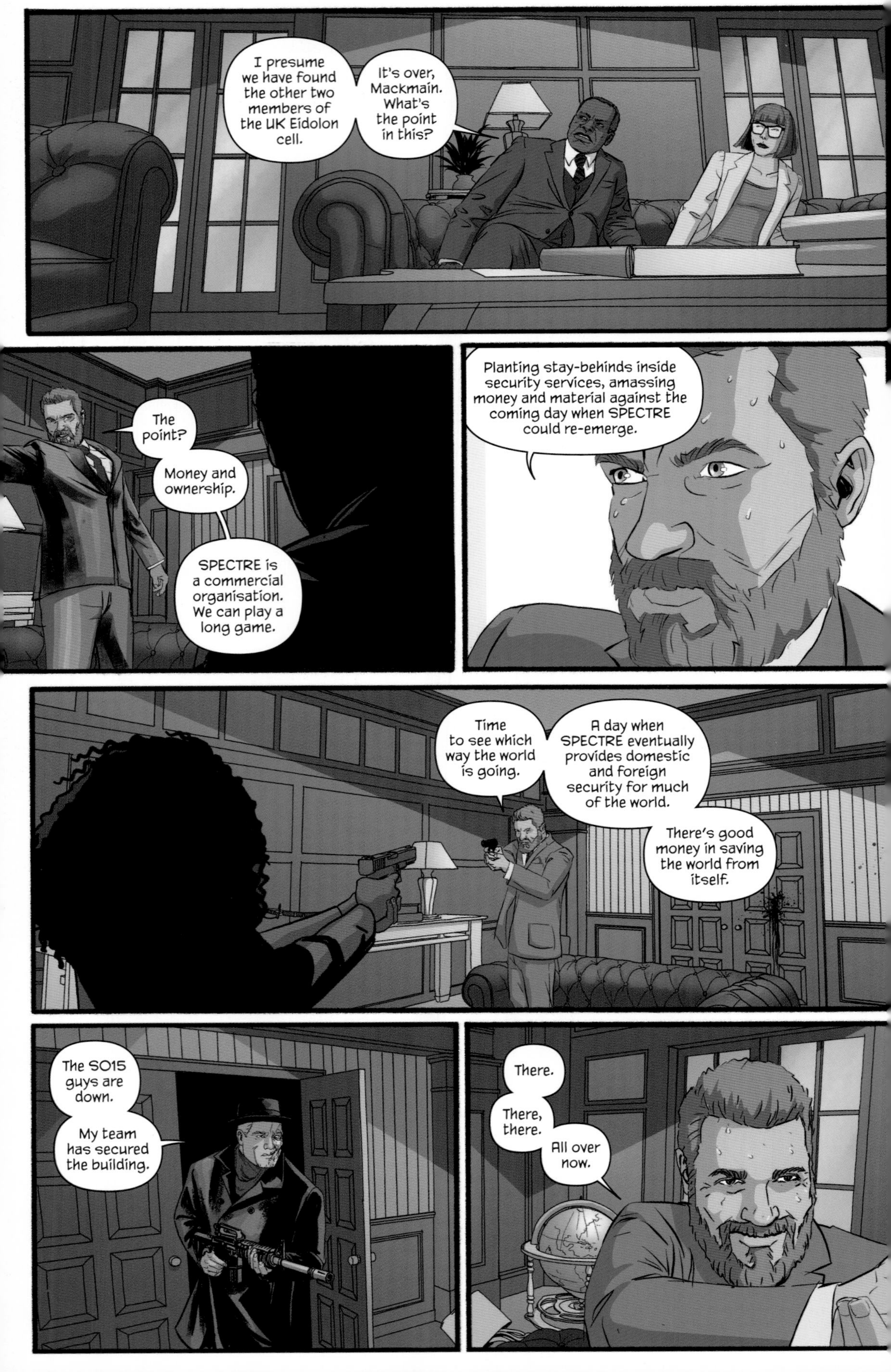
I presume we have found the other two members of the UK Eidolon cell.
It's over, Mackmain. What's the point in this?
The point?
Money and ownership.
SPECTRE is a commercial organisation. We can play a long game.
Planting stay-behinds inside security services, amassing money and material against the coming day when SPECTRE could re-emerge.
Time to see which way the world is going.
A day when SPECTRE eventually provides domestic and foreign security for much of the world.
There's good money in saving the world from itself.
The SO15 guys are down.
My team has secured the building.
There.
There, there.
All over now.

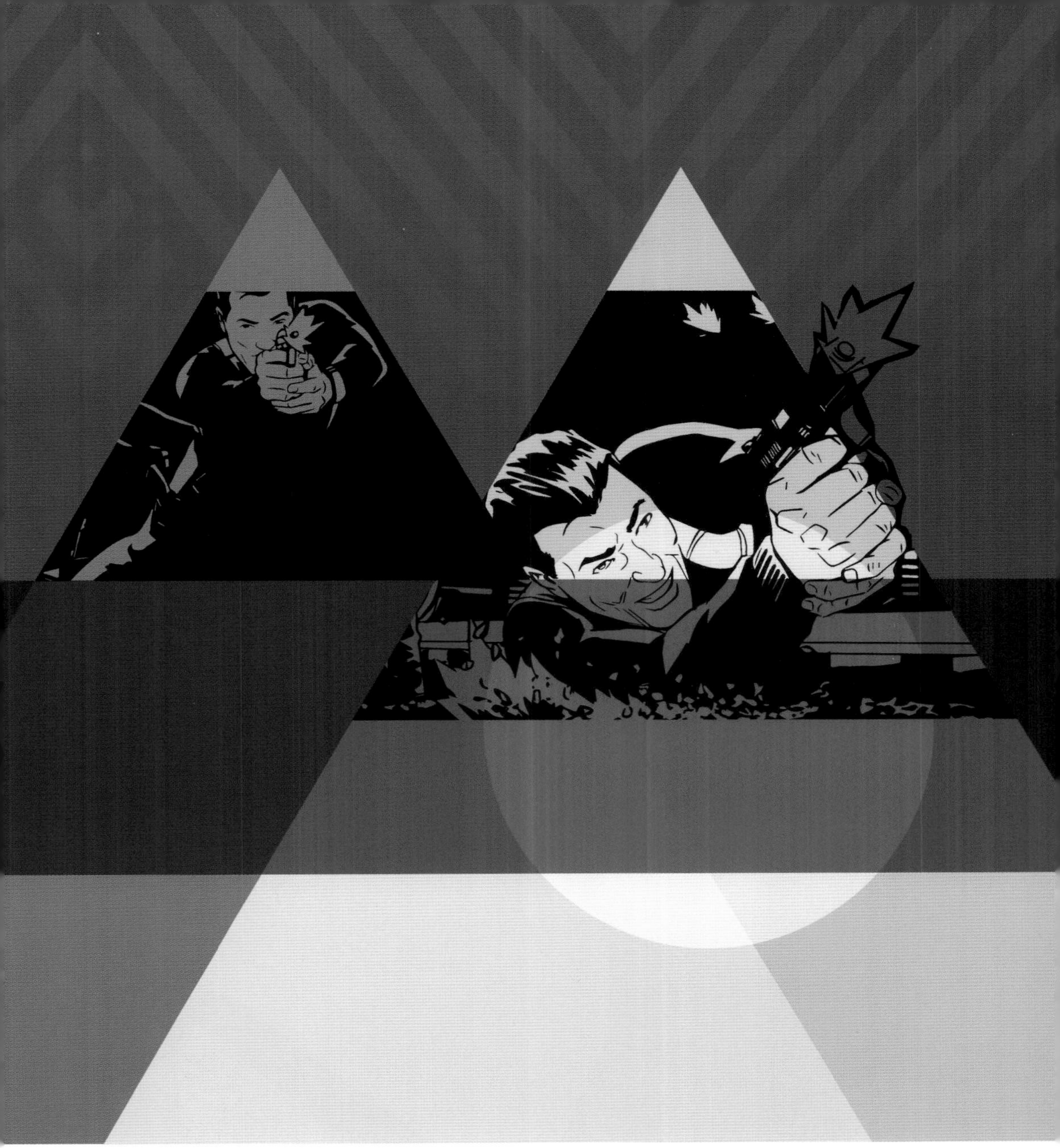

issue eleven

issue #11 main cover by **DOM REARDON**

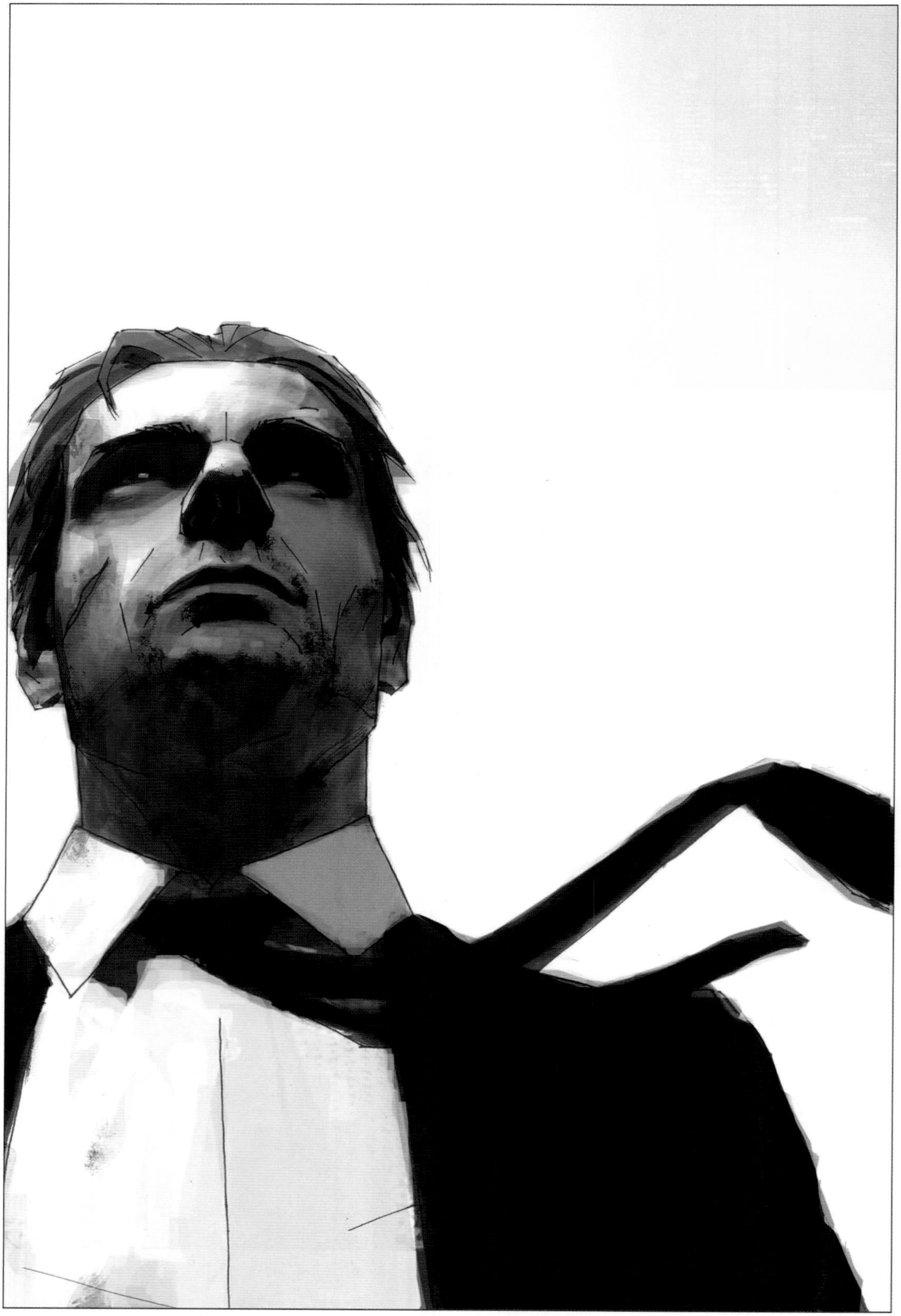

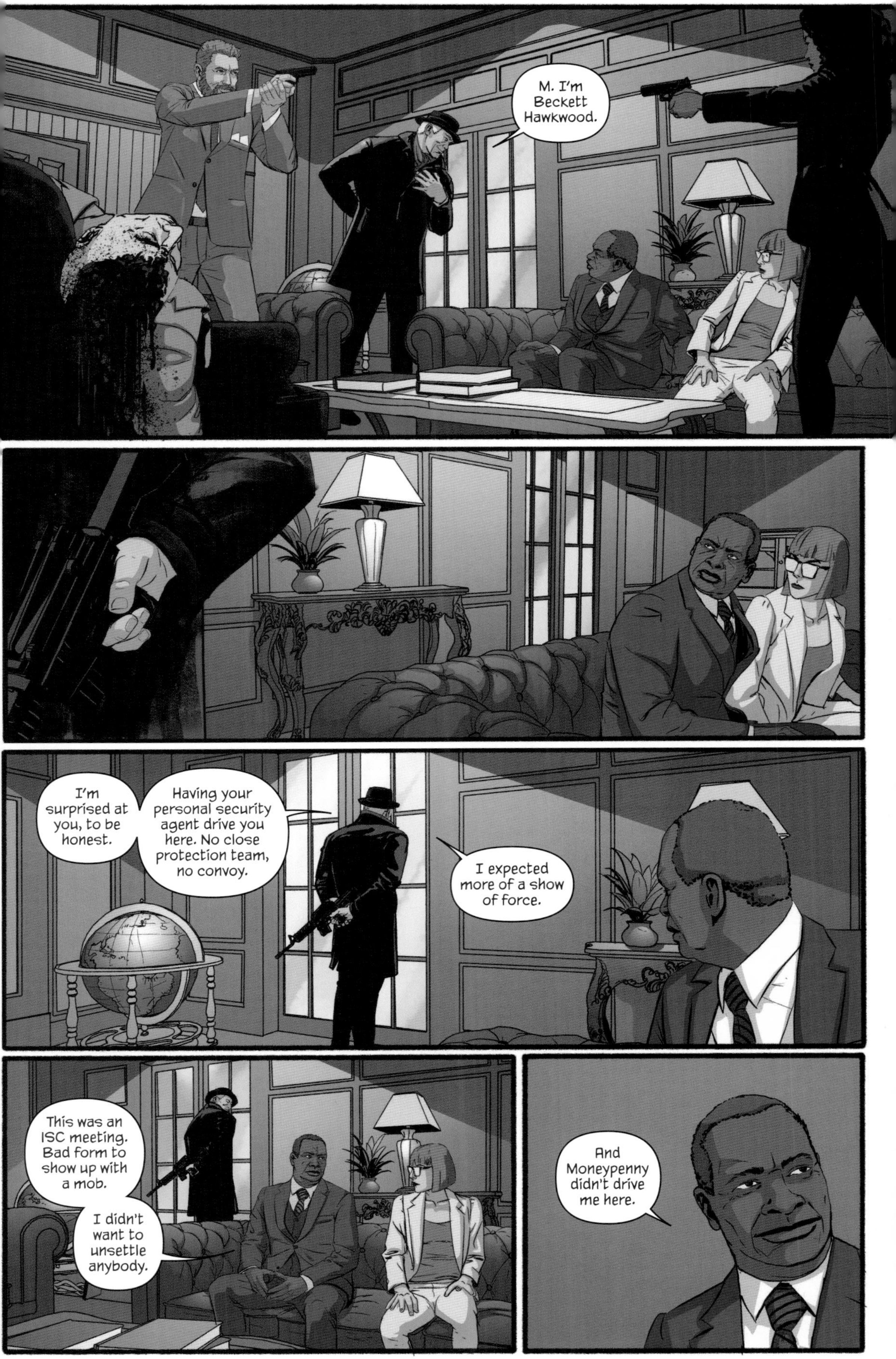
M. I'm Beckett Hawkwood.
I'm surprised at you, to be honest.
Having your personal security agent drive you here. No close protection team, no convoy.
I expected more of a show of force.
This was an ISC meeting. Bad form to show up with a mob.
I didn't want to unsettle anybody.
And Moneypenny didn't drive me here.

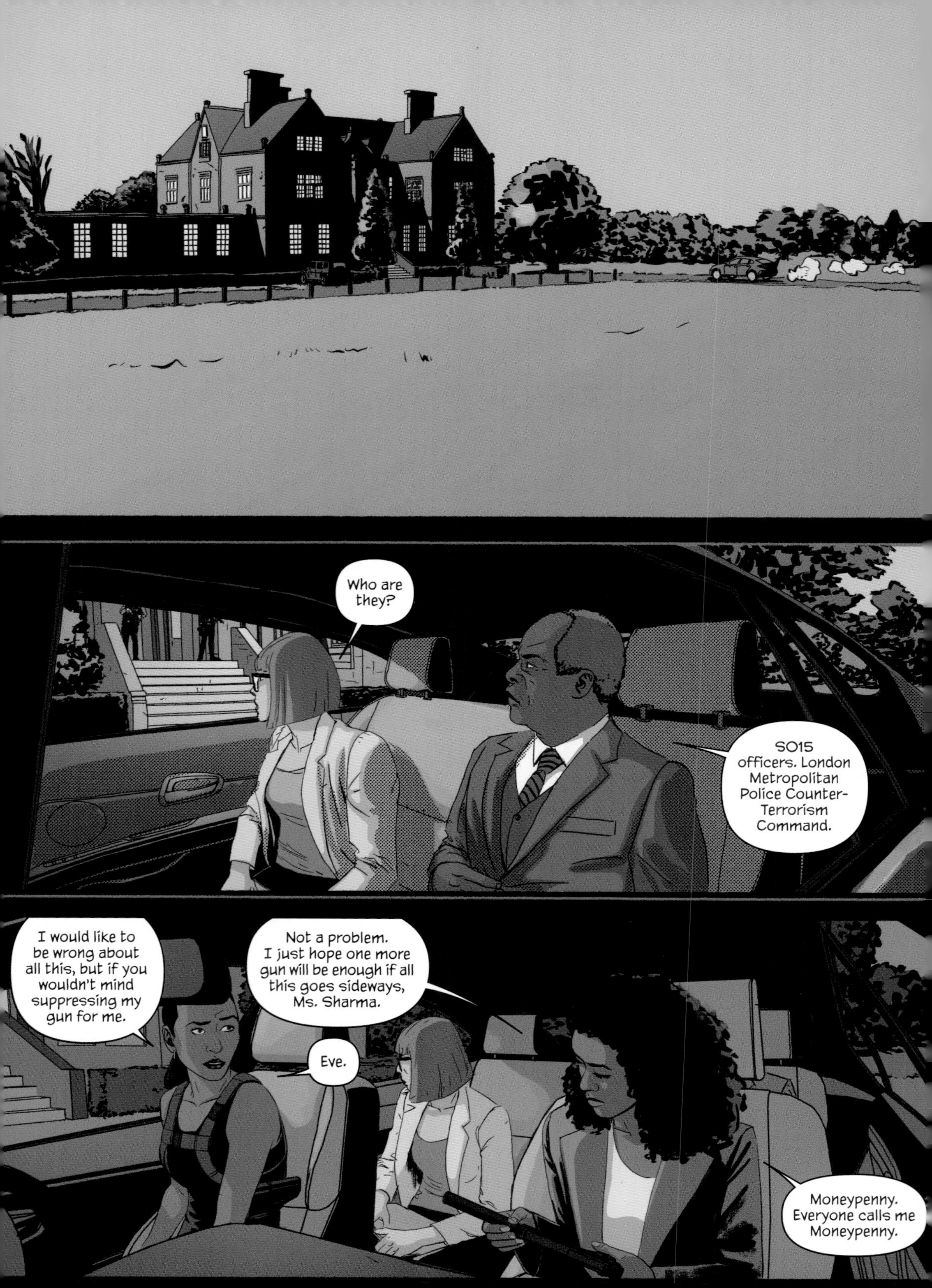
Who are they?
SO15 officers. London Metropolitan Police Counter-Terrorism Command.
I would like to be wrong about all this, but if you wouldn't mind suppressing my gun for me.
Not a problem. I just hope one more gun will be enough if all this goes sideways, Ms. Sharma.
Eve.
Moneypenny. Everyone calls me Moneypenny.

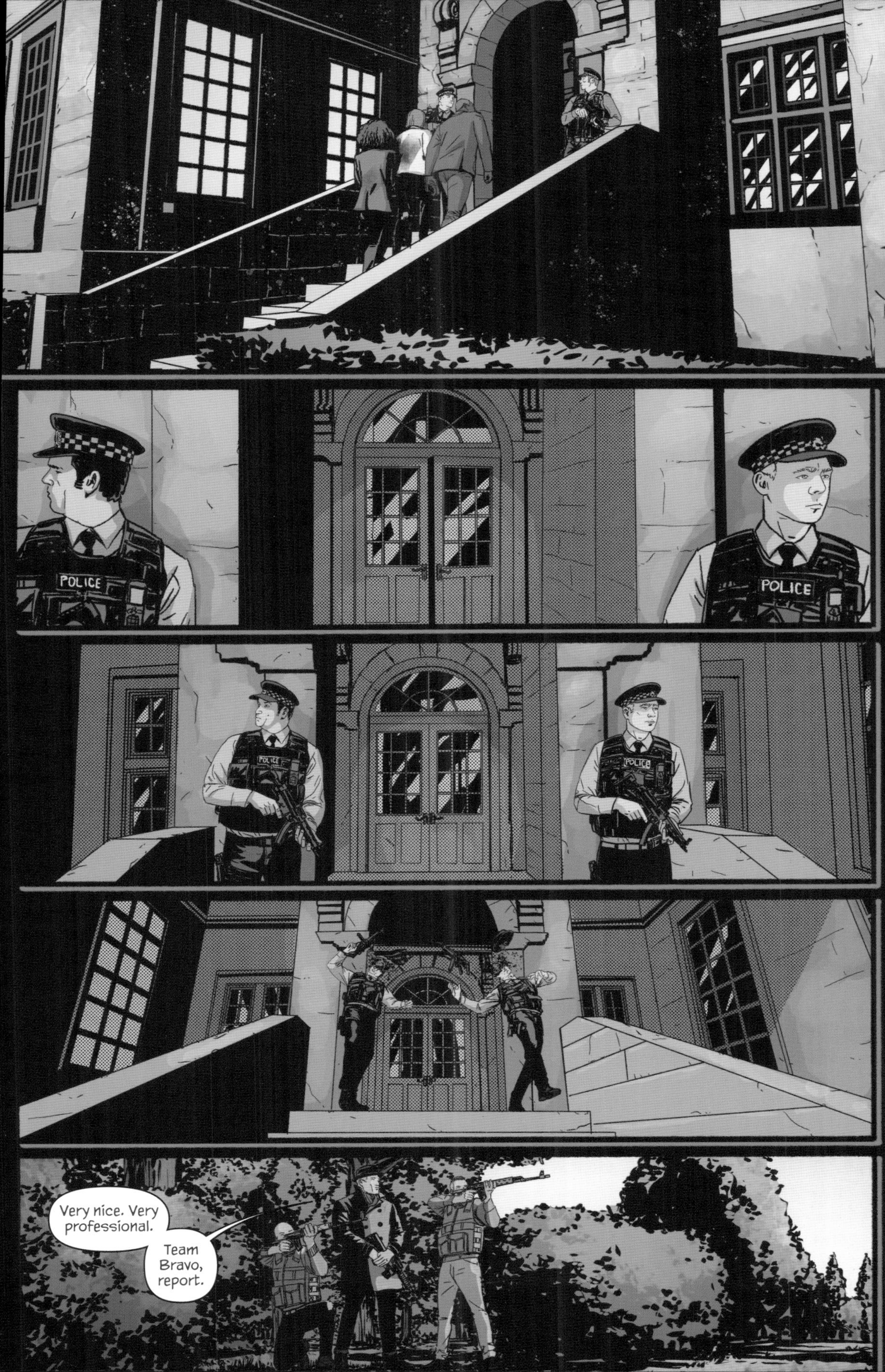
POLICE
POLICE
Very nice. Very professional.
Team Bravo, report.

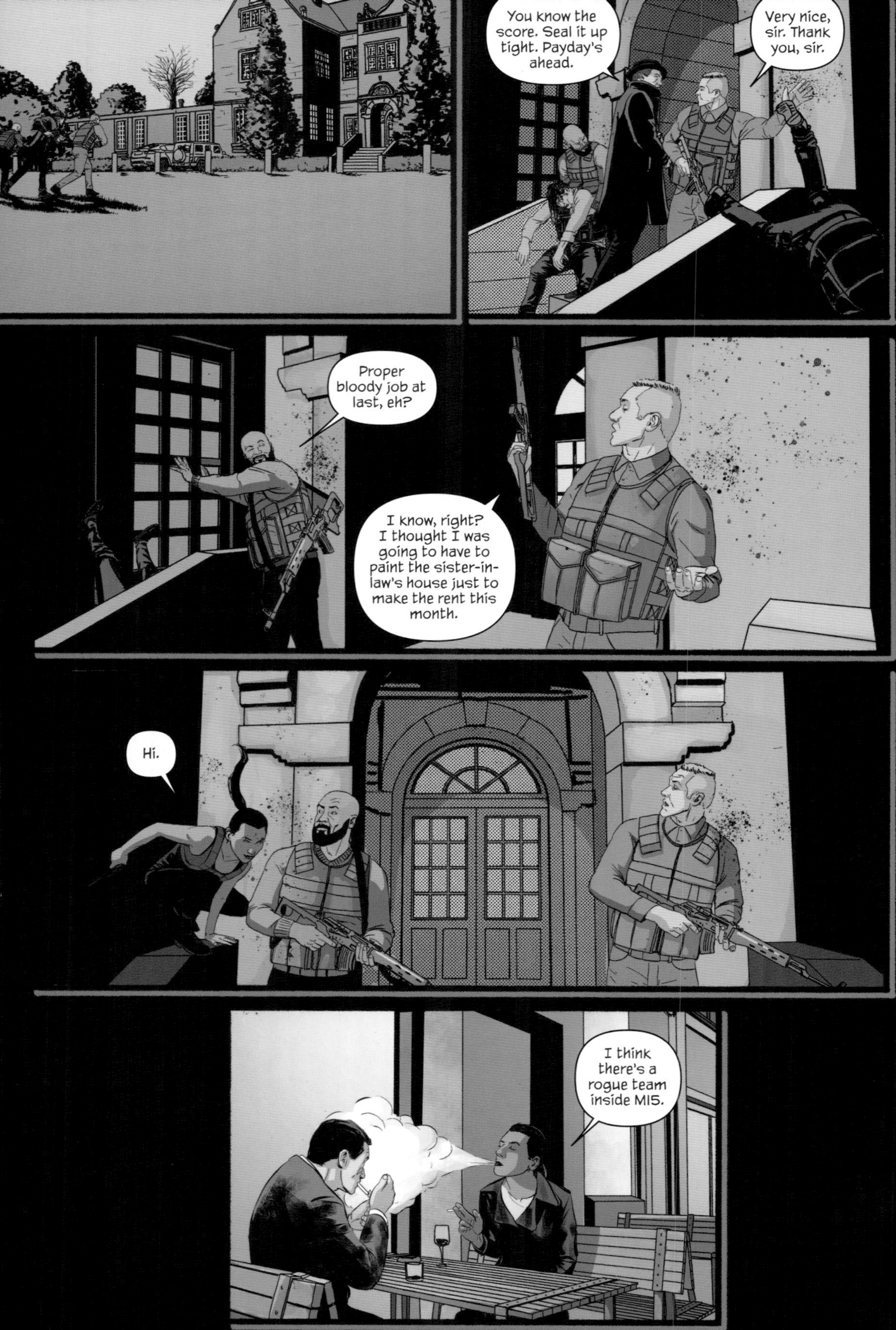
You know the score. Seal it up tight. Payday's ahead.
Very nice, sir. Thank you, sir.
Proper bloody job at last, eh?
I know, right? I thought I was going to have to paint the sister-in-law's house just to make the rent this month.
Hi.
I think there's a rogue team inside MI5.

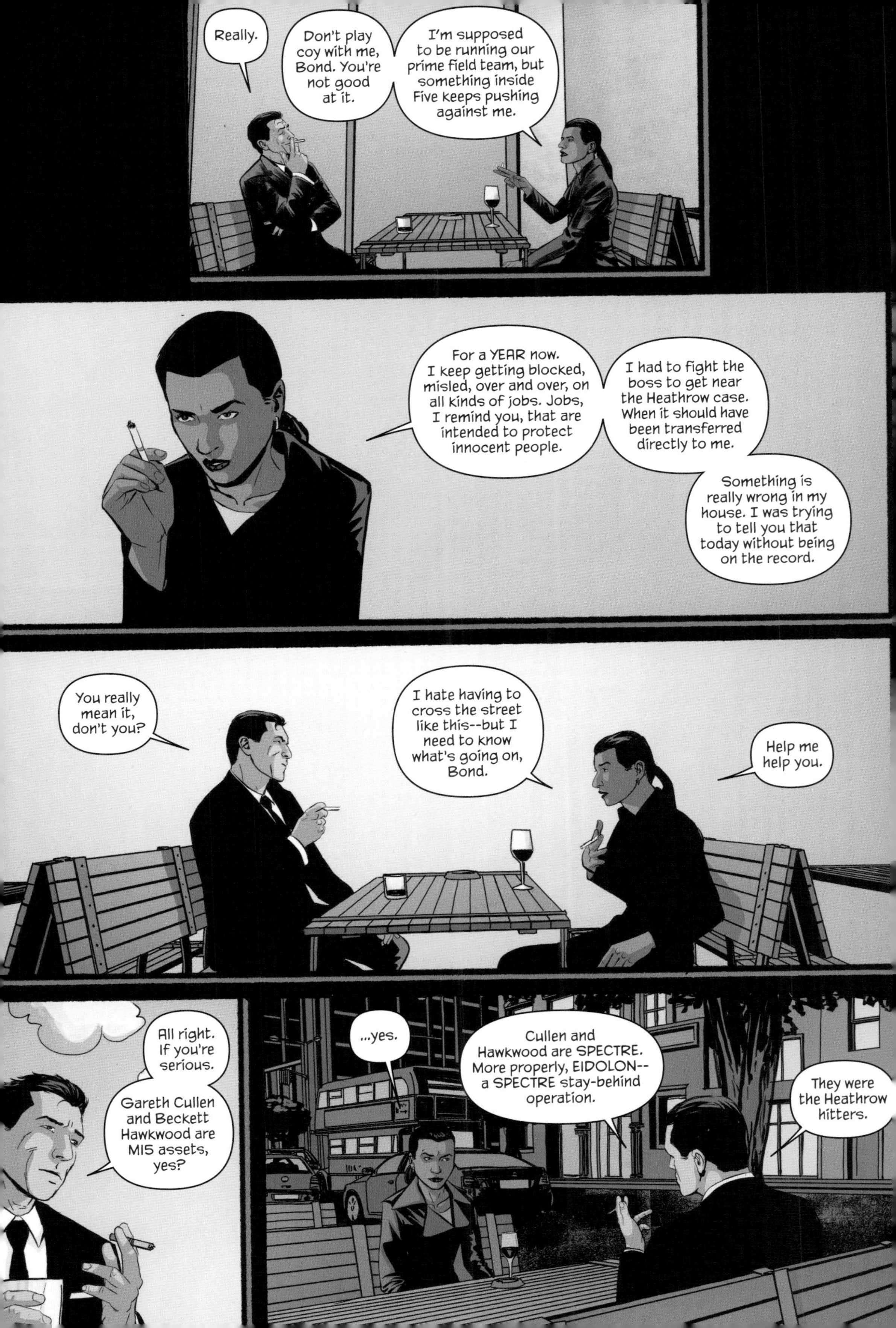
Really.
Don't play coy with me, Bond. You're not good at it.
I'm supposed to be running our prime field team, but something inside Five keeps pushing against me.
For a YEAR now. I keep getting blocked, misled, over and over, on all kinds of jobs. Jobs, I remind you, that are intended to protect innocent people.
I had to fight the boss to get near the Heathrow case. When it should have been transferred directly to me.
Something is really wrong in my house. I was trying to tell you that today without being on the record.
You really mean it, don't you?
I hate having to cross the street like this--but I need to know what's going on, Bond.
Help me help you.
All right. If you're serious.
Gareth Cullen and Beckett Hawkwood are MI5 assets, yes?
...yes.
Cullen and Hawkwood are SPECTRE. More properly, EIDOLON--a SPECTRE stay-behind operation.
They were the Heathrow hitters.

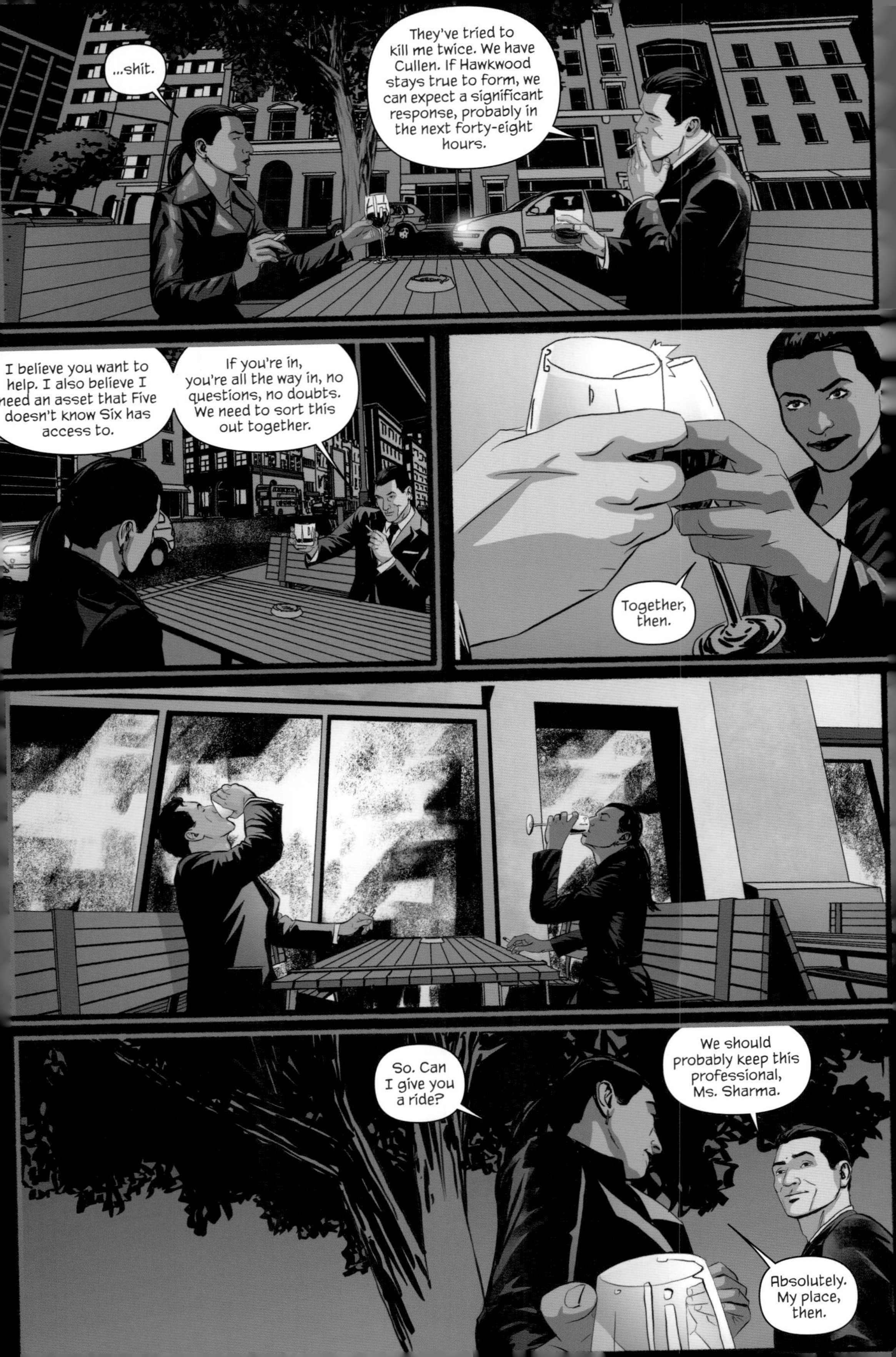
...shit.
They've tried to kill me twice. We have Cullen. If Hawkwood stays true to form, we can expect a significant response, probably in the next forty-eight hours.
I believe you want to help. I also believe I need an asset that Five doesn't know Six has access to.
If you're in, you're all the way in, no questions, no doubts. We need to sort this out together.
Together, then.
So. Can I give you a ride?
We should probably keep this professional, Ms. Sharma.
Absolutely. My place, then.

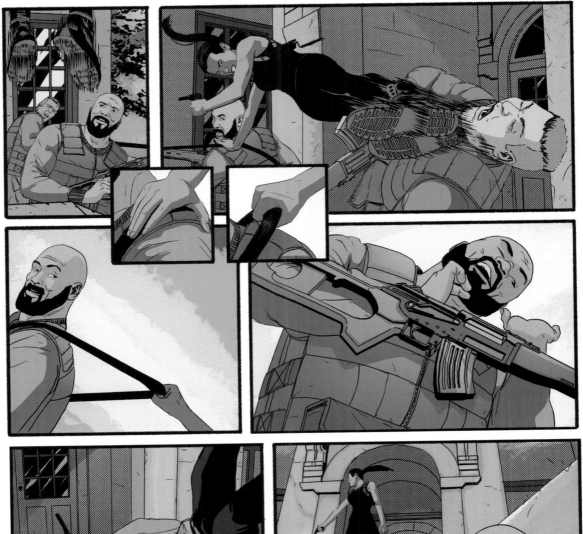

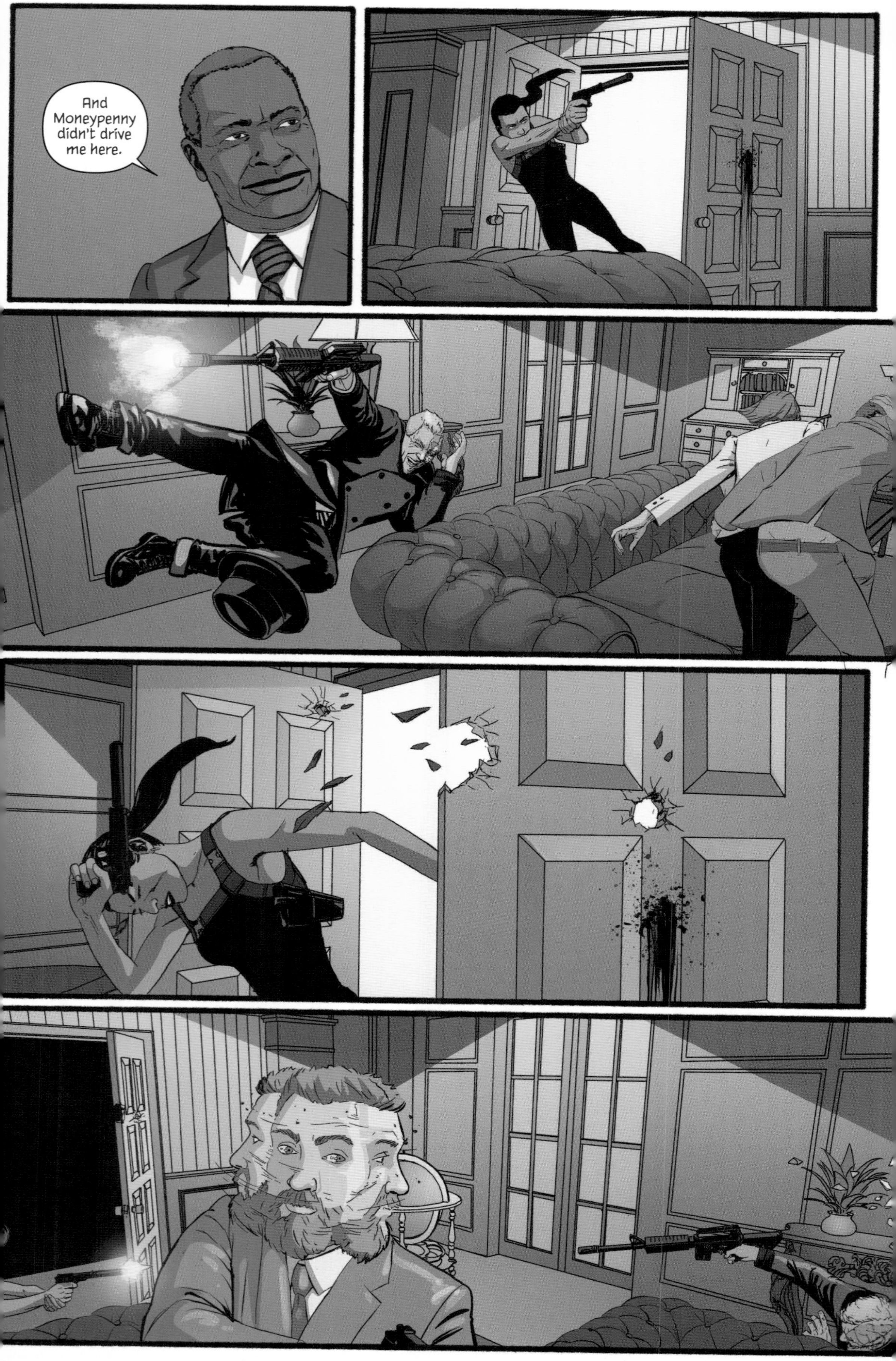
And Moneypenny didn't drive me here.

It's time.

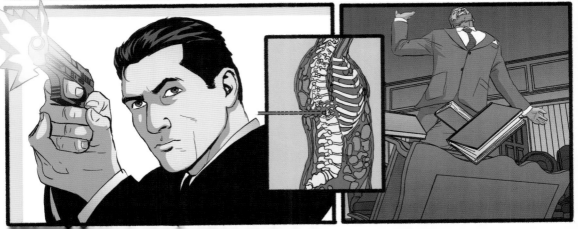

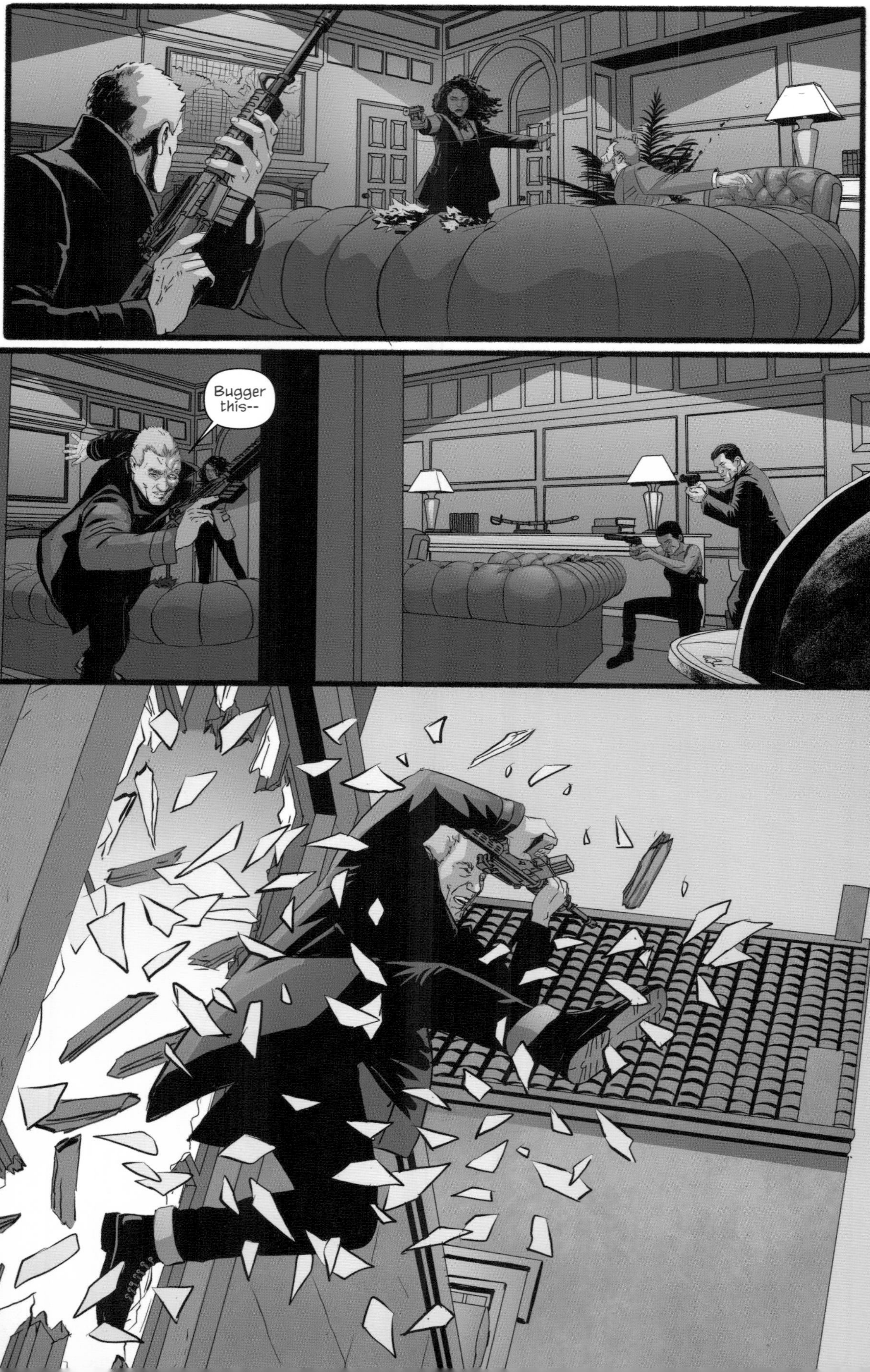
Bugger this--

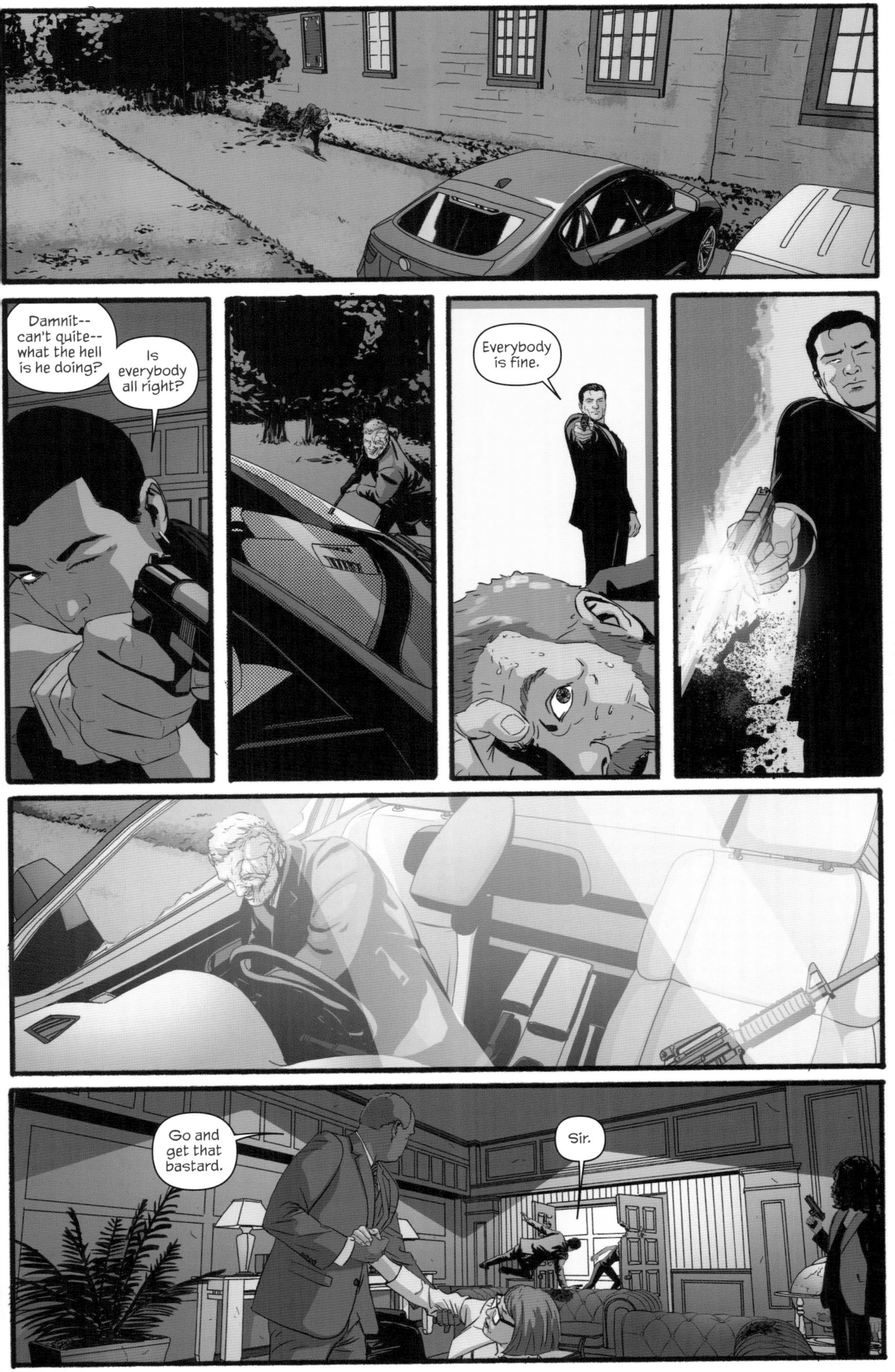
Damnit--
can't quite--
what the hell
is he doing?
Is
everybody
all right?
Everybody
is fine.
Go and
get that
bastard.
Sir.

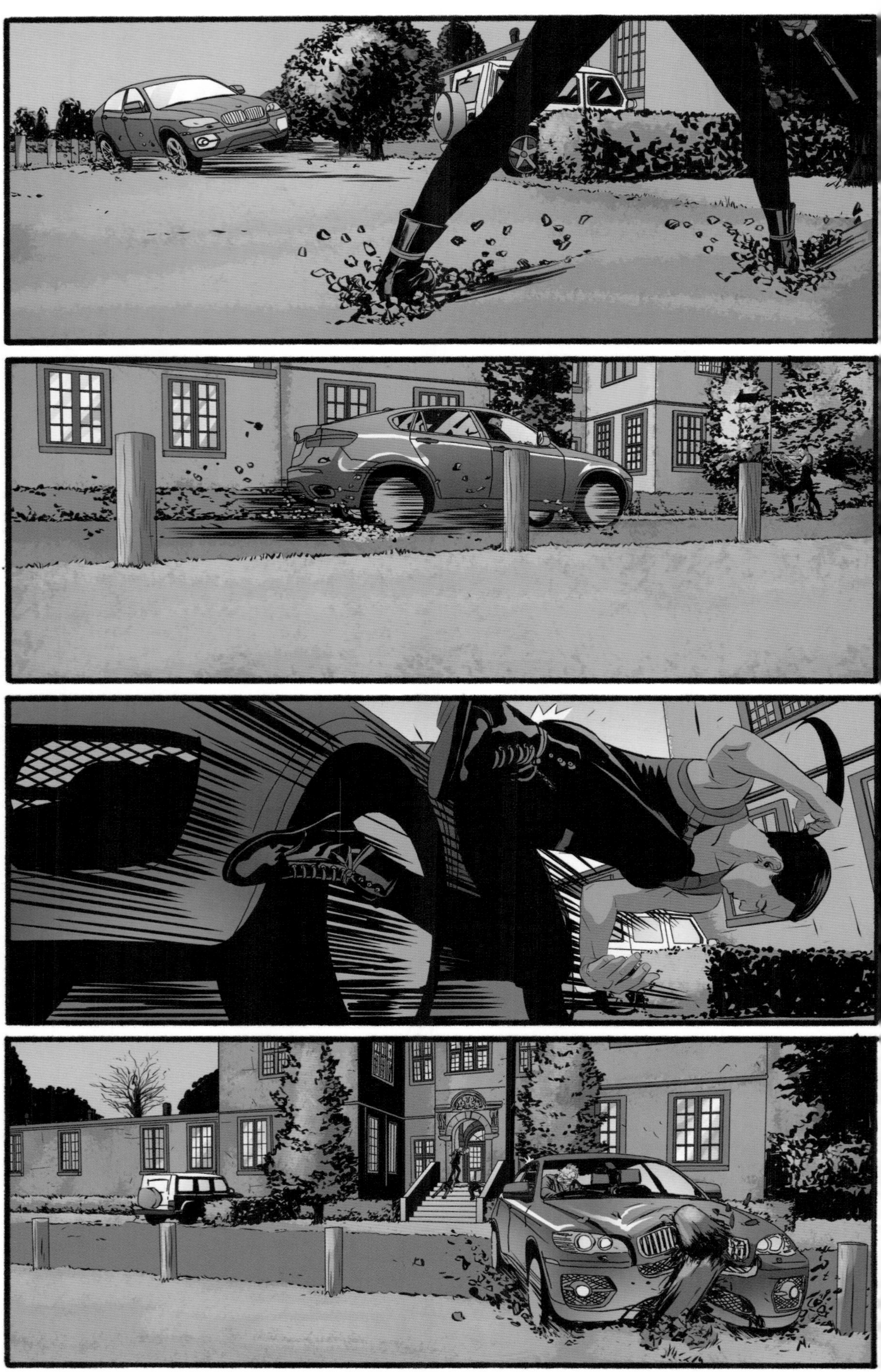

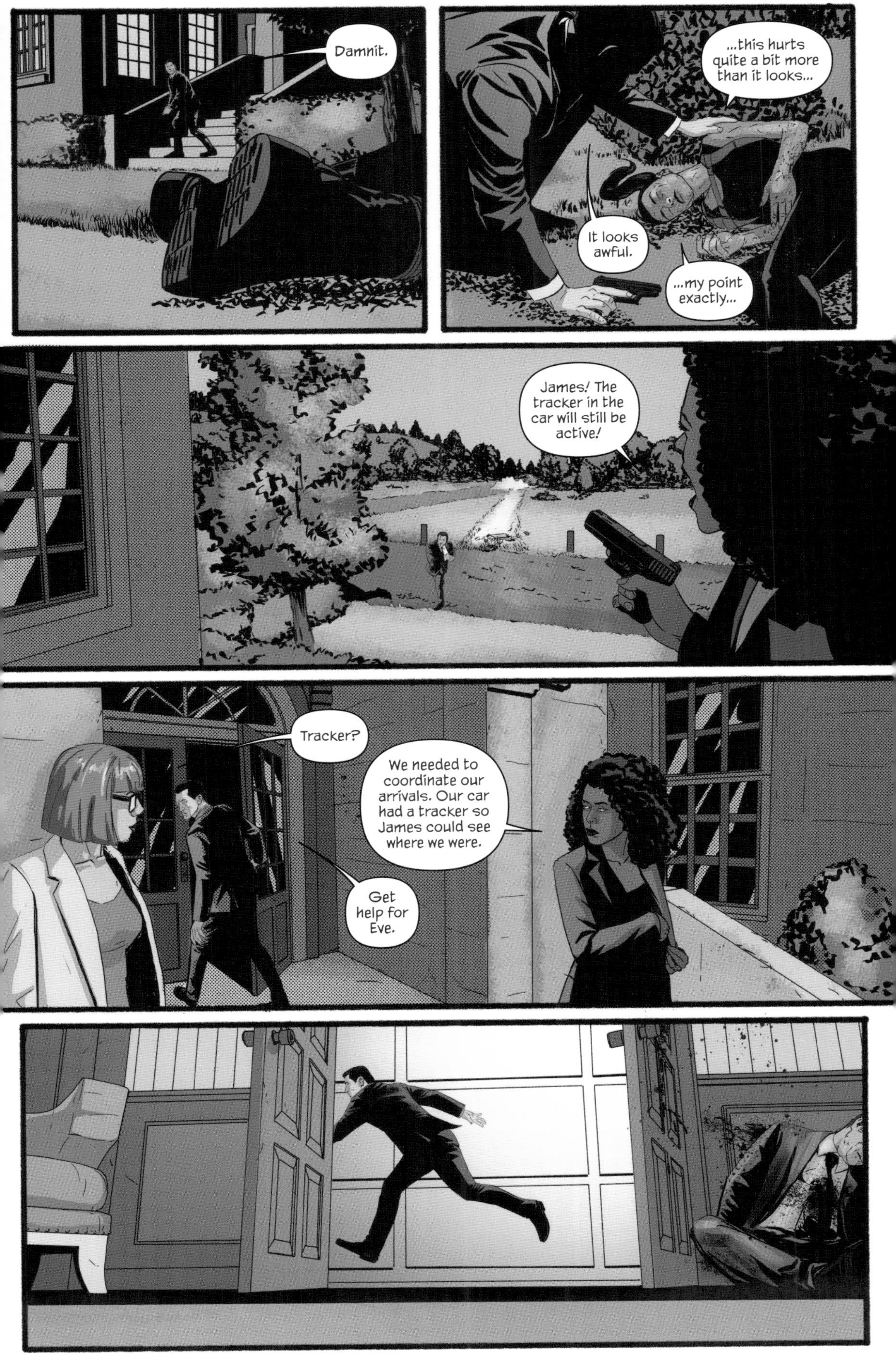
Damnit.
...this hurts quite a bit more than it looks...
It looks awful.
...my point exactly...
James! The tracker in the car will still be active!
Tracker?
We needed to coordinate our arrivals. Our car had a tracker so James could see where we were.
Get help for Eve.

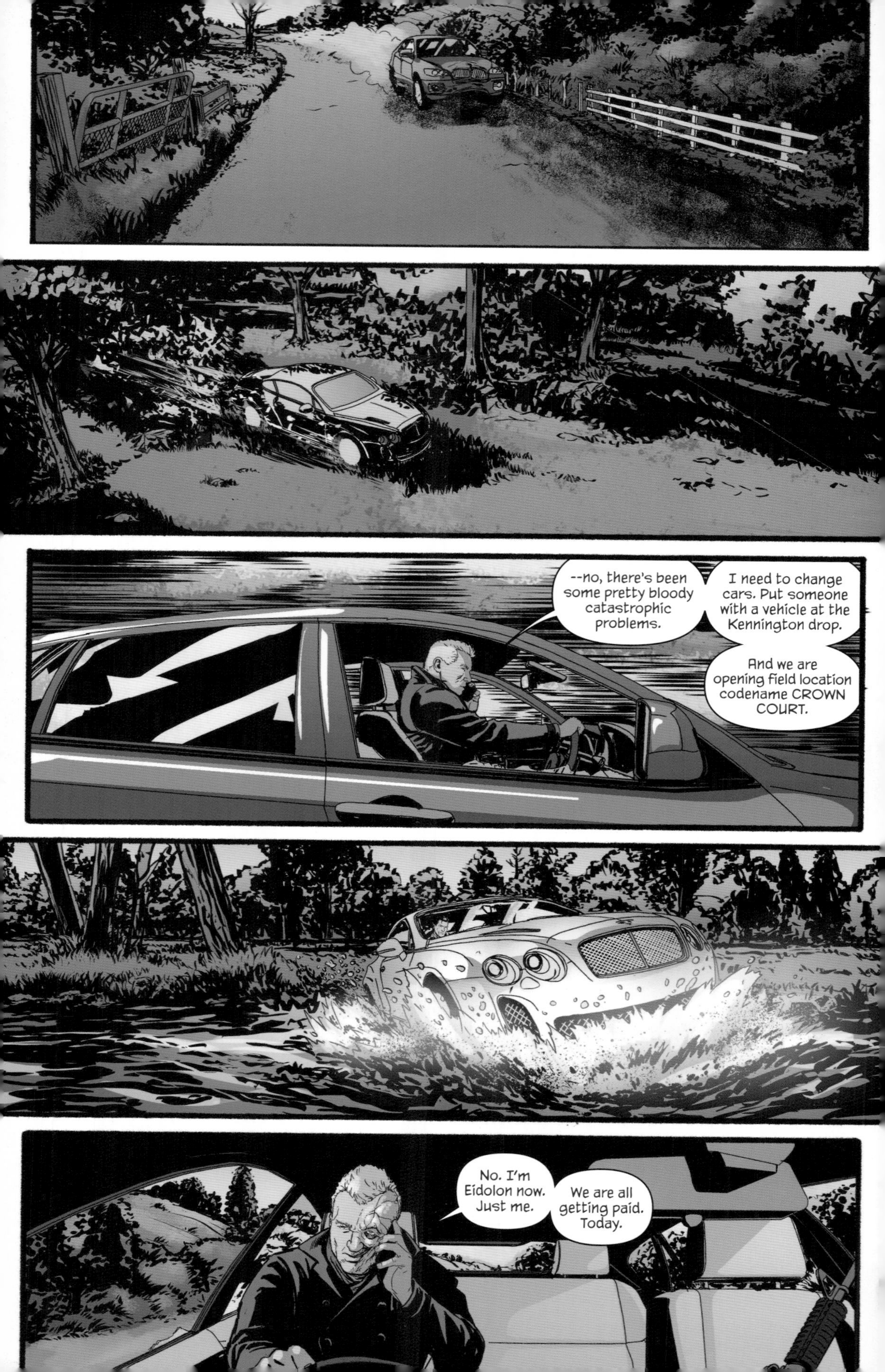
--no, there's been some pretty bloody catastrophic problems.
I need to change cars. Put someone with a vehicle at the Kennington drop.
And we are opening field location codename CROWN COURT.
No. I'm Eidolon now. Just me.
We are all getting paid. Today.

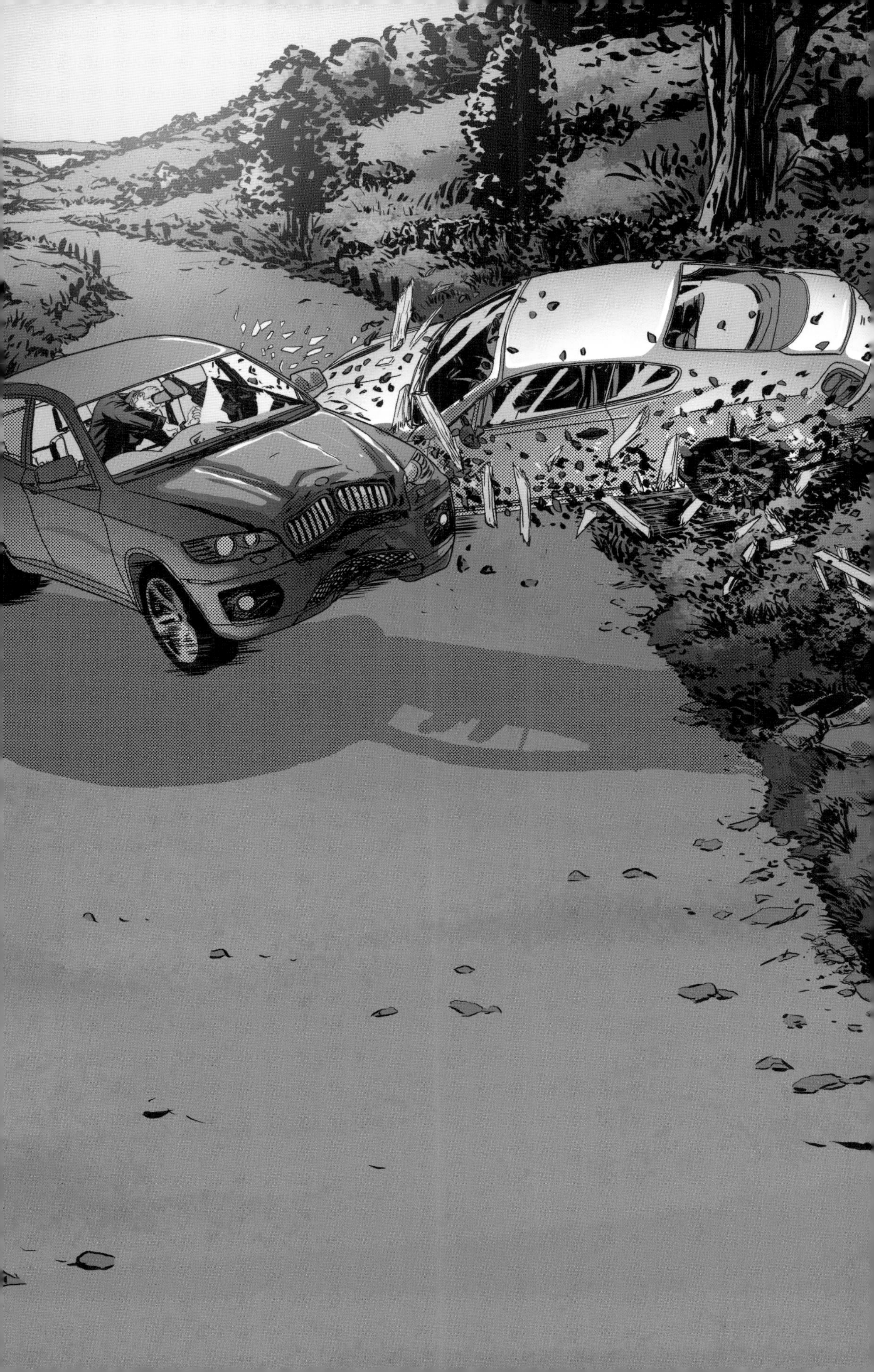

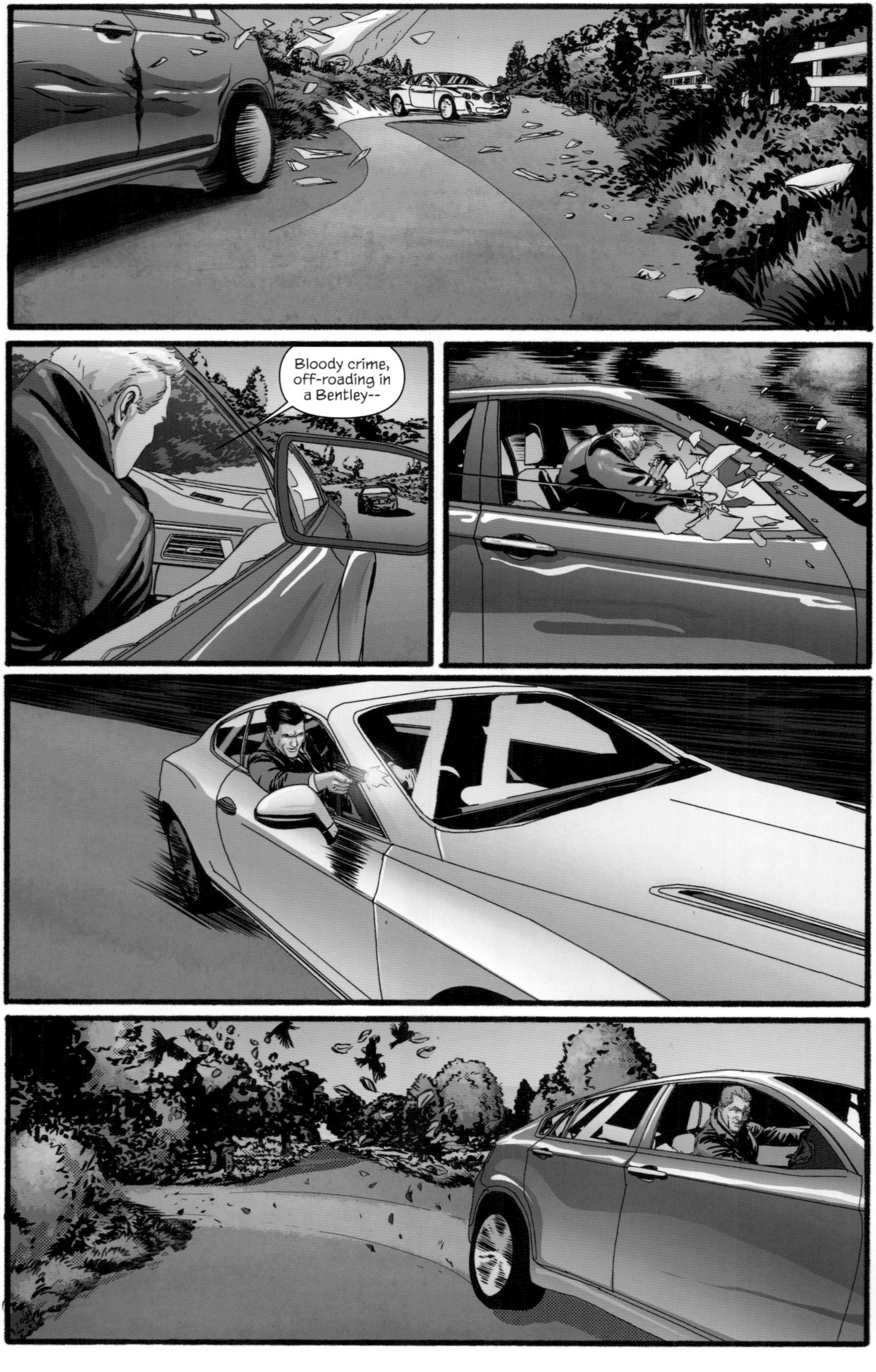
Bloody crime, off-roading in a Bentley--

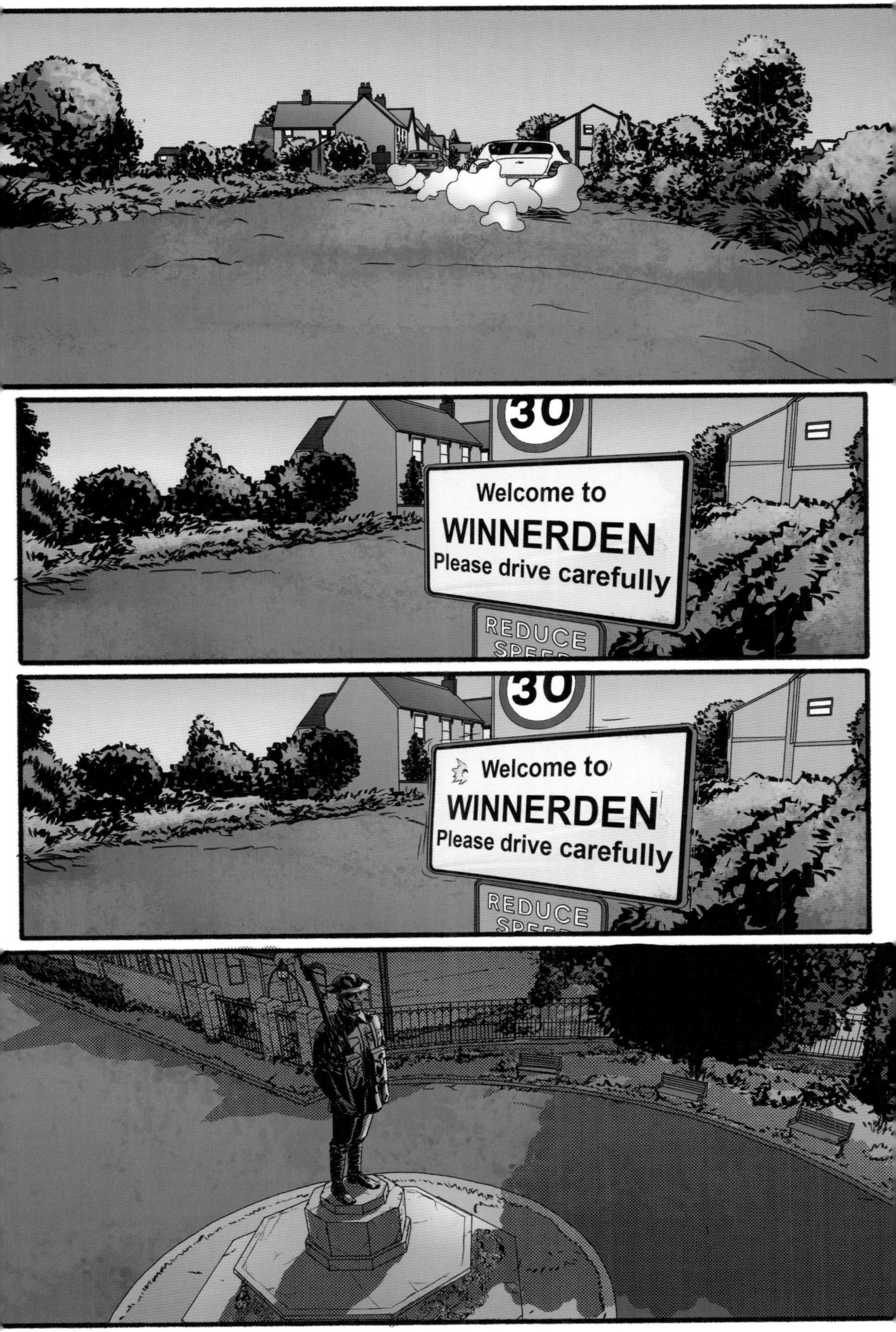
30
Welcome to
WINNERDEN
Please drive carefully
REDUCE
30
Welcome to
WINNERDEN
Please drive carefully
REDUCE

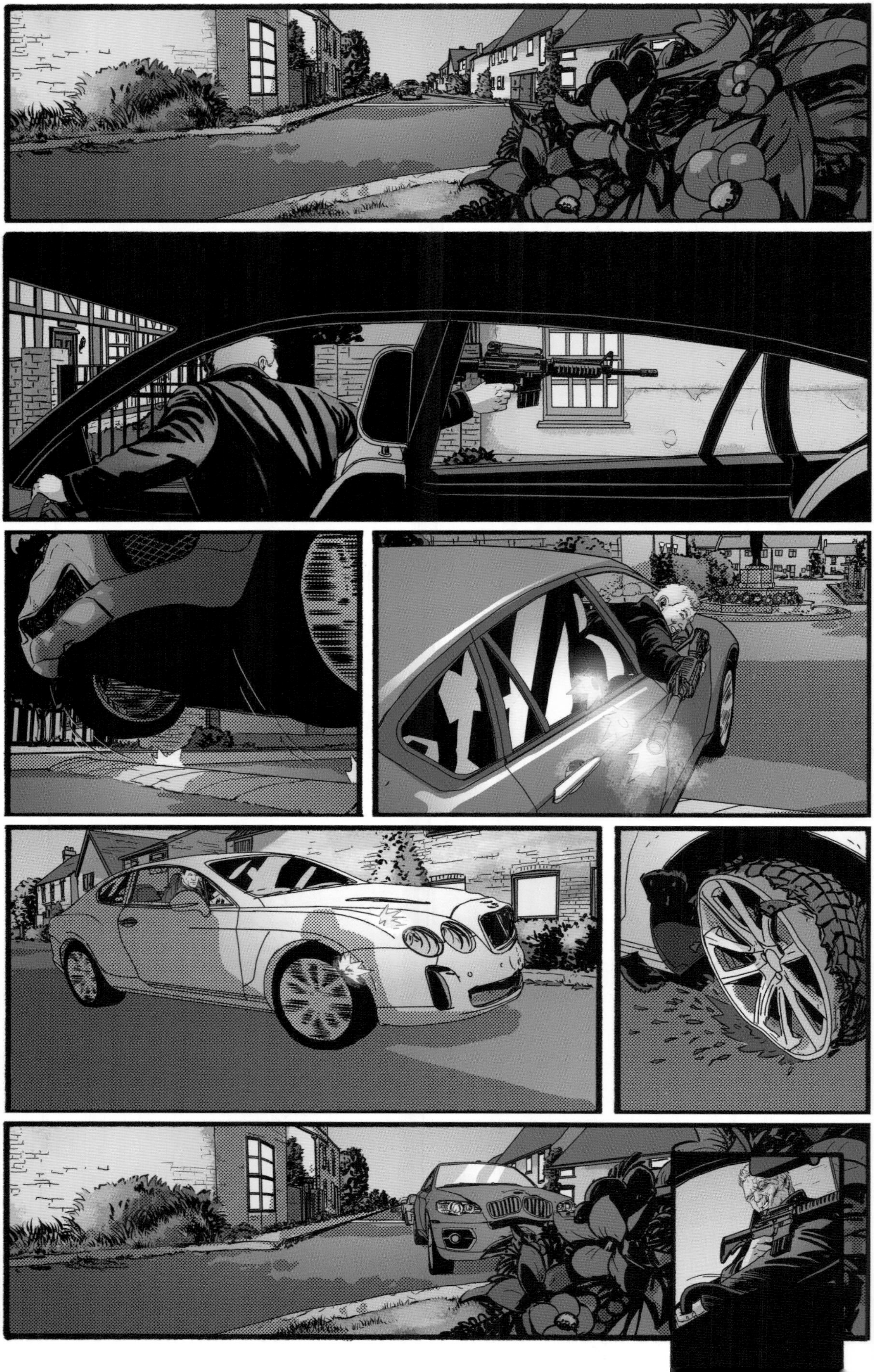

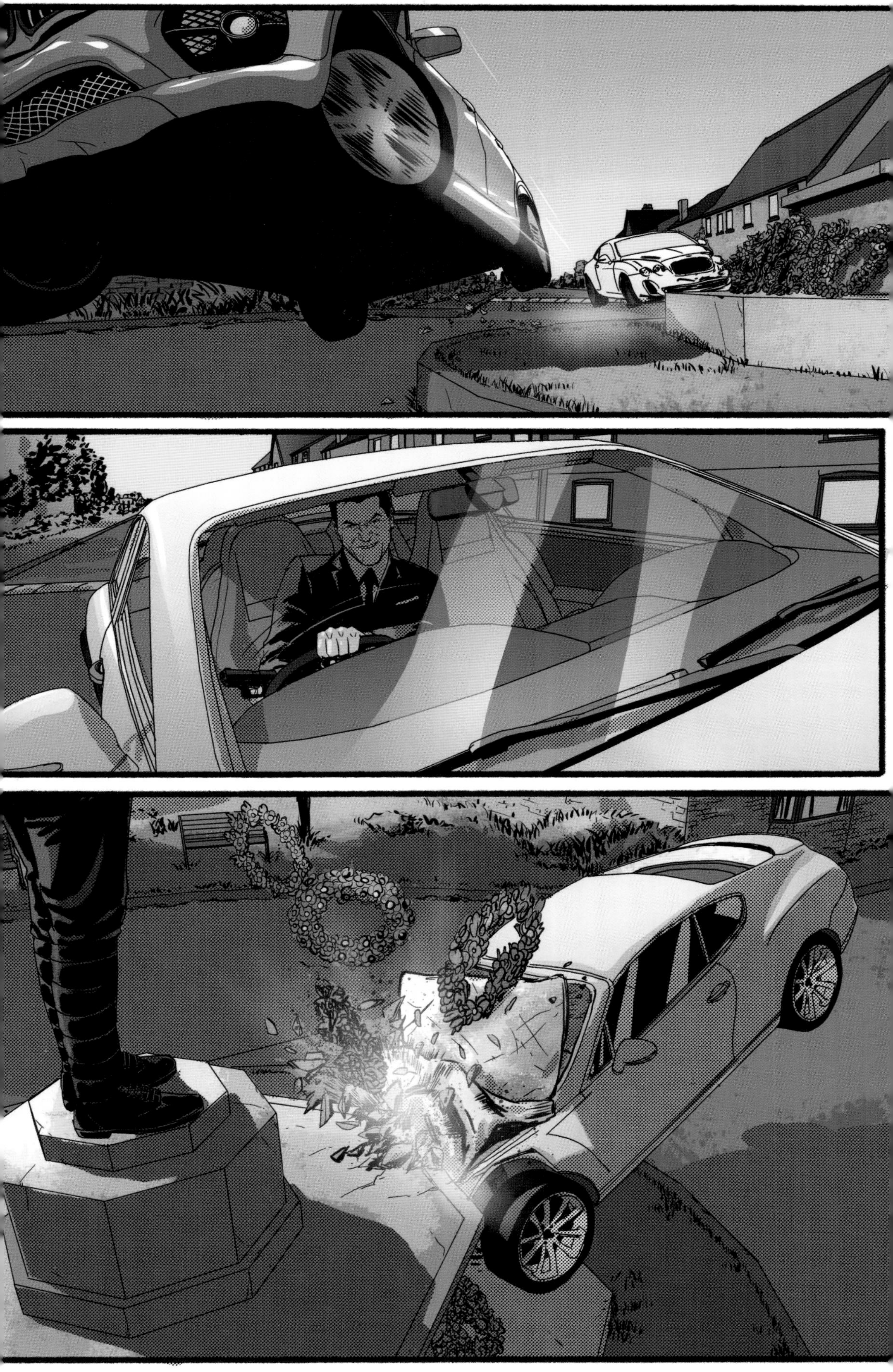

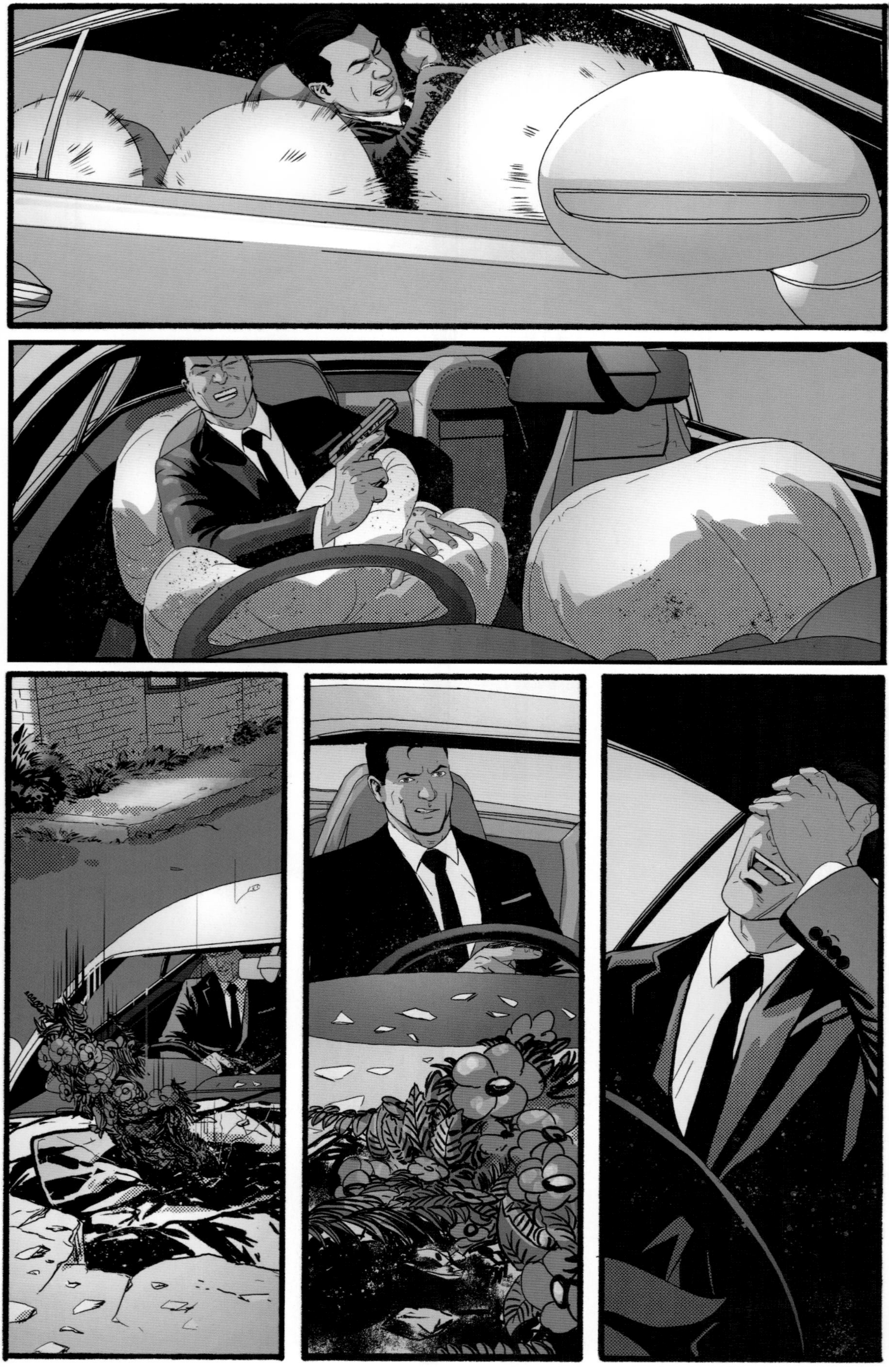

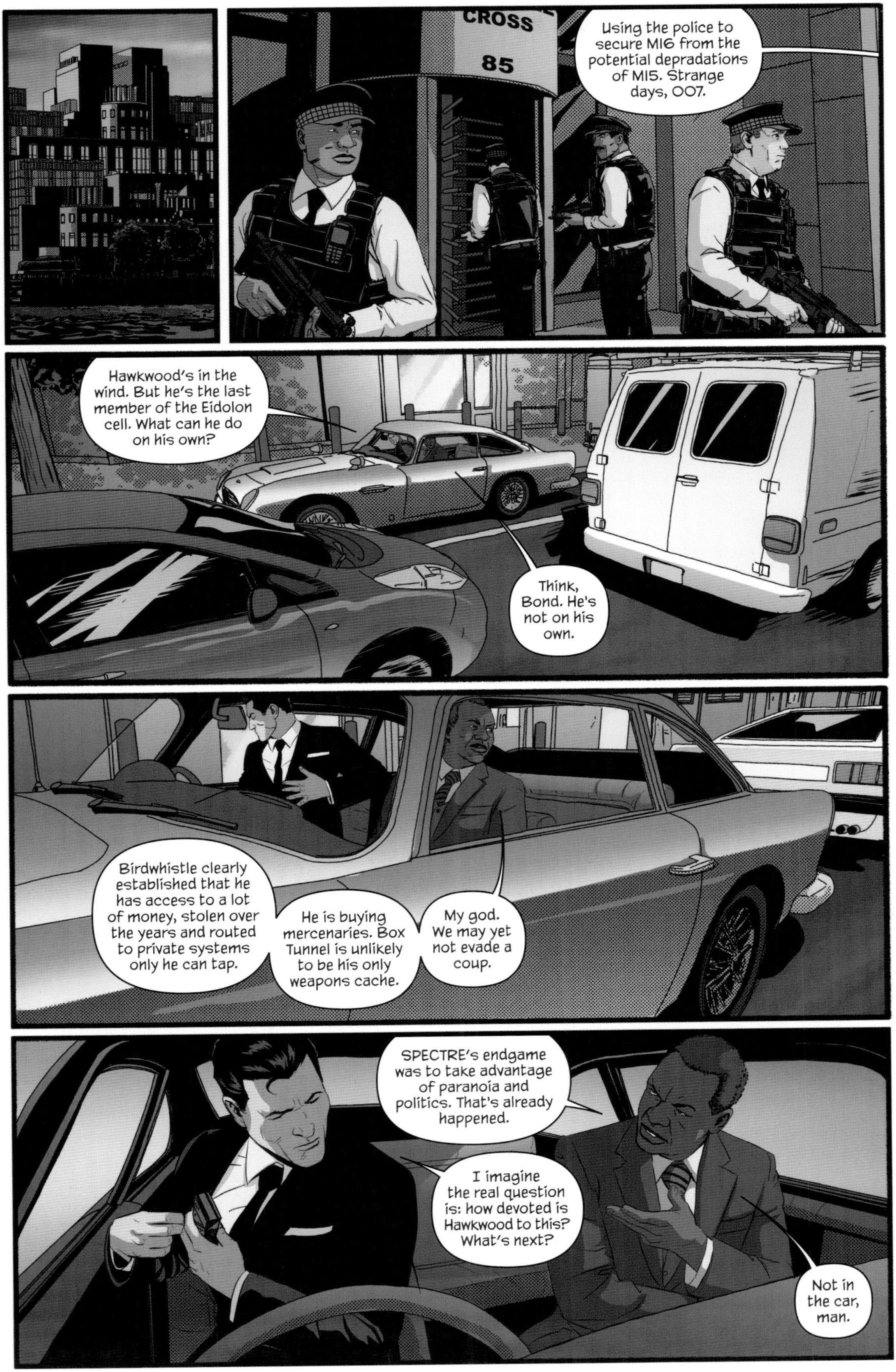
CROSS
85
Using the police to secure MI6 from the potential depradations of MI5. Strange days, 007.
Hawkwood's in the wind. But he's the last member of the Eidolon cell. What can he do on his own?
Think, Bond. He's not on his own.
Birdwhistle clearly established that he has access to a lot of money, stolen over the years and routed to private systems only he can tap.
He is buying mercenaries. Box Tunnel is unlikely to be his only weapons cache.
My god. We may yet not evade a coup.
SPECTRE's endgame was to take advantage of paranoia and politics. That's already happened.
I imagine the real question is: how devoted is Hawkwood to this? What's next?
Not in the car, man.

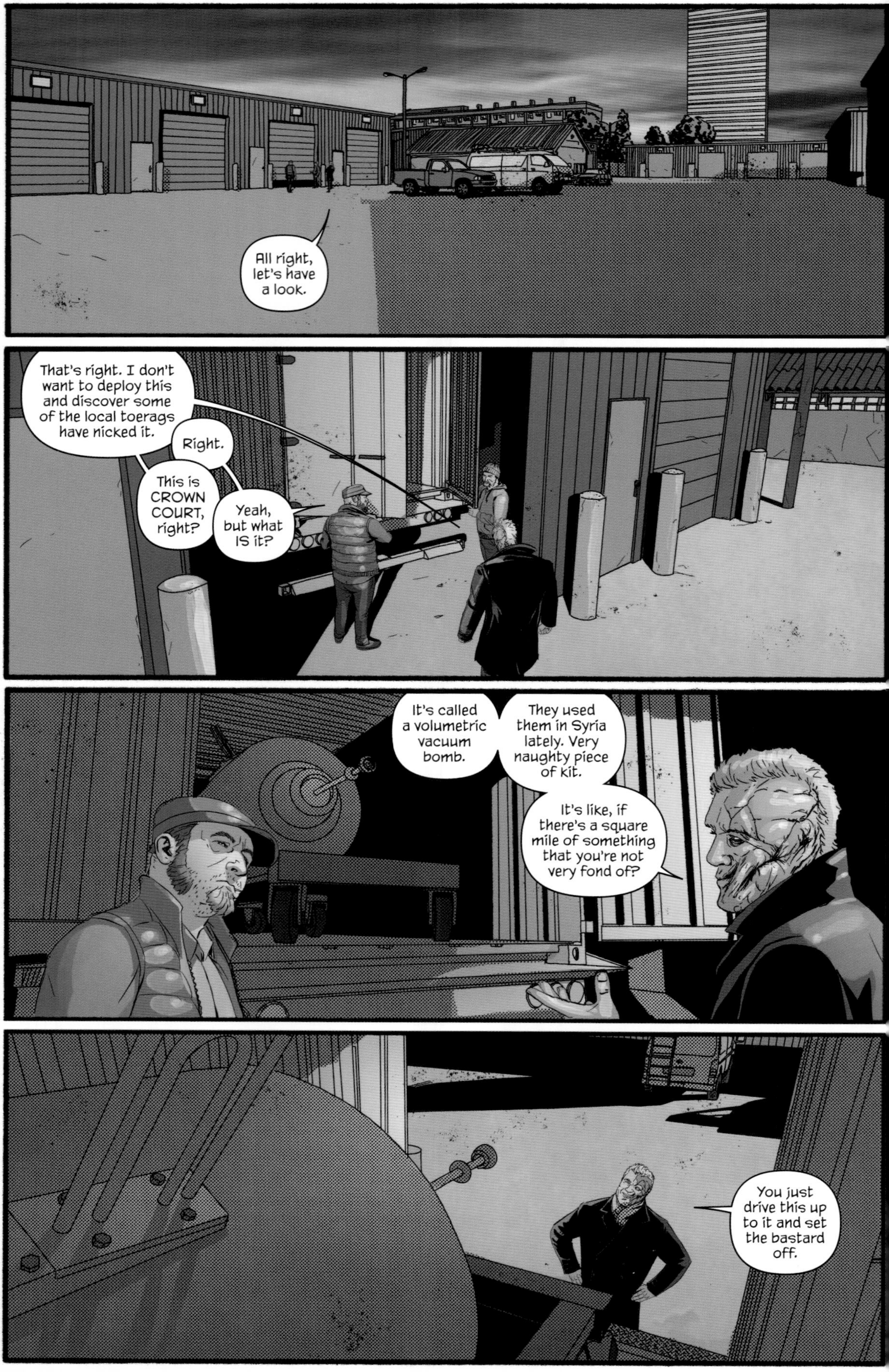
All right, let's have a look.
That's right. I don't want to deploy this and discover some of the local toerags have nicked it.
Right.
This is CROWN COURT, right?
Yeah, but what IS it?
It's called a volumetric vacuum bomb.
They used them in Syria lately. Very naughty piece of kit.
It's like, if there's a square mile of something that you're not very fond of?
You just drive this up to it and set the bastard off.

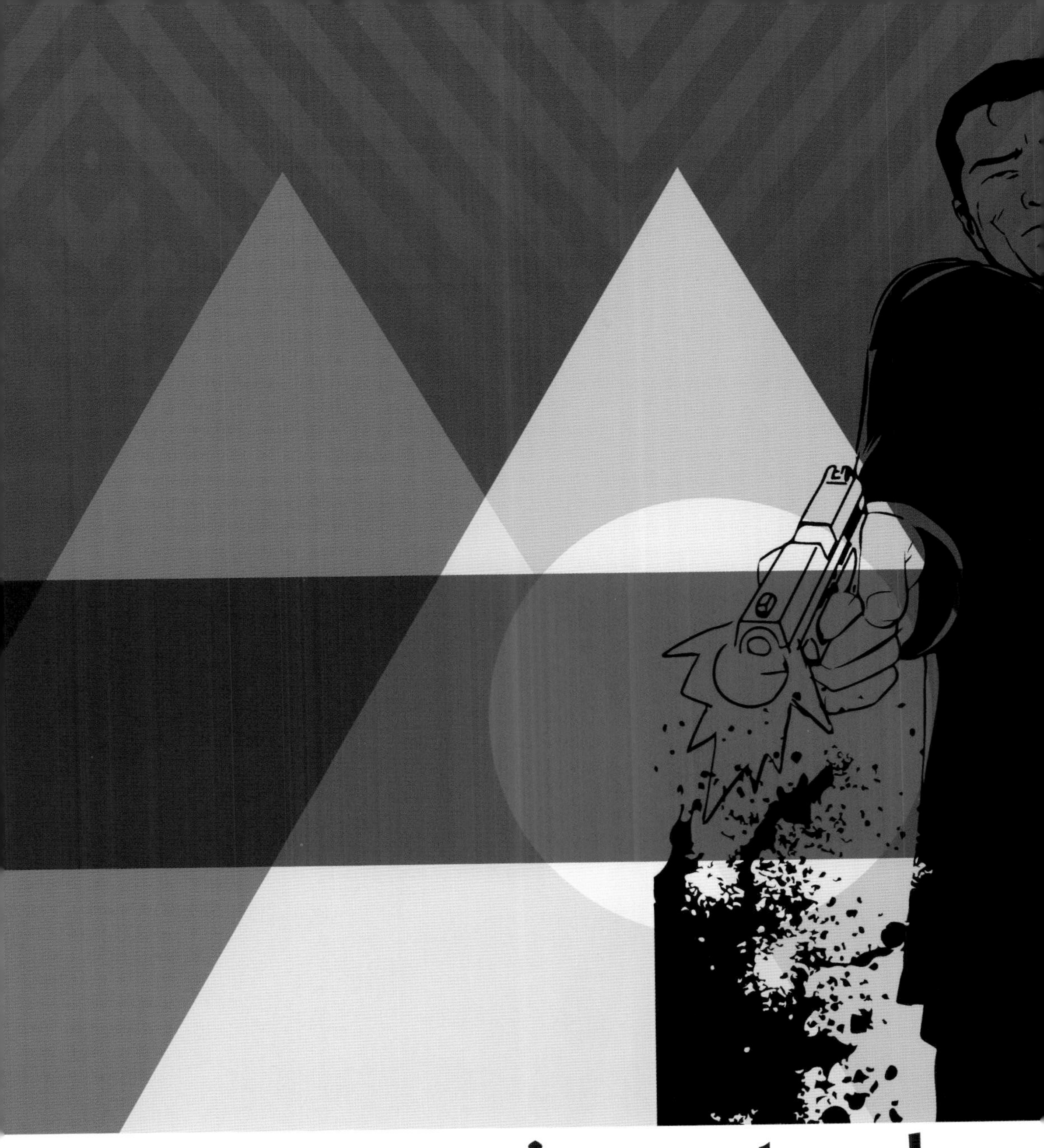

issue twelve

issue #12 main cover by **DOM REARDON**

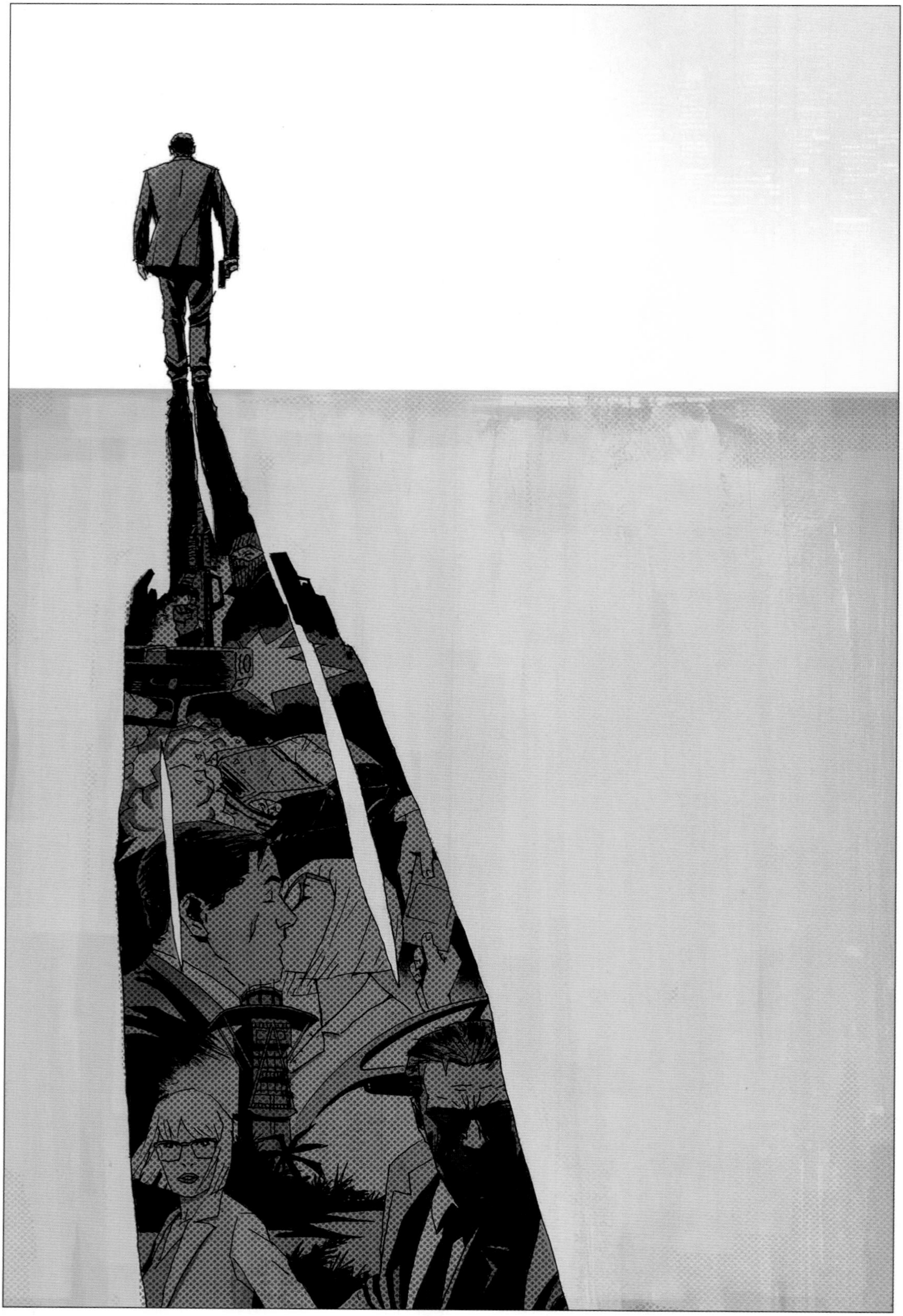

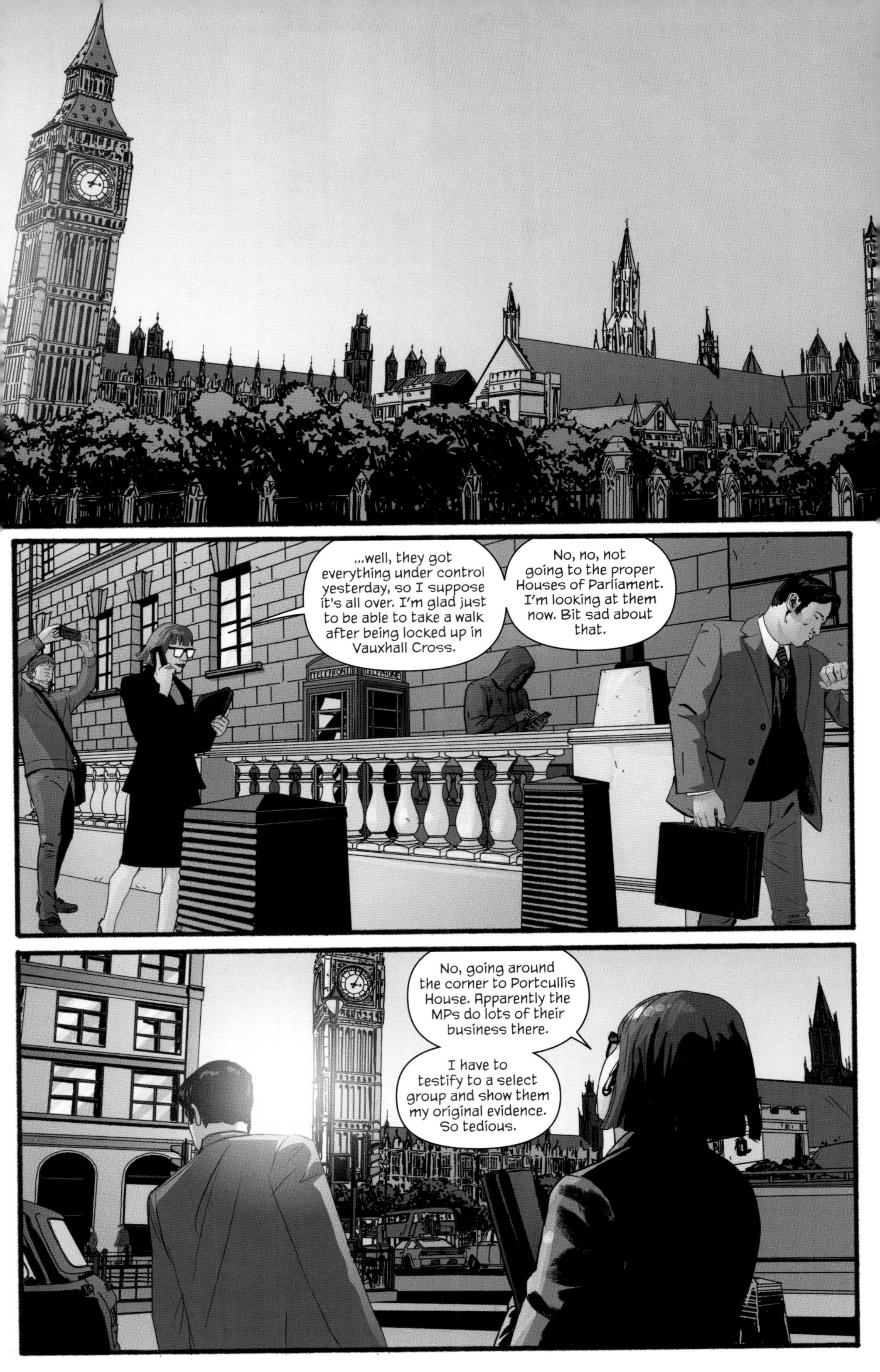
...well, they got everything under control yesterday, so I suppose it's all over. I'm glad just to be able to take a walk after being locked up in Vauxhall Cross.
No, no, not going to the proper Houses of Parliament. I'm looking at them now. Bit sad about that.
TELEPHONE
No, going around the corner to Portcullis House. Apparently the MPs do lots of their business there.
I have to testify to a select group and show them my original evidence. So tedious.

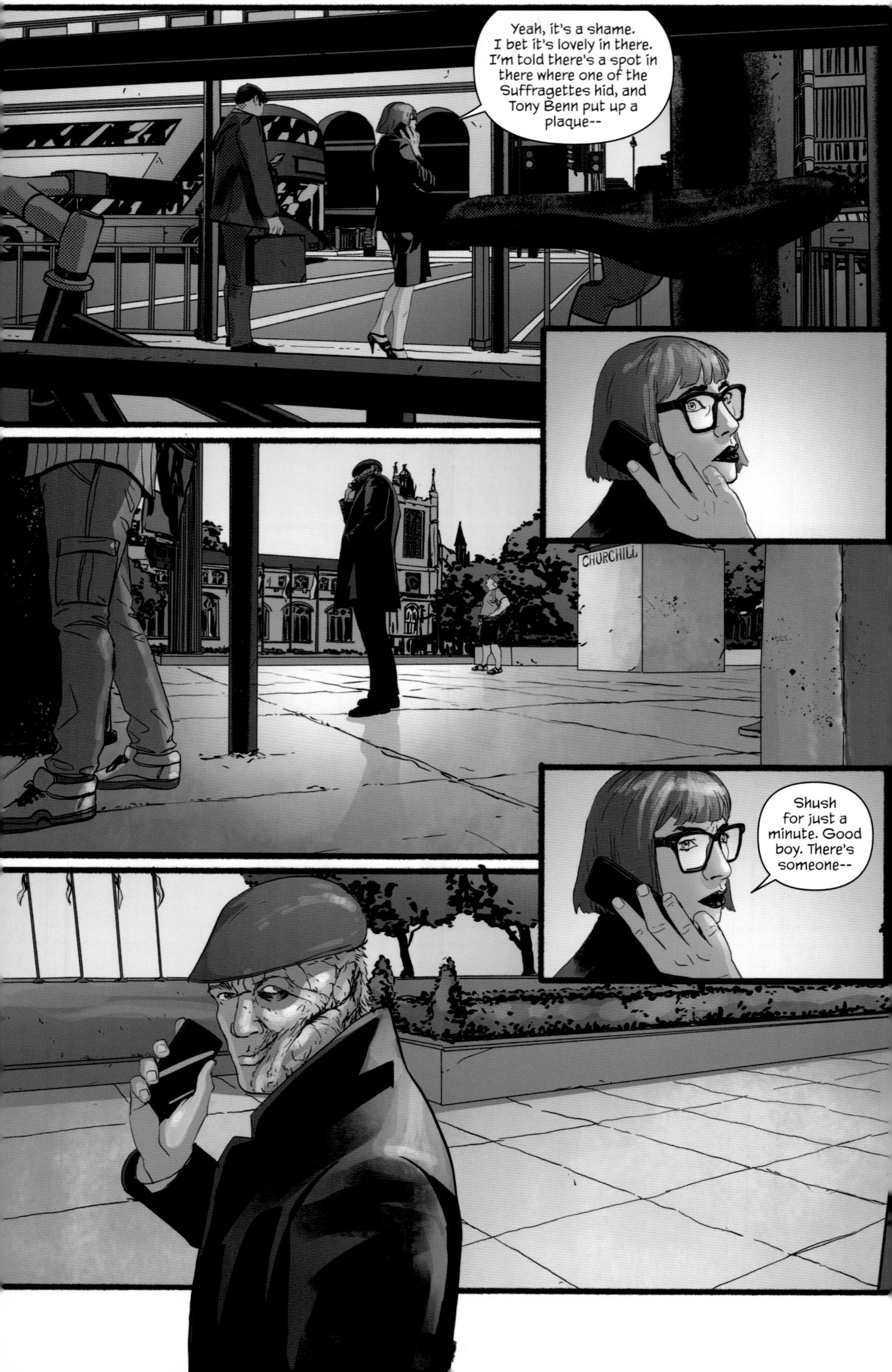

Yeah, it's a shame. I bet it's lovely in there. I'm told there's a spot in there where one of the Suffragettes hid, and Tony Benn put up a plaque--
CHURCHILL
Shush for just a minute. Good boy. There's someone--

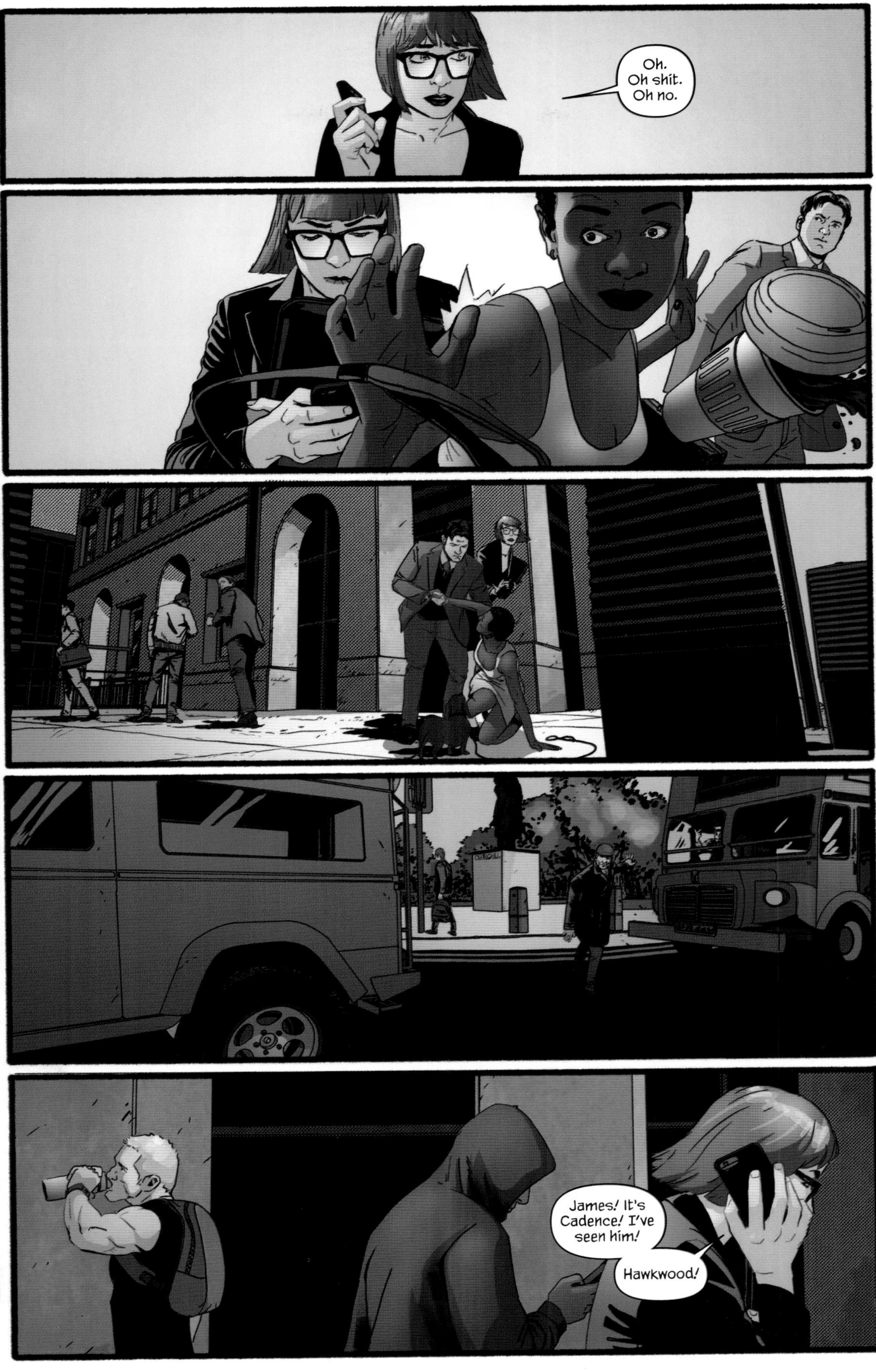
Oh.
Oh shit.
Oh no.
James! It's Cadence! I've seen him!
Hawkwood!

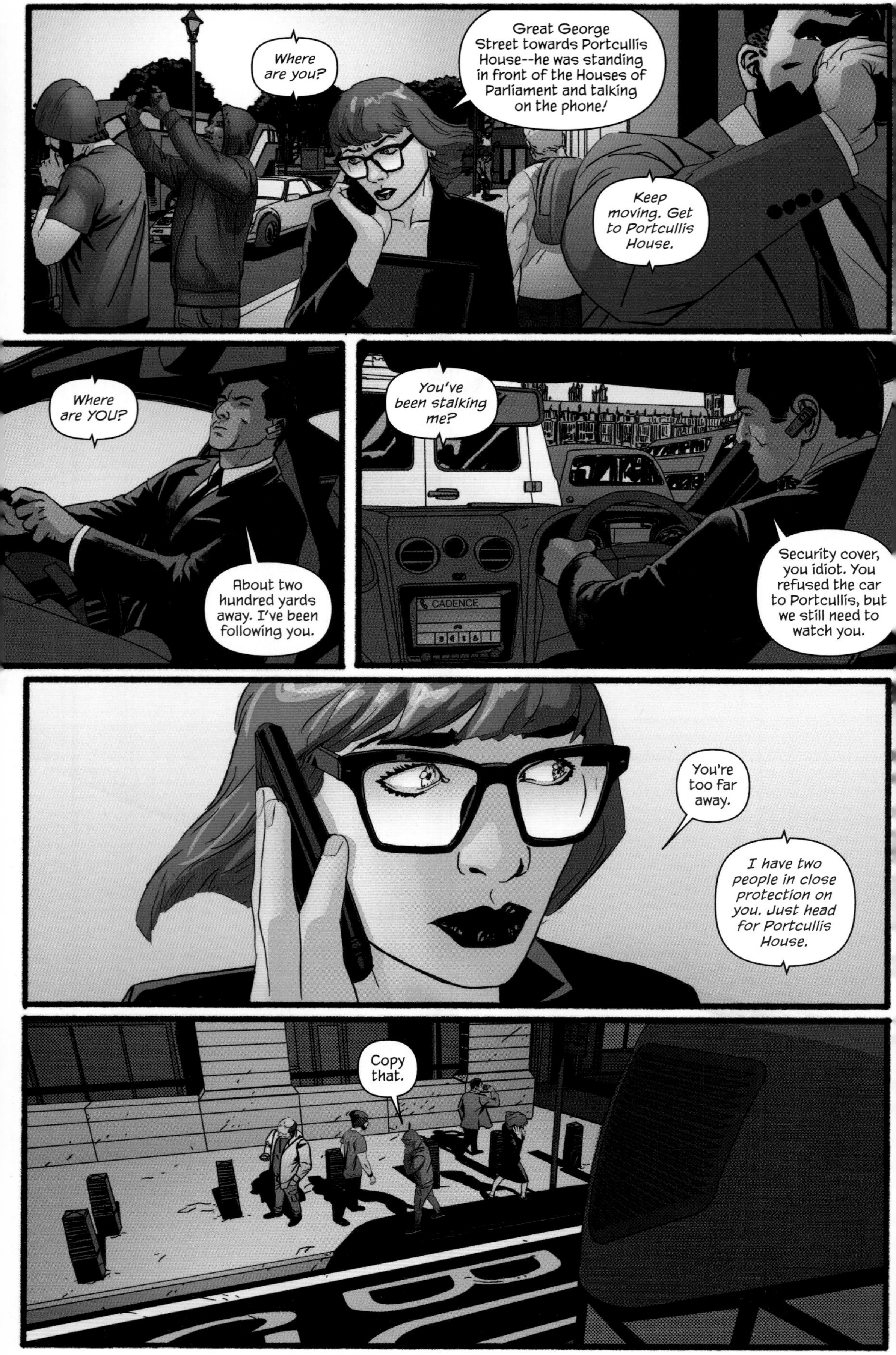
Where are you?
Great George Street towards Portcullis House--he was standing in front of the Houses of Parliament and talking on the phone!
Keep moving. Get to Portcullis House.
Where are YOU?
About two hundred yards away. I've been following you.
You've been stalking me?
CADENCE
Security cover, you idiot. You refused the car to Portcullis, but we still need to watch you.
You're too far away.
I have two people in close protection on you. Just head for Portcullis House.
Copy that.

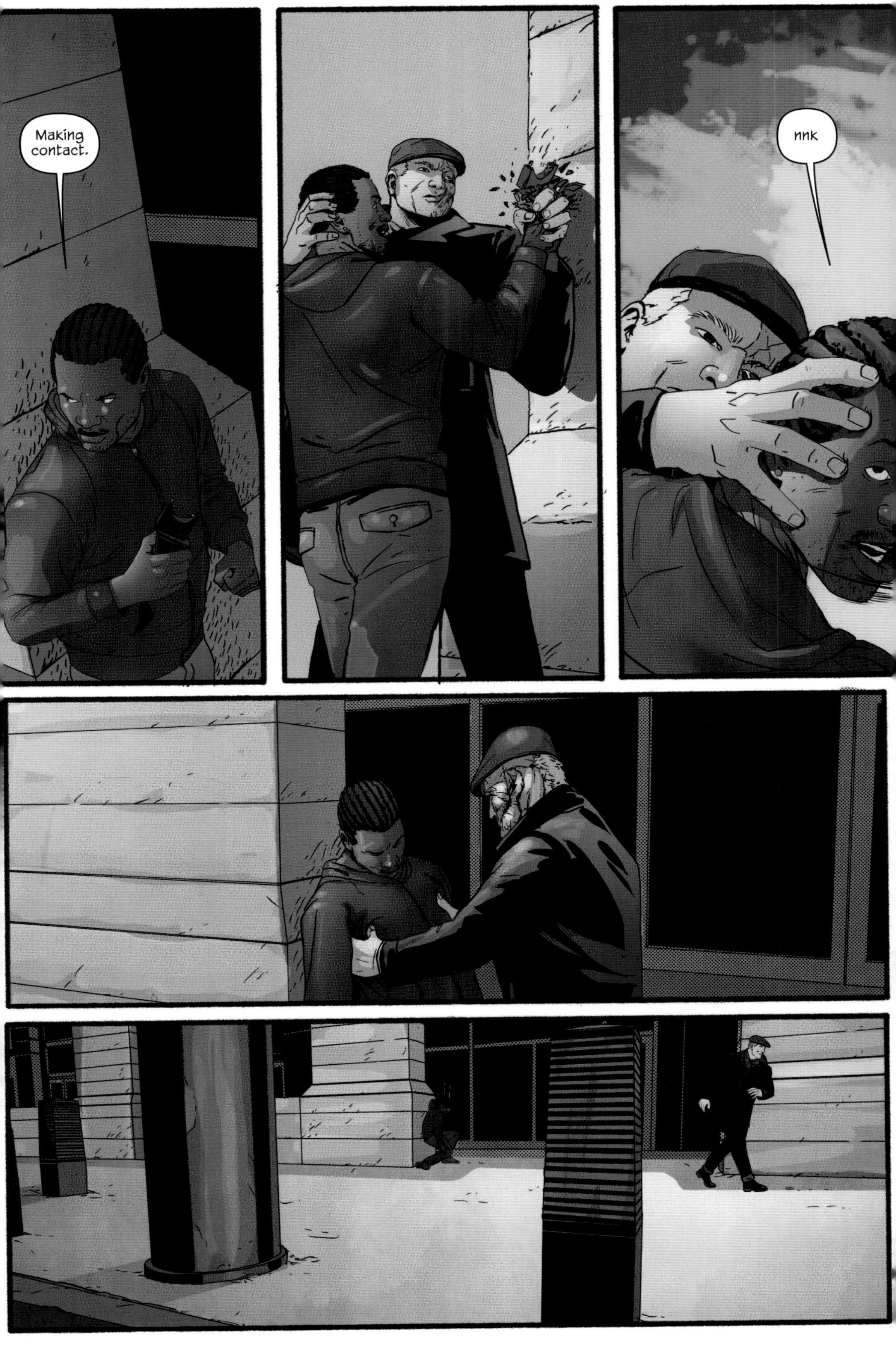
Making contact.
nnk

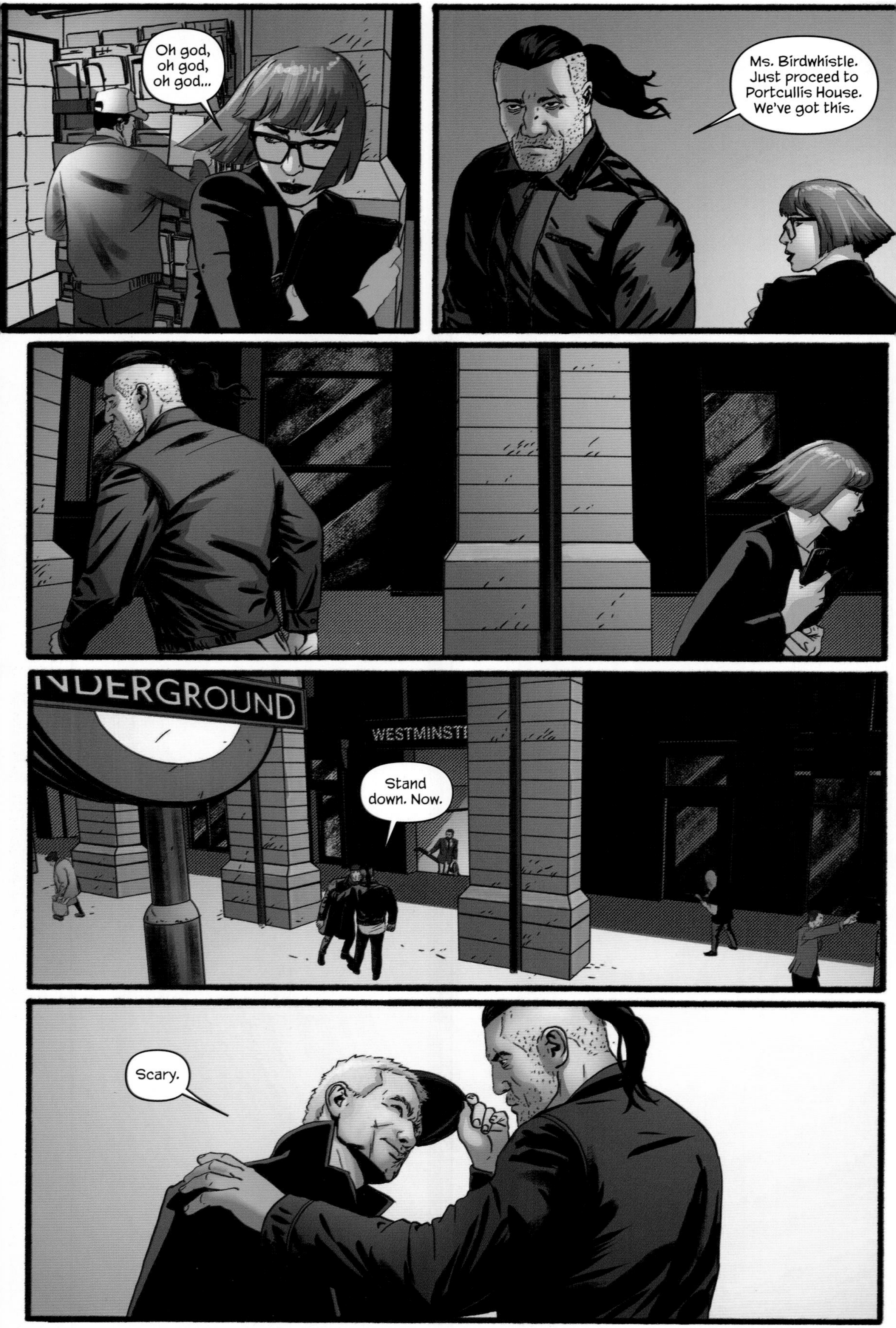
Oh god, oh god, oh god...
Ms. Birdwhistle. Just proceed to Portcullis House. We've got this.
NDERGROUND
WESTMINST
Stand down. Now.
Scary.

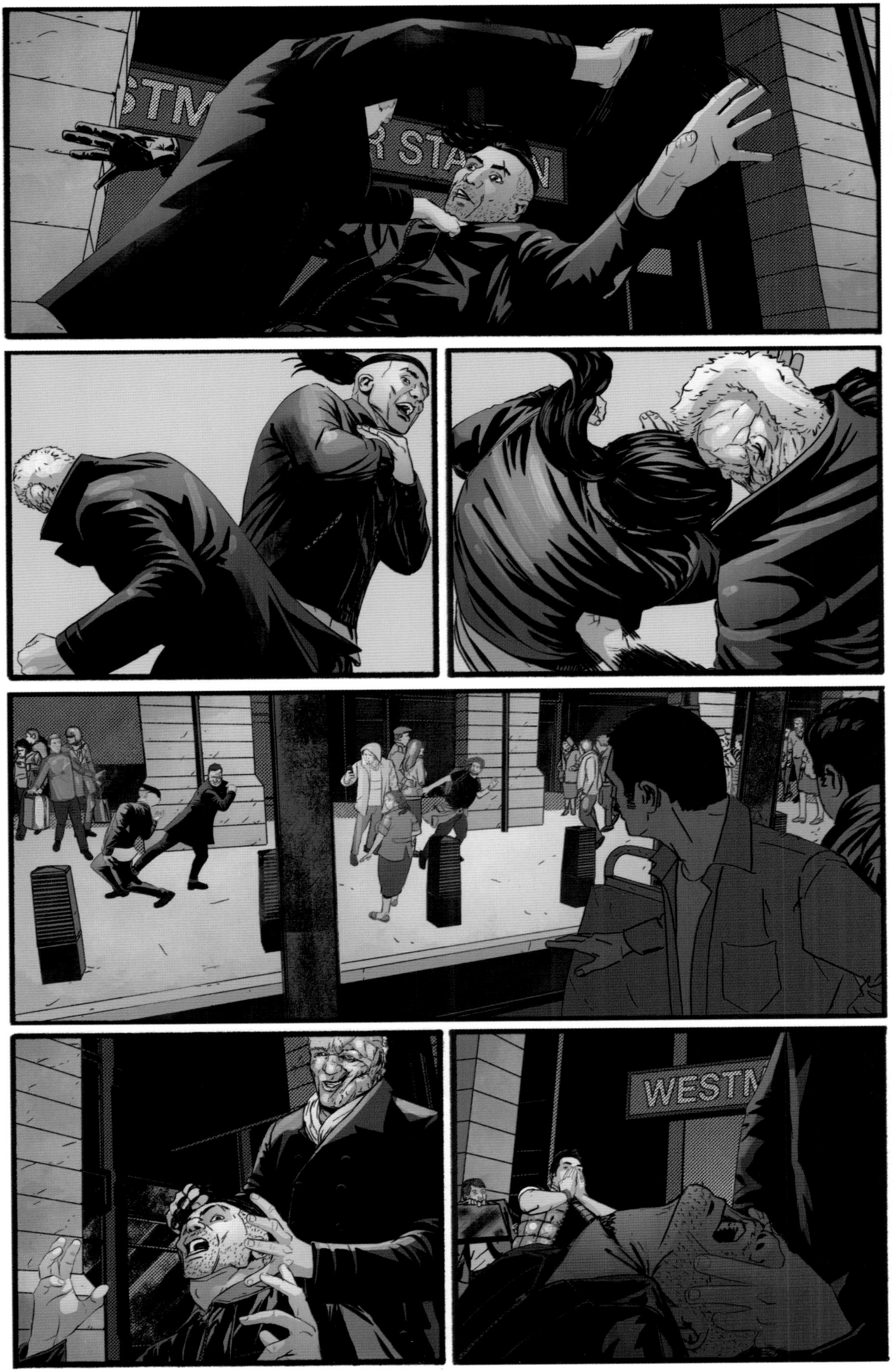
WESTM

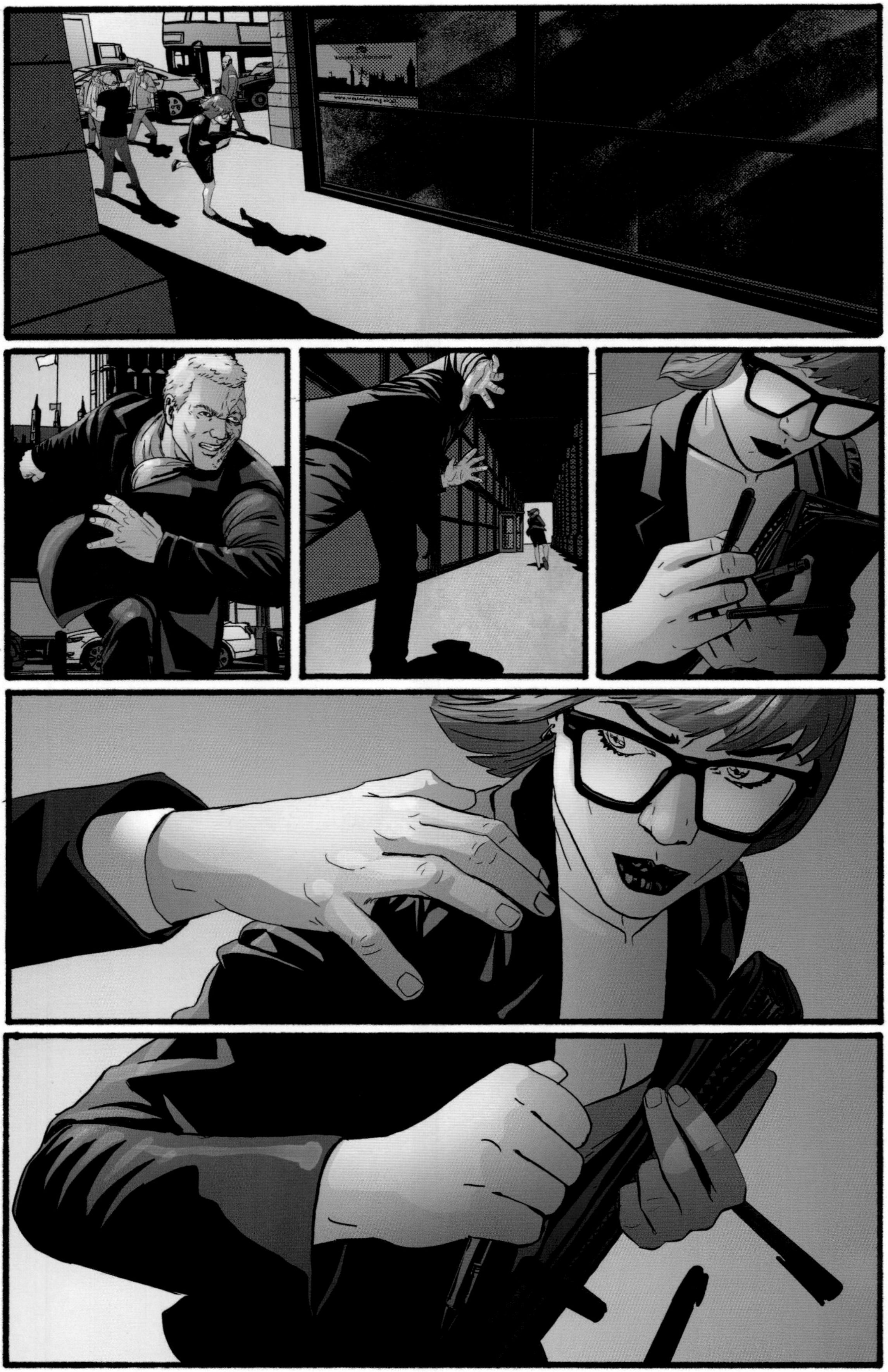

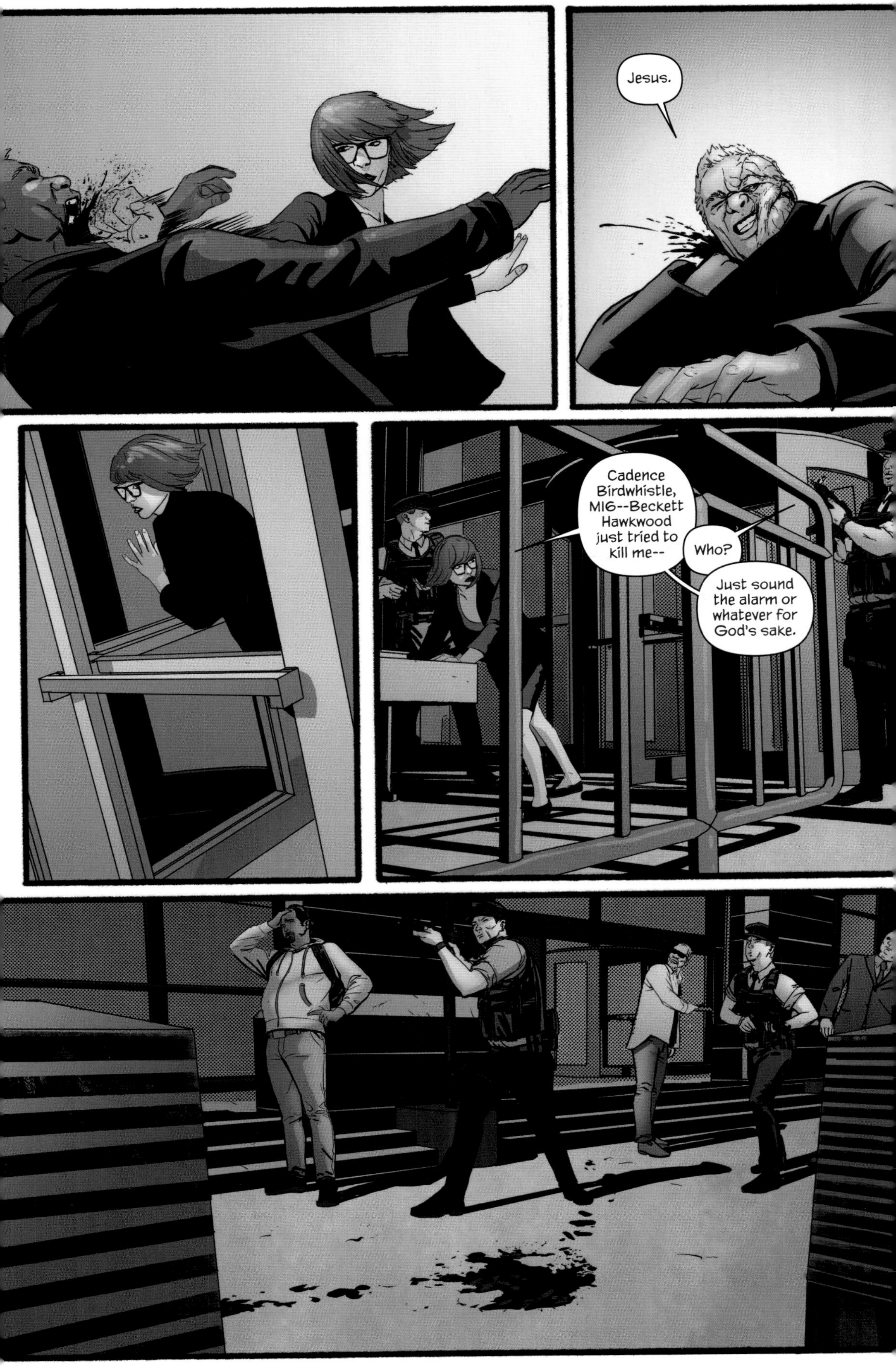
Jesus.
Cadence Birdwhistle, MI6--Beckett Hawkwood just tried to kill me--
Who?
Just sound the alarm or whatever for God's sake.

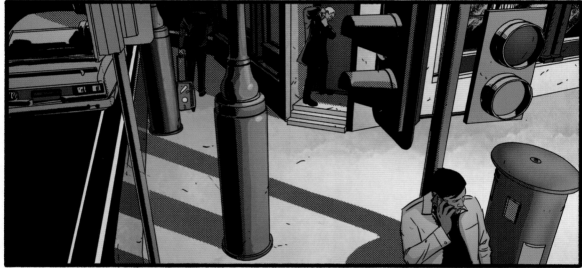

Oi!
Over here,
chief!

--yes, I applaud
the fast lockdown of
the immediate area,
but I want to still be
able to drive through
it, so please let
them know--

--wait.
I have eyes on
Hawkwood. He's
moving.

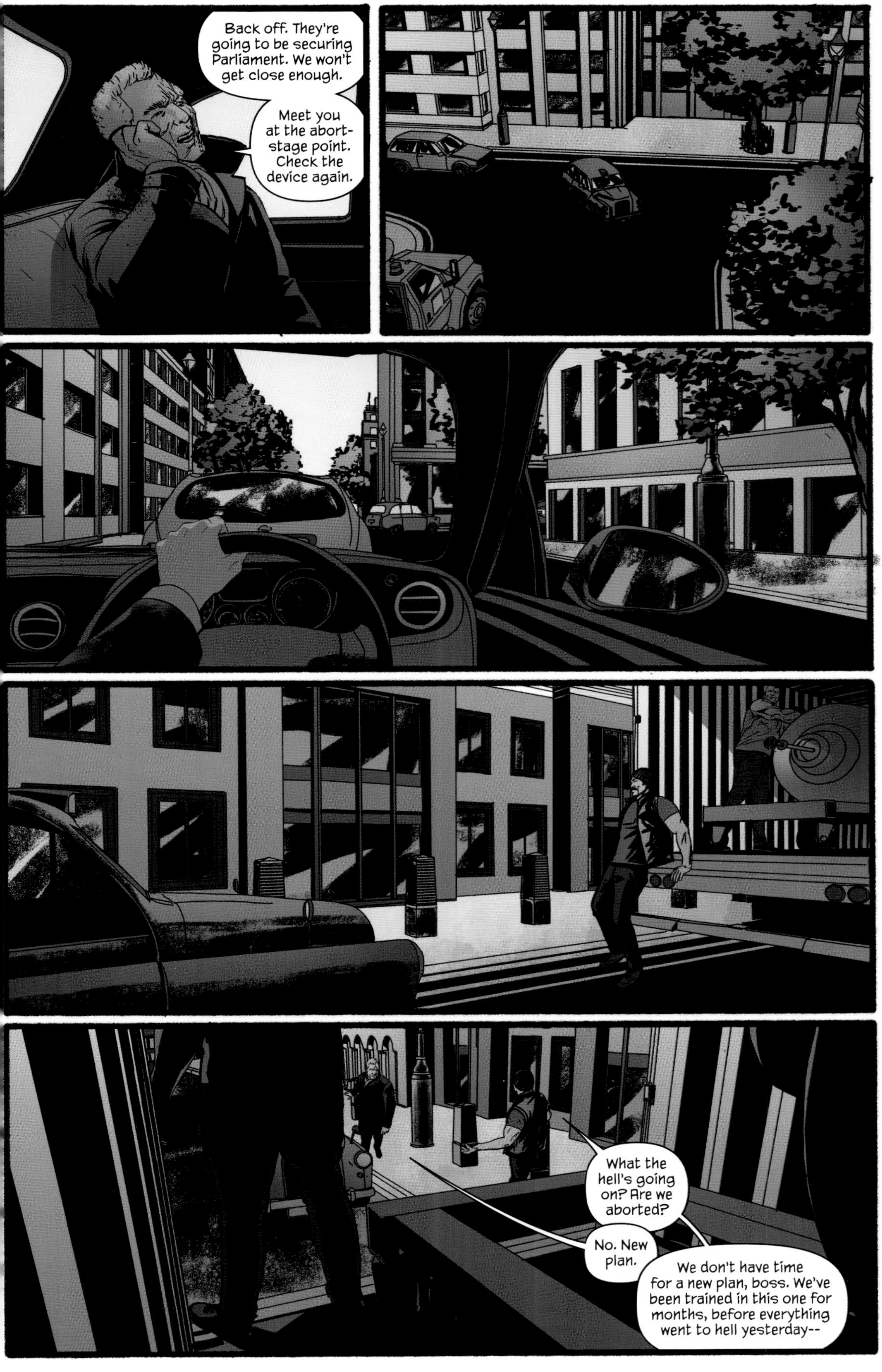
Back off. They're going to be securing Parliament. We won't get close enough.
Meet you at the abort-stage point. Check the device again.
What the hell's going on? Are we aborted?
No. New plan.
We don't have time for a new plan, boss. We've been trained in this one for months, before everything went to hell yesterday--

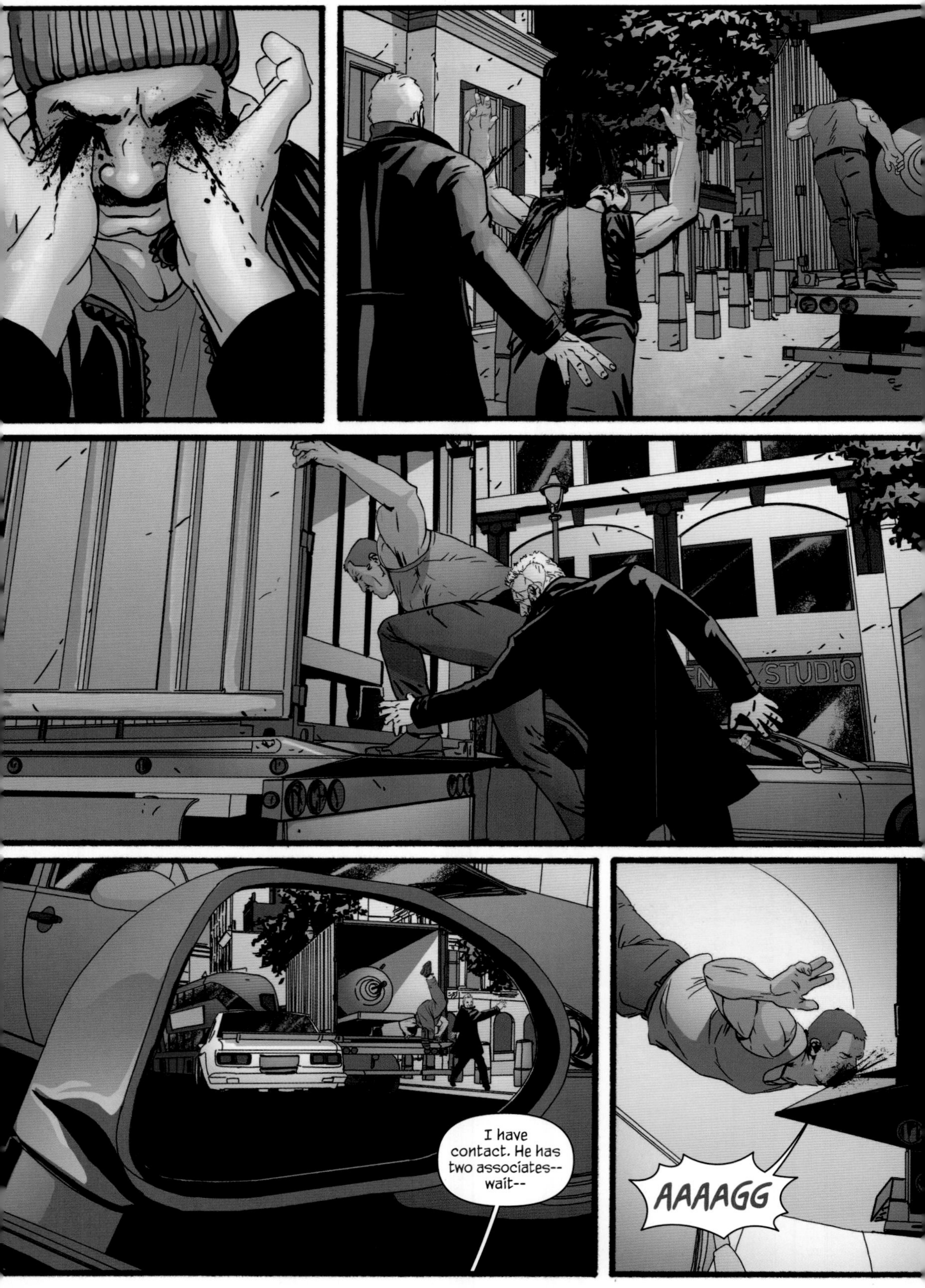
STUDIO
I have contact. He has two associates-- wait--
AAAAGG

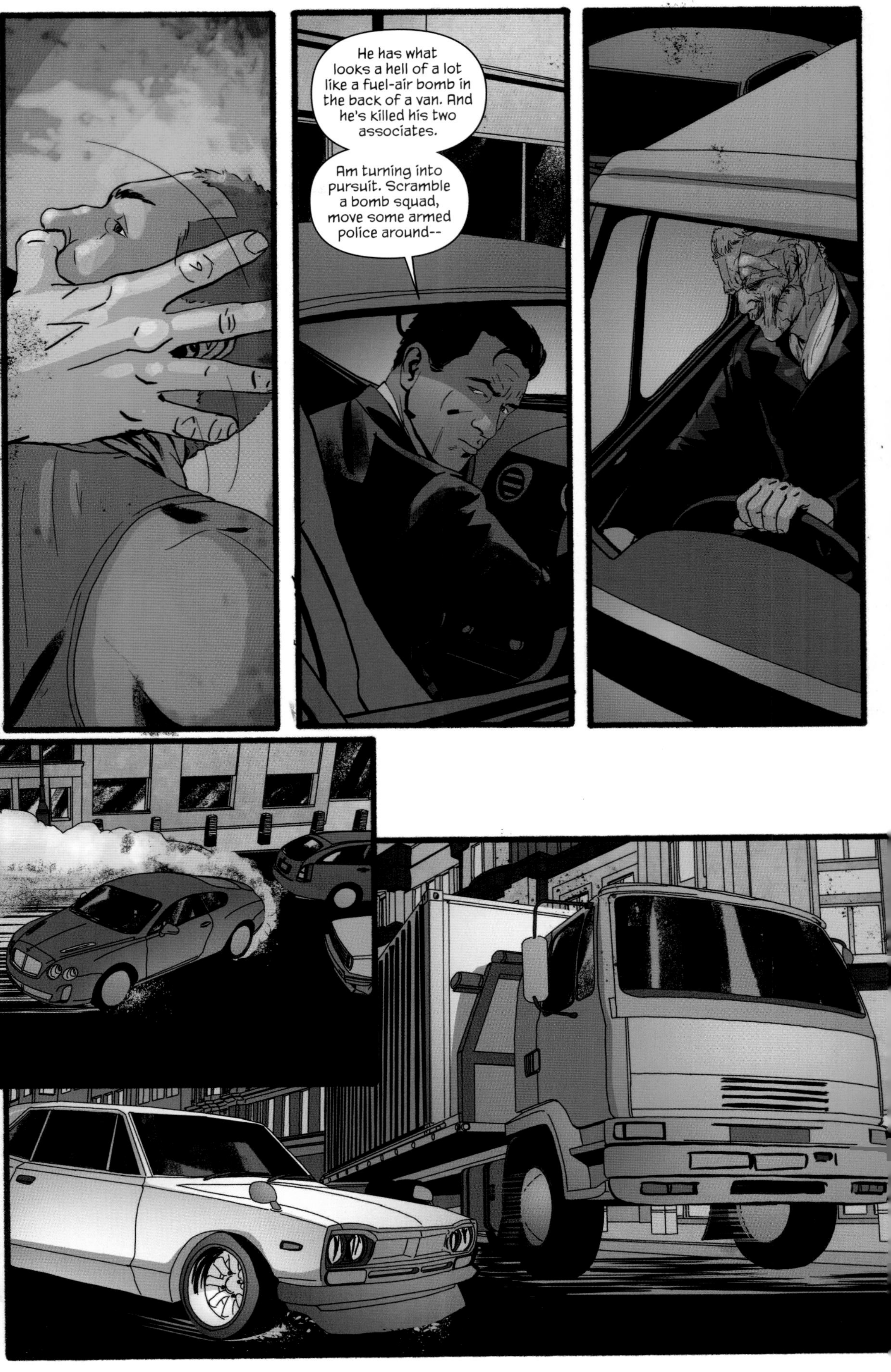
He has what looks a hell of a lot like a fuel-air bomb in the back of a van. And he's killed his two associates.
Am turning into pursuit. Scramble a bomb squad, move some armed police around--

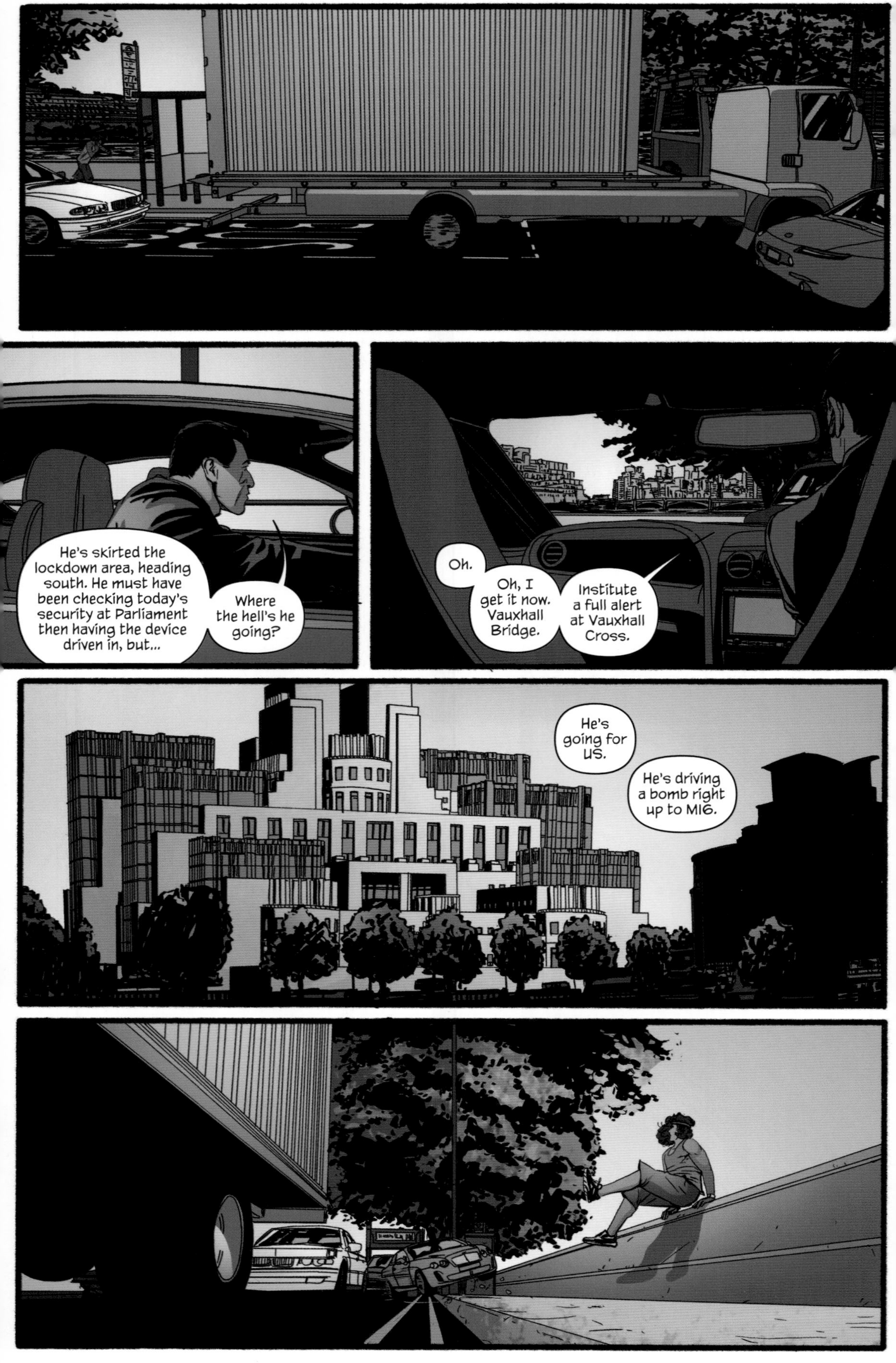
He's skirted the lockdown area, heading south. He must have been checking today's security at Parliament then having the device driven in, but...
Where the hell's he going?
Oh.
Oh, I get it now. Vauxhall Bridge.
Institute a full alert at Vauxhall Cross.
He's going for US.
He's driving a bomb right up to MI6.

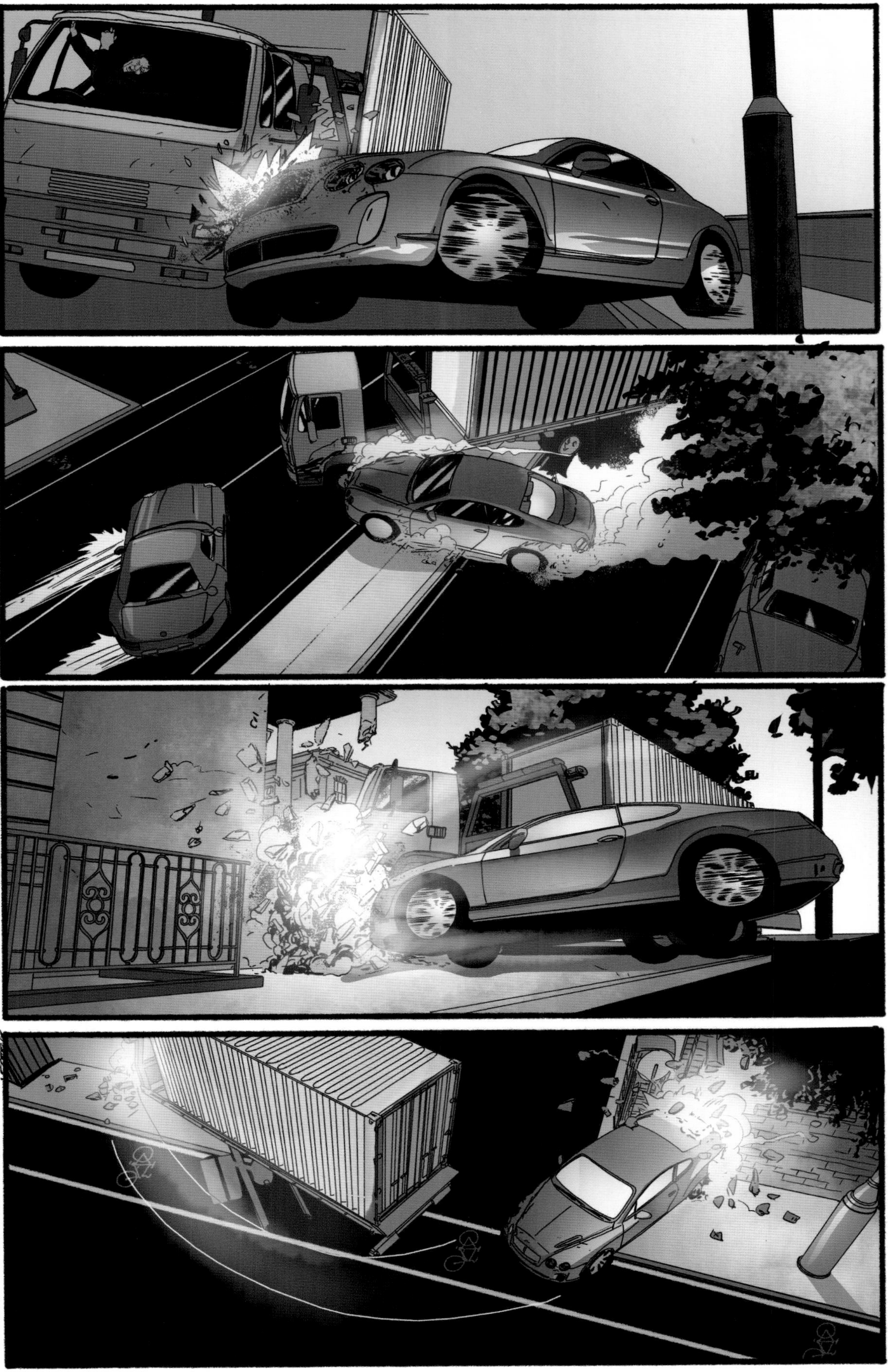

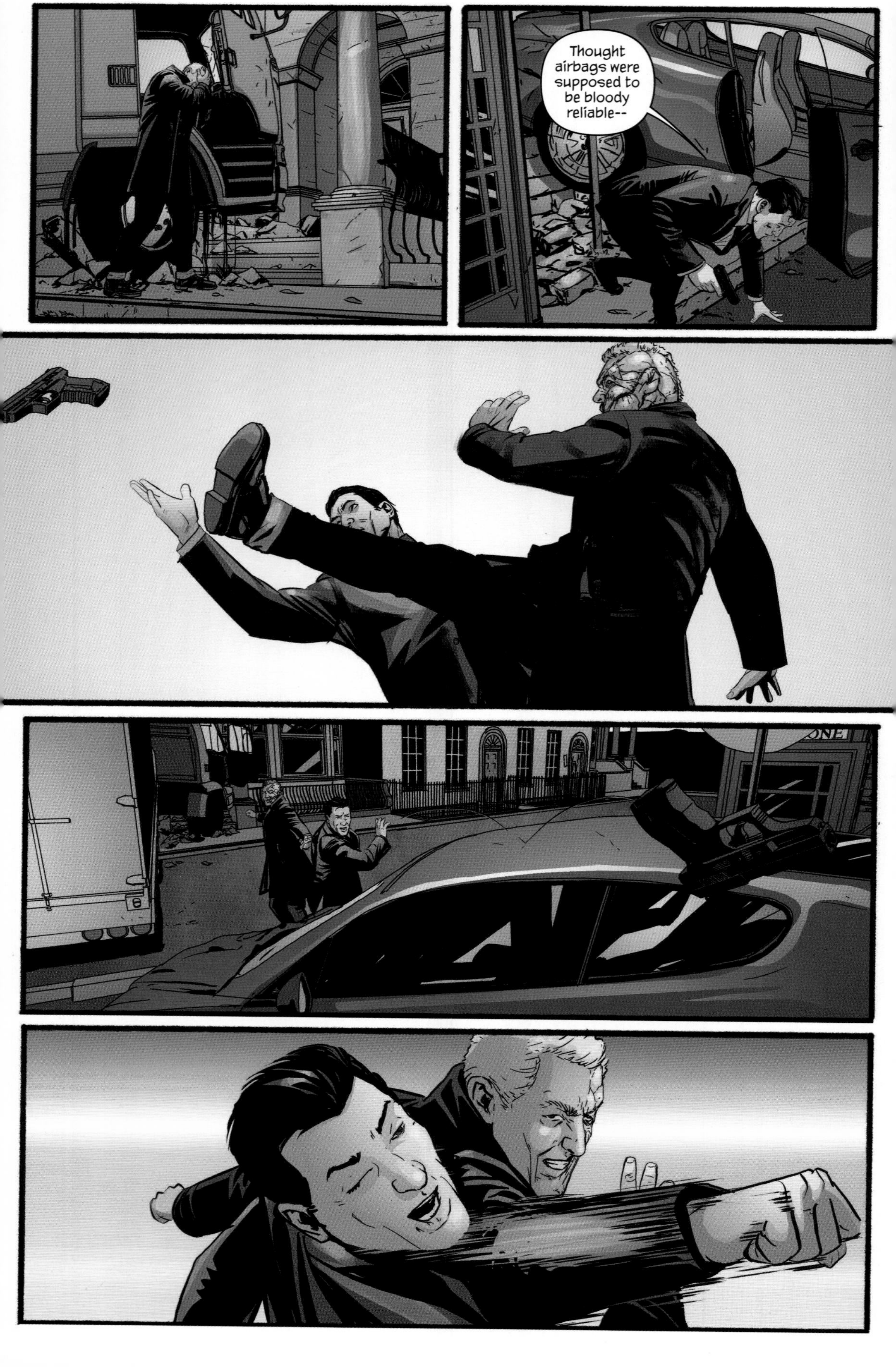
Thought airbags were supposed to be bloody reliable--

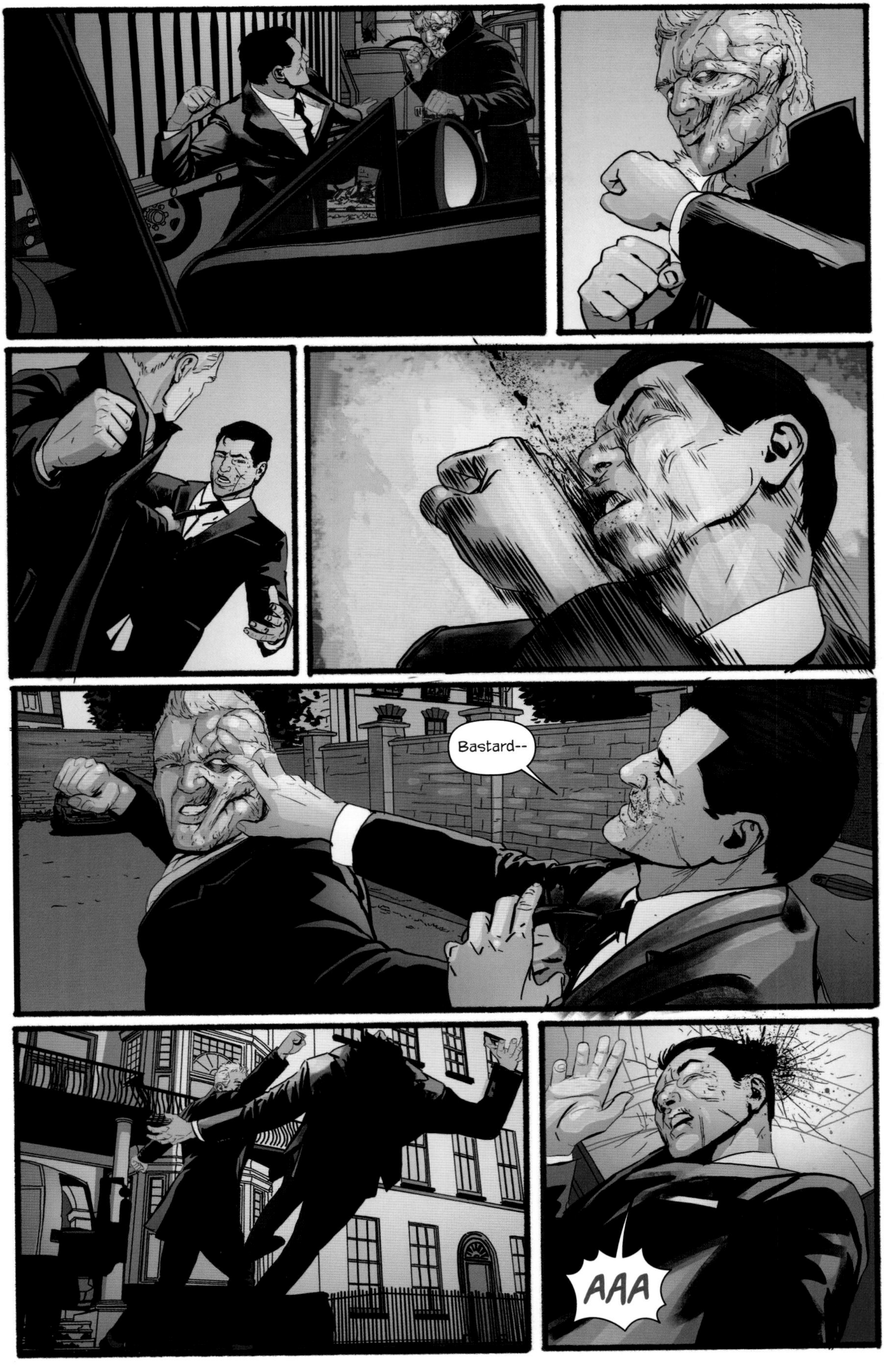
Bastard--
AAA

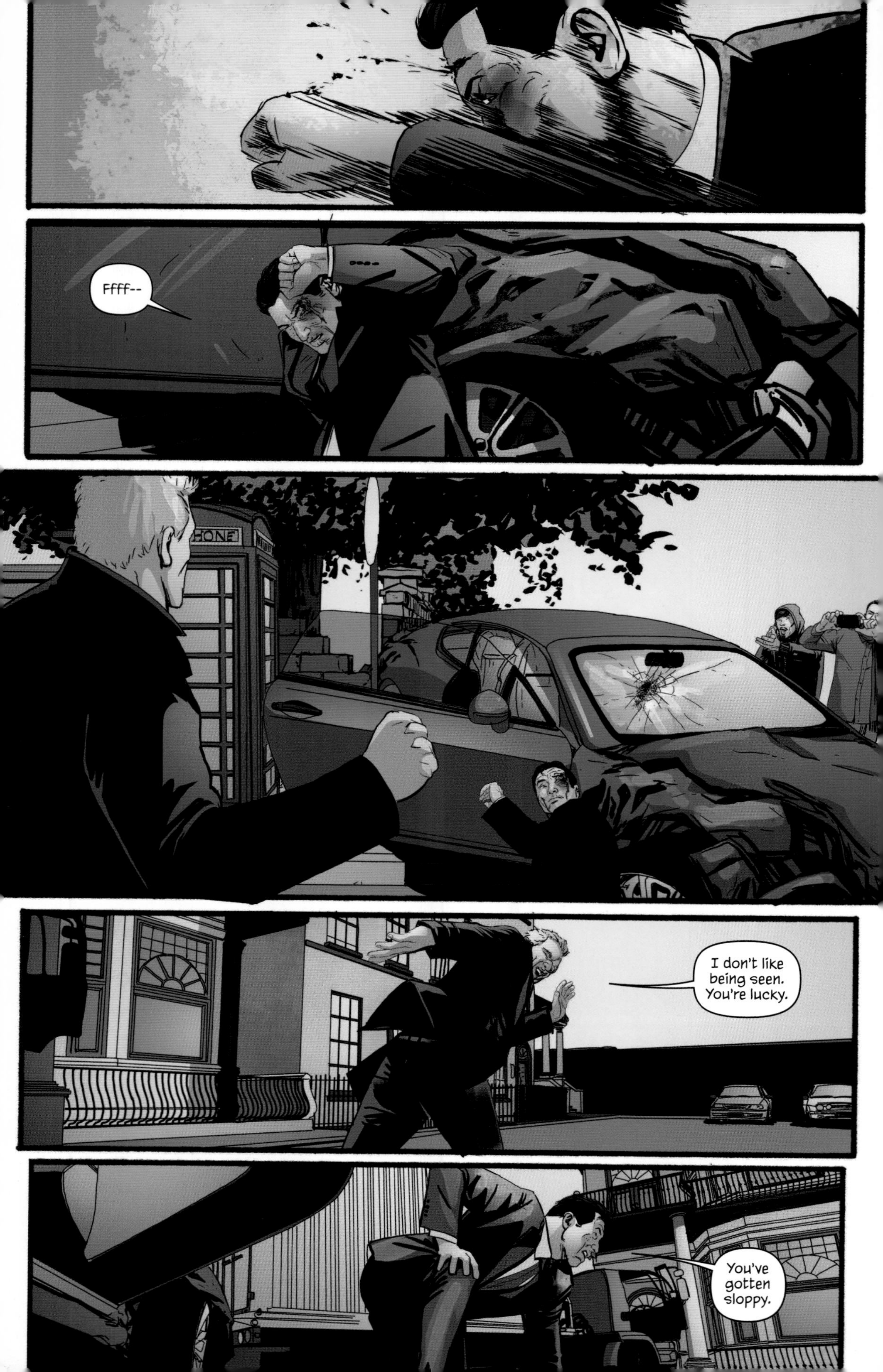
FFFF--
PHONE
I don't like being seen. You're lucky.
You've gotten sloppy.

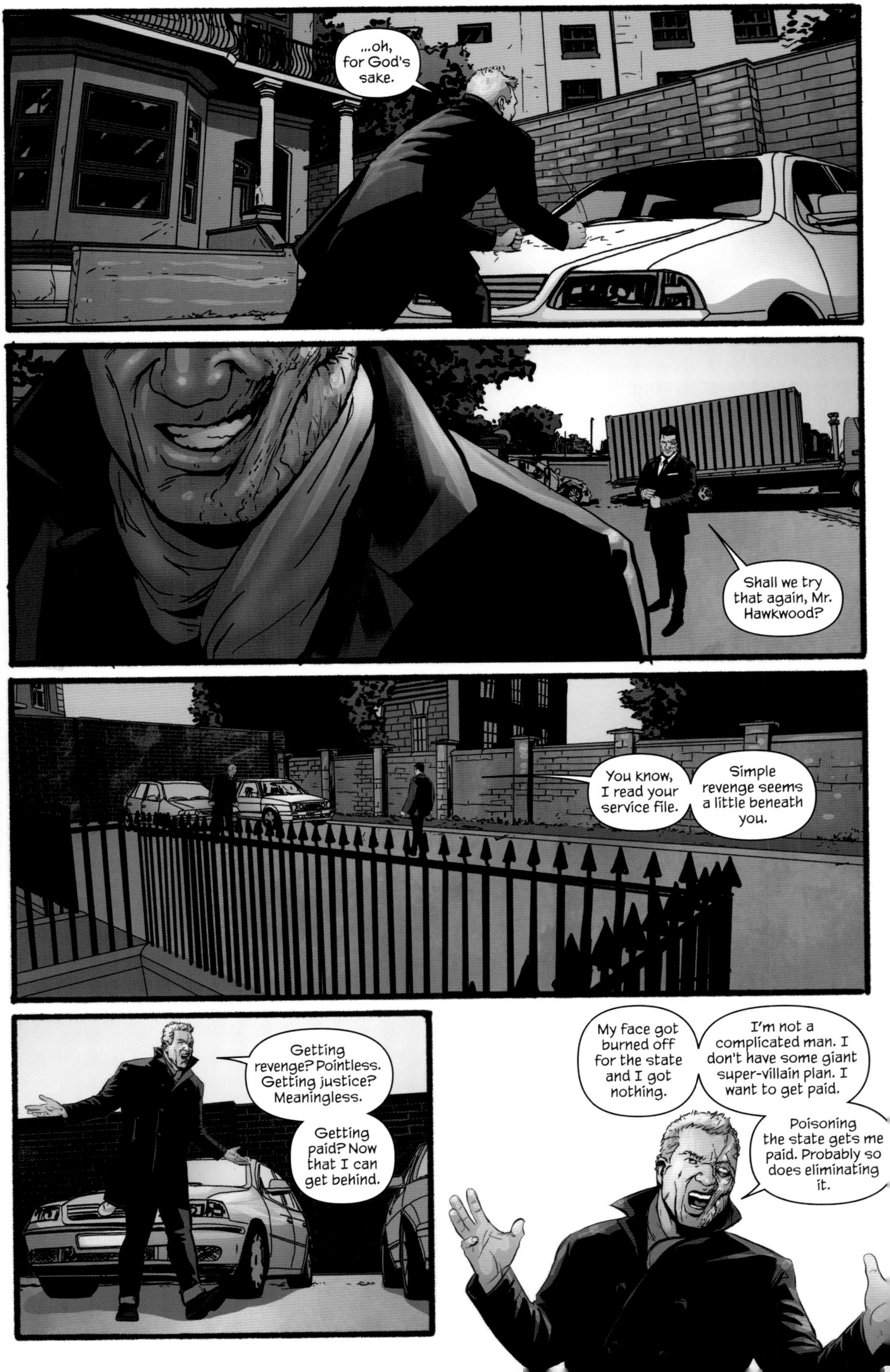
...oh, for God's sake.
Shall we try that again, Mr. Hawkwood?
You know, I read your service file.
Simple revenge seems a little beneath you.
Getting revenge? Pointless. Getting justice? Meaningless.
Getting paid? Now that I can get behind.
My face got burned off for the state and I got nothing.
I'm not a complicated man. I don't have some giant super-villain plan. I want to get paid.
Poisoning the state gets me paid. Probably so does eliminating it.

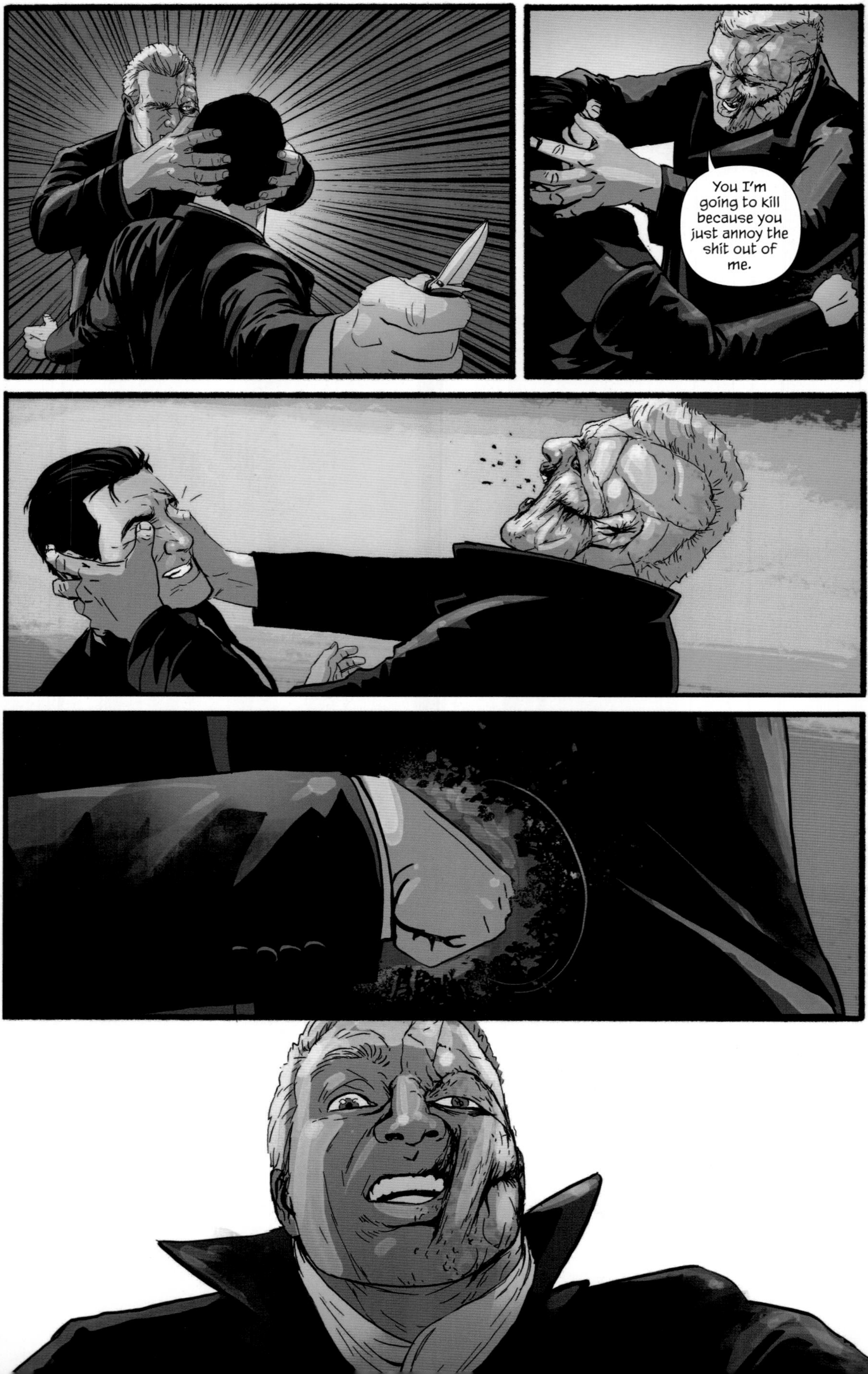
You I'm going to kill because you just annoy the shit out of me.

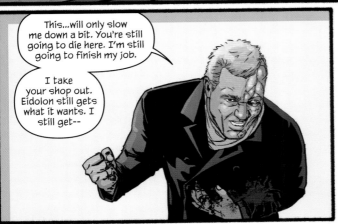

This...will only slow me down a bit. You're still going to die here. I'm still going to finish my job.

I take your shop out. Eidolon still gets what it wants. I still get--

Police and security service back-up will be here any moment, Mr. Hawkwood.

You're losing. In the next few ticks of the clock, you will have lost entirely.

And, of this moment, nobody knows what's happening here.

There's a war hero. And a bomb. Nobody needs to know that you were resentful and damaged enough to stoop to being paid.

Nobody needs to know anything other than what I tell them.

Do you understand me?

No.

You can die a hero and get respect. Or you can live as a criminal, a terrorist, a failure and a traitor.

You're a brave man. You know what to do.

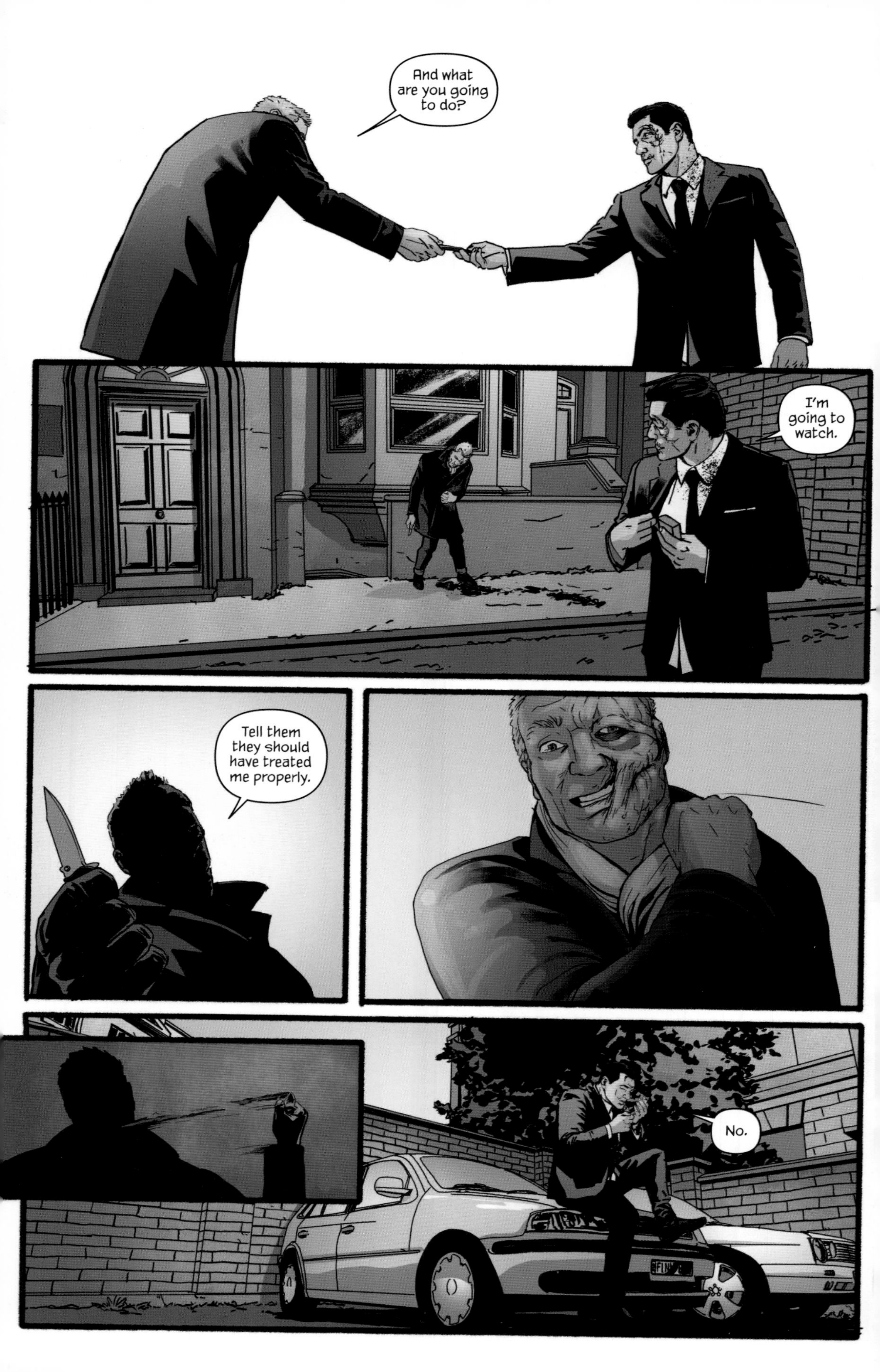
And what are you going to do?
I'm going to watch.
Tell them they should have treated me properly.
No.

ELLIS · MASTERS
IAN FLEMING'S
JAMES BOND 007

VARGR

"...this James Bond comic by Warren Ellis and Jason Masters is the best contemporary take on 007."
– Brian K Vaughan (writer of Saga)

DYNAMITE

JAMES BOND: VARGR HC & TPB

Warren Ellis | writer
Jason Masters | artist
Guy Major | colorist
Simon Bowland | letterer

Collecting issues 1-6
HC: 9781606909010
TPB: 9781524104801
IN STORES NOW!

IAN FLEMING PUBLICATIONS LIMITED

DYNAMITE®
dynamite.com

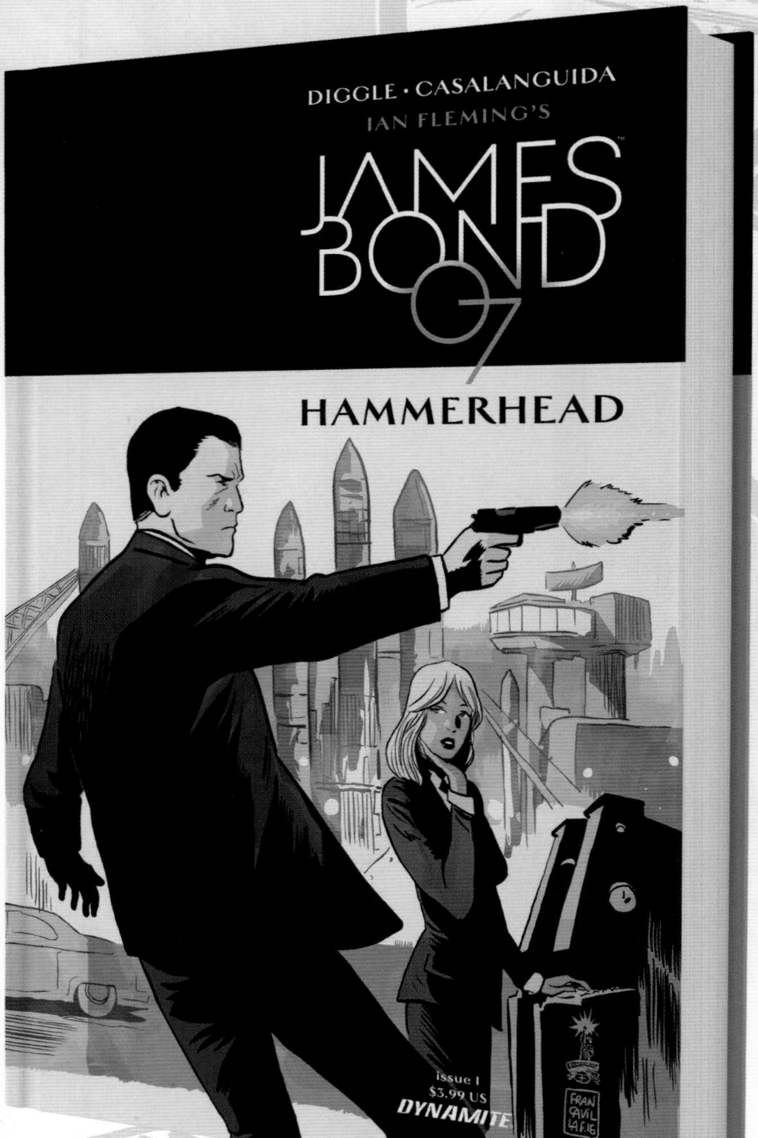
DIGGLE • CASALANGUIDA
IAN FLEMING'S
JAMES BOND 007
HAMMERHEAD
issue 1
$3.99 US
DYNAMITE

PRAISE FOR ANDY DIGGLES' JAMES BOND: HAMMERHEAD

"Diggle is an accomplished crime writer and a very good fit for the series."
– Bleeding Cool

"Visceral action, solid storytelling."
– SciFi Pulse

"I just read it and it's a dream. RECOMMENDED!"
– Mark Miller
(writer of Old Man Logan)

"Taut and beautiful. Andy is perhaps my favourite writer of spy work in Western comics, so this is perfect. Luca gets a wonderful modern noir mood to it."
– Kieron Gillen
(writer of The Wicked + The Divine)

"It's like watching the best modern Bond movies. Great stuff"
– Bryan Hitch
(writer of Justice League)

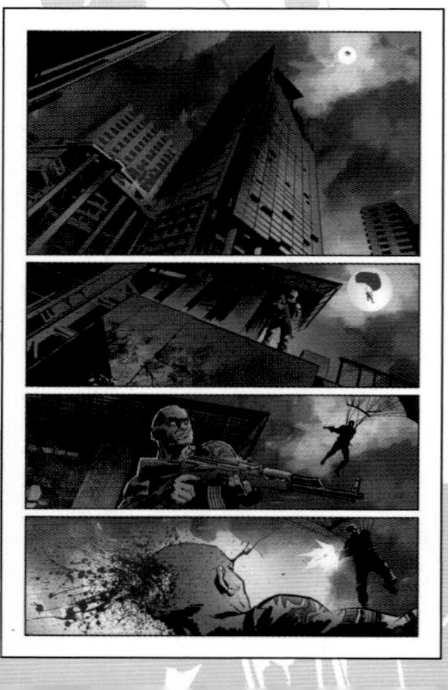

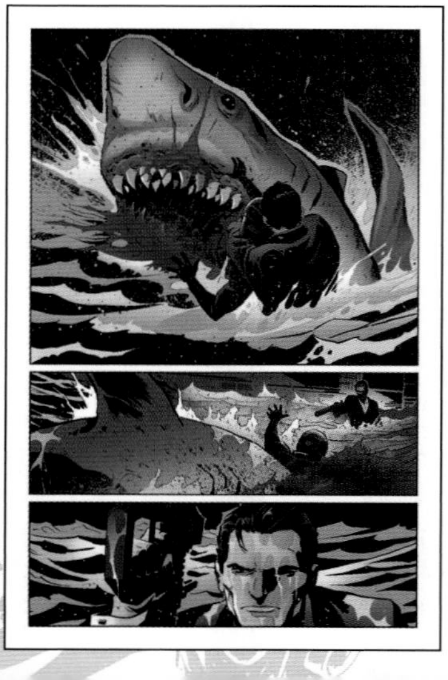

JAMES BOND: HAMMERHEAD
HARDCOVER

Andy Diggle | writer
Luca Casalanguida | artist
Chris Blythe | colorist
Simon Bowland | letterer
Francesco Francavilla | cover

Collecting issues 1-6
ISBN: 9781524103224
IN STORES NOW!

Ian Fleming
IAN FLEMING PUBLICATIONS LIMITED

DYNAMITE
dynamite.com

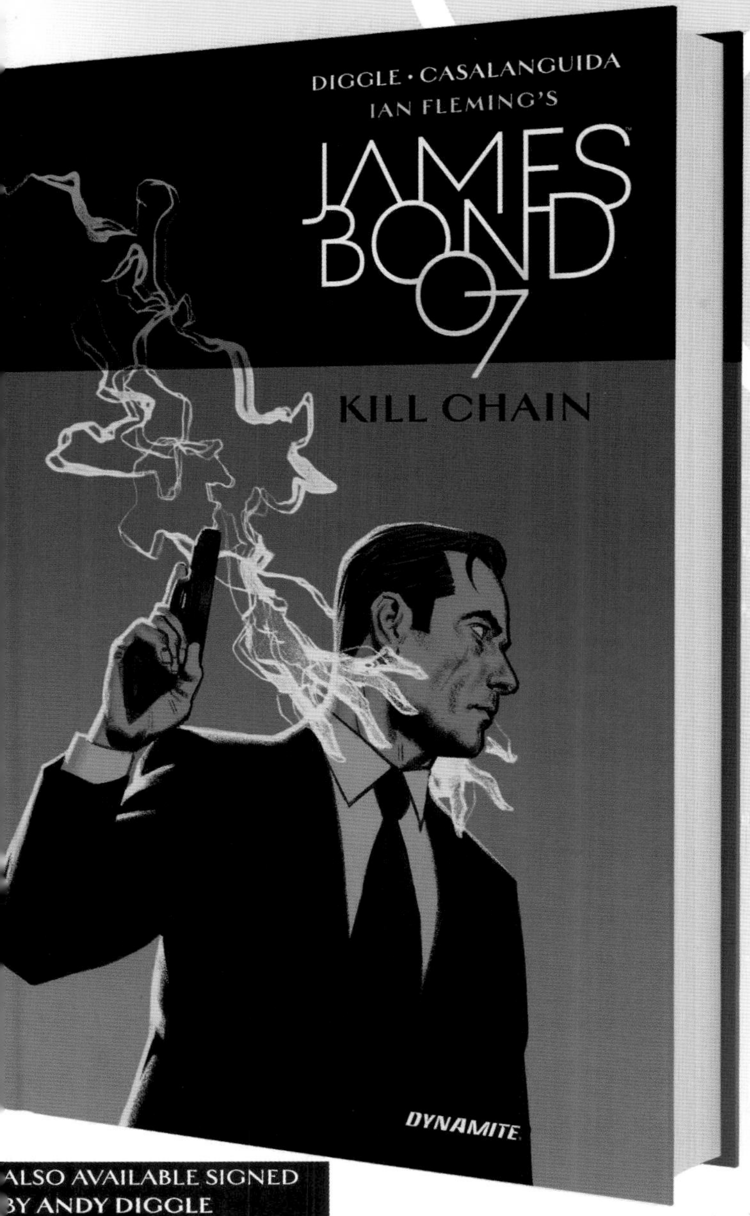
DIGGLE · CASALANGUIDA
IAN FLEMING'S
JAMES BOND 007
KILL CHAIN
DYNAMITE

PRAISE FOR ANDY DIGGLE'S JAMES BOND: KILL CHAIN

"The creative team behind Hammerhead [delivers] yet another must have comic."
– SnapPow

"The art is spot on and delivers on every front."
– Comic Buzz

"A well set up mystery with all the hallmarks of a Bond classic."
– Multiversity Comics

"This is pure Bond in the classic Fleming sense for me visually and it's just striking."
– The Fandom Post

"An action fest fans should enjoy."
– Adventures in Poor Taste

"Dynamite Entertainment continues to show that when it comes to James Bond, nobody does it better."
– Comic Crusaders

ALSO AVAILABLE SIGNED BY ANDY DIGGLE

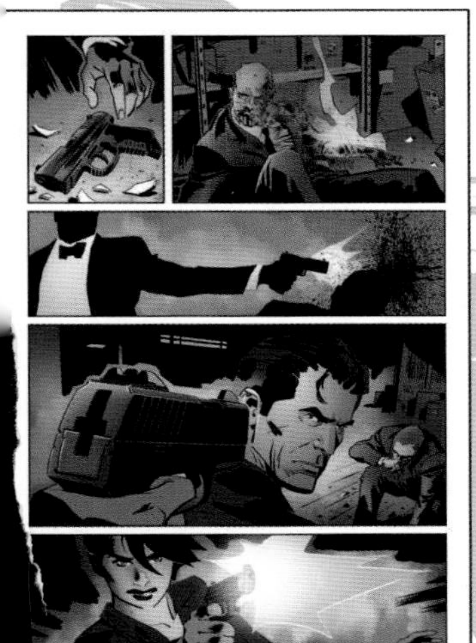

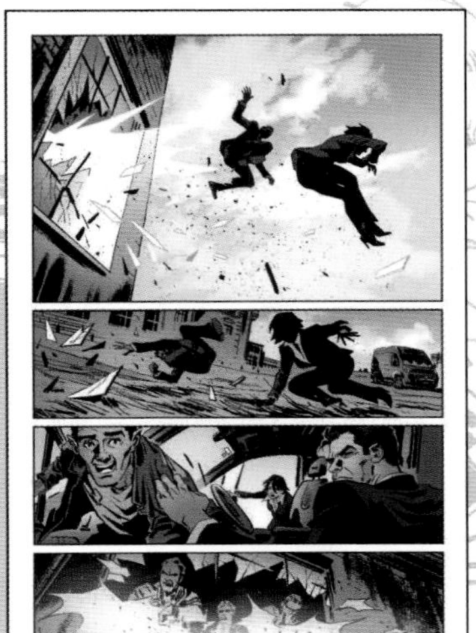

JAMES BOND: KILL CHAIN
HARDCOVER

Andy Diggle | writer
Luca Casalanguida | artist
Chris Blythe | colorist
Simon Bowland | letterer
Greg Smallwood | cover

Collecting issues 1-6
ISBN: 9781524105952
IN STORES APRIL 2018

IAN FLEMING PUBLICATIONS LIMITED

DYNAMITE
dynamite.com

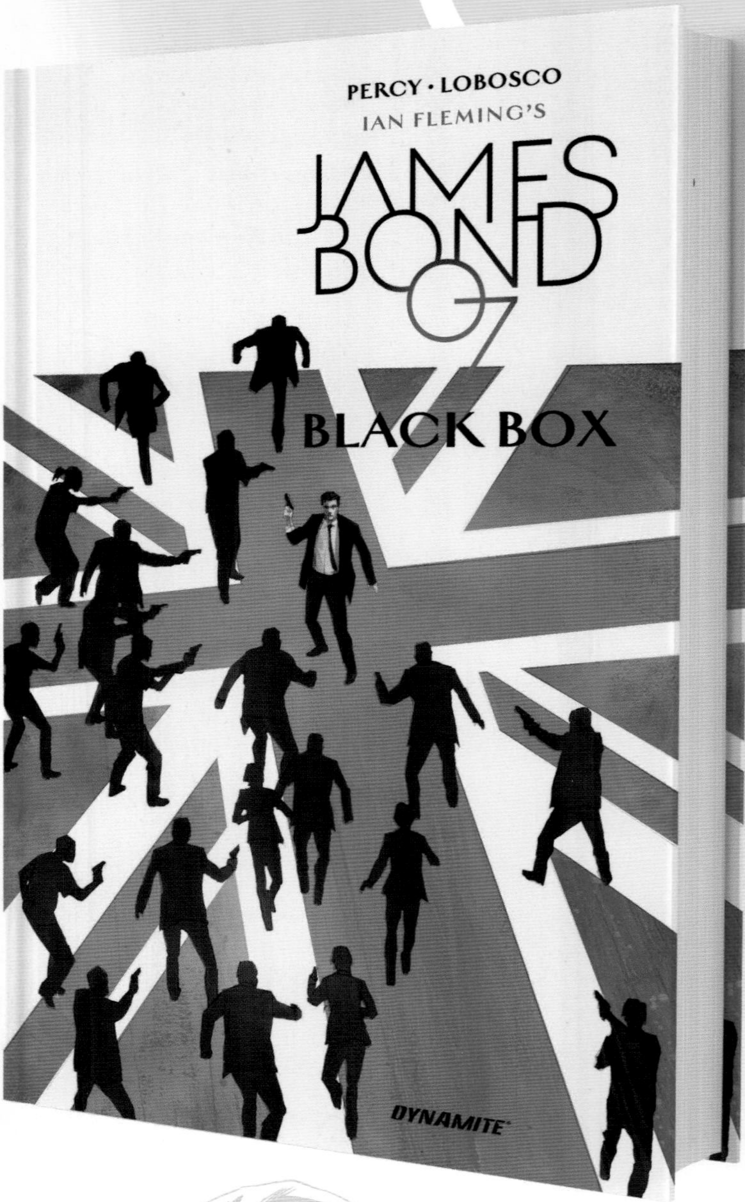
PERCY · LOBOSCO
IAN FLEMING'S
JAMES BOND 007
BLACK BOX
DYNAMITE

PRAISE FOR BENJAMIN PERCY'S JAMES BOND: BLACK BOX

"Percy goes big and sleek for his opening... Artist Rapha Lobosco, whose pencils look like a stylish cross between Howard Chaykin and Eduardo Risso, keeps pace with Percy's brisk script and... distances the new volume from the previous ones with plenty of his own singular panache. If you are unsure of this new volume, just think of it as a new director and production team taking over the returning cast because James Bond #1 is too fun to just dismiss outright."
– NEWSARAMA

"Percy's got the voice right for Bond and Lobosco definitely has some really strong design work here with characters and locations."
– THE FANDOM POST

JAMES BOND: BLACK BOX
HARDCOVER

Benjamin Percy | writer
Rapha Lobosco | artist
Chris O'Halloran | colorist
Simon Bowland | letterer
Dominic Reardon | cover

Collecting issues 1-6
ISBN: 9781524104092
IN STORES NOW!

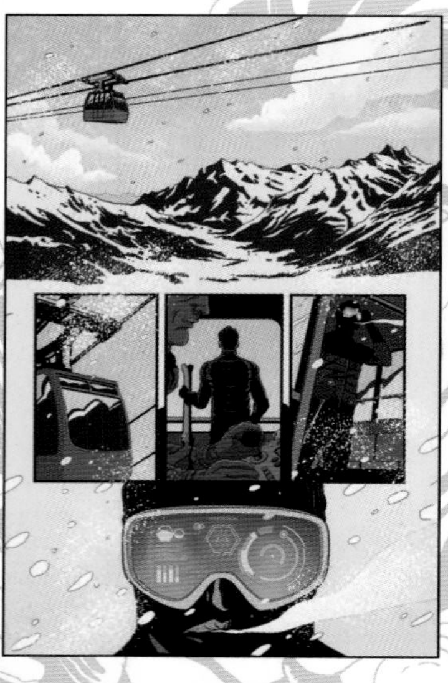

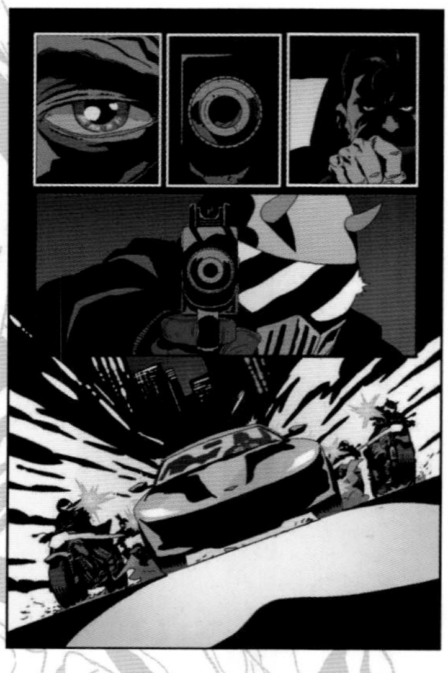

IAN FLEMING PUBLICATIONS LIMITED

DYNAMITE
dynamite.com